THE
EDINBURGH
BOOK
OF
DAYS

MICHAEL T.R.B. TURNBULL

For my Grandfather, Bruce Turnbull, senior bailie

Acknowledgements: Thanks are due to Henry Steuart Fothringham OBE for sharing his compendious knowledge on the records of the Convenery and incorporated trades of Edinburgh, along with the generous help and advice afforded me by Richard Hunter and his team at the Edinburgh City Archives. I am grateful to Julian Russell for allowing me to make use of his transcription of a letter from Father Richard Augustine Hay and to the staff of the National Library of Scotland and the Public Library's Edinburgh Room – a fathomless cornucopia of information on Edinburgh. Finally, I am most grateful to the Editor of *The Scotsman* for allowing me to quote from past issues of this magnificent publication and its antecedents.

Sources

Anon., *A Diurnal of Remarkable Occurrents* (Edinburgh: Maitland Club, 1833)
Arnot, H., *The History of Edinburgh* (Edinburgh, 1788)
Chambers, R. (ed.), *The Book of Days*, 2 vols (Edinburgh: W & R Chambers, 1863)
Chambers, R., *Traditions of Edinburgh* (Edinburgh: W & R Chambers, 1868)
Dalyell, J.G. (ed.), *The Diarey of Robert Birrel 1532-1605 in Fragments of Scotish History* (Edinburgh, 1798)
Darling, W., *A Book of Days* (London: The Richards Press, 1951)
Gilbert, W.M. (ed.), *Edinburgh in the Nineteenth Century* (Edinburgh: J & R Allan, 1901)
Nicoll, J., *A Diary of Public Transactions 1650-67* (Edinburgh: Bannatyne Club, 1836)
Extracts from the Records of the Burgh of Edinburgh (*ERBE*), 1403-1680

Further references are accredited throughout the text.

First published 2011

The History Press

The Mill, Brimscombe Port

Stroud, Gloucestershire, GL5 2QG

www.thehistorypress.co.uk

British Library Cataloguing in Publication Data.

A catalogue record for this book is available from the British Library.

ISBN 978 0 7524 5841 0

Typesetting and origination by The History Press

Printed in Great Britain

January 1st

1661: King Charles II, on his accession, had written to the presbytery of Edinburgh, emphasising his determination to support the presbyterian form of church government established by law in Scotland. The Presbyterians had always been averse to the observation of particular days, which they deemed highly superstitious, perhaps even impious. When required to observe the Royal birthday, they answered 'That they kept with strictness the holy Christian Sabbath: that they would keep no other holiday. That, on the most cogent reasons, they did not observe Christmas nor Easter.' (Arnot, *The History of Edinburgh*)

1863: Till few years ago in Scotland, the custom of the wassail bowl at the passing away of the old year might be said to be still in comparative vigour. On the approach of twelve o'clock, a hot pint was prepared – that is, a kettle or flagon full of warm, spiced and sweetened ale, with an infusion of spirits. When the clock had struck the knell of the departing year, each member of the family drank of this mixture with a general hand-shaking, and perhaps a dance round the table, with the addition of a song. (Chambers, *The Book of Days*)

January 2nd

1877: On this day Father, later Canon, Edward Hannan, as Chaplain of St Patrick's Catholic Young Men's Society (CYMS), which he had founded, was recorded in the minutes to have enquired about a group of young Irishmen who had formed Hibernian Football Club. He asked for information on the Club, as he said 'it appeared it was outside our direction'. He wished to meet the members with a view to 'bringing them within our influence'. At a meeting of the CYMS on 20 February 1877, it was recorded that Father \ had had 'a conversation recently with some members of the Hibernian Football Club with respect to their placing themselves under the control of the Council' of the CYMS. It was noted on 27 February 1877 that officers of the Club were willing to come under the control and patronage of the council to be guided by Father Hannan, who would provide facilities and finance for the players. From being a casual grouping of young men who enjoyed a kick-about, Father Hannan gave Hibernian FC a formal structure and financial security. (*Scottish Catholic Archives*: GD82/812)

January 3rd

1503: The provost, bailies and council took action against the possible outbreak of the plague, which had been rife some years before. They ordered a proclamation to be made that all beggars without benefit of regular alms should leave the burgh and not return under pain of death. All persons found begging would be punished: in the case of men, they would have a hand cut off; in the case of women, they would be branded on the cheek and banished. Similarly, any young man or woman found in the burgh without regular employment or other financial support would be liable to the same punishments. (*Extracts from the Records of the Burgh of Edinburgh (ERBE)*)

———•◆•———

1694: On this day the council debated the public scandal where several young women, pretending to sell lemons and oranges and other fruits, went through Edinburgh as common whores or thieves. They therefore ordained that no woman should walk through the streets and up to gentlemen's rooms carrying fruit-baskets, under pain of prosecution and imprisonment in the Correction House. On 12 January 1700 the bailies recommended that common thieves and whores should be marked on the nose by cutting out a piece of the left side of the nose with a branding-iron made for that purpose. (*ERBE*)

January 4th

1859: Newspaper advertisements, with their artful rhetoric, reveal so much about how life is lived. Some advertisements printed in *The Scotsman* on this day read:

PORTRAITS: The much-admired Patent Portraits are taken in any weather, and are warranted to stand in any climate — at Hay's, 68 & 70 Princes' Street, Edinburgh, for the Stereoscope, Lockets, Brooches, Cases, &c., Portraits on Paper, Plain or Coloured. Portraits and Pictures of all kinds COPIED. Prices from 2s. 6d. Upwards. Opinions of The Press: 'The remarkable Likenesses in the Galleries of Messrs G. & D. Hay evince the success of these artists in the highest departments of the photographic art.' — *Edinburgh Courant.* 'The untouched photographs of Messrs G. & D. Hay, Edinburgh, may be noticed, rivalling as they do, in clearness and delicacy, the finest productions of their class.' — *Times.*

Pier and Mantelpiece Mirrors and Console Tables, in Extensive Variety, and every species of Ornamental Carving and Gilding Designed, Made and Exhibited on the Premises of Messrs J. & J. Ciceri, Mantica, & TORRE, Late Ciceri & Pini, 81 Leith Street — Mirrors Packed and Guaranteed Safe at Destination.

James Cooke's Livery Stables, Meuse Lane, St Andrew Square. Private Broughams, Phaetons, Dog-Carts, Gigs, and Saddle-Horses, &c., on Hire Daily. N.B. — Horses Broke for Single and Double Harness.

January 5th

1593: Because of public commotion and disorder, the council decided on this day in January that there should be a more thorough watch and guard kept within the town. The bailies would recruit forty well-armed men to be on duty for a month, night and day and construct a wooden watch-house or guardhouse at the Mercat Cross. Other precautions taken at the time of these 'Papist plots' was a drummer stationed for three days on the High Street; exercises at the shooting-butts; a watchman located in St Giles' steeple between December and June; a trumpeter and a herald paid to proclaim publicly that all papists should leave the town. (*ERBE*)

———•◆•———

1596: A proclamation was made, declaring perpetual peace between Scotland and England, and that none of the Borderers should invade each other, under the pain of death. Nevertheless, the general musters were still proclaimed to be held the following 2 February. (*Diarey of Robert Birrel*)

———•◆•———

1859: 'Wind and Weather Predictions for 1859: The well-known and popular Captain Peter Turner, commander of the tourists' steamer on the Caledonian Canal, requests us to give our readers the benefit of a regular estimate of the weather that may be expected in Great Britain and Ireland during the year 1859.' (*The Scotsman*)

January 6th

1859: 'A meeting of the County Prison Board was held. The number of prisoners in custody was 394 — 192 of whom were females, and 267 being in separate confinement. The number in custody at this same date last year was 287, of whom 130 were women. The total number of commitments to the prison in December was 351, there being 89 commitments to the prison cells. The monthly average of prisoners in custody during December was 365, and 8 to the prison cells, the daily average of prisoners in the jail during the year being 354.' (*The Scotsman*)

'Assaulting A Policeman. —At the Police Court, before Bailie Forrester, four men, all Irish labourers, were charged with assaulting a policeman in the High Street on New Year's Day. One had obstructed a body of militiamen proceeding to the Castle, and was given in charge to the policeman, upon which his companions and himself joined in a brutal attack on the officer, knocking him down and kicking him violently.' (*The Scotsman*)

January 7th

1857: A concerned member of the public had a letter printed in *The Scotsman* on this day:

To the Editor: Sir, — It appears that this year, in Scotland, two deaths and several cases of serious stabbing have arisen from this ancient but foolish practice of 'first-footing' at the commencement of New-Year's morning — and indeed, unfortunately, there is seldom a New Year in Scotland without such fatal results. But besides such cases, which attract more public attention, the practice always gives rise to a large amount of evil in drunkenness and debauchery, and through the licence and excitement of the occasion, is often most corrupting even to previously respectable young men and women of the working classes. How much better in every way it would be if the greetings and rejoicings of the day were delayed till daylight, when evil deeds would be less likely to be committed, and the many innocent and instructive means of holiday recreation now generally provided might be enjoyed in sobriety. No doubt the practice has much abated of late years from what it was in former times, but it still exists to such an extent as to be a very serious evil — I am, &c. 'A Citizen'.

January 8th

1998: It was announced that generous grants from a number of funds would enable the Cramond Lioness to go on public display as the centrepiece of 'Pax Romana', an exhibition at the City Art Centre. Some 4ft 6ins long and 2ft high, the sandstone sculpture, dating from the second or early third century, depicts a lioness eating a man and was discovered by Robert Graham, the local ferryman. It was excavated from the Almond river-bed by archaeologists in January 1997 and is thought to have been part of twin sculptures on the tomb of a Roman official. Emperor Antoninus Pius' troops built a 6-acre fort and associated harbour at the mouth of the River Almond in AD 142. This was abandoned from the time of the construction of Hadrian's Wall, but the Emperor Septimus Severus and his son Caracalla came to Cramond between AD 208-11, when they re-established the Roman fort. From the evidence of inscribed stones discovered at Cramond, the fort was garrisoned by soldiers from various parts of the Roman Empire: the Second Legion Augusta (from Wales), the Fifth Cohort of Gauls (from ancient France) and the First Cohort of Tungri (from the Ardennes).

January 9th

1604: On this day Alistair MacGregor of Glenstrae was brought to Edinburgh. He had been captured by the Laird of Arkynles but escaped and was then caught by the Earl of Argyle. The Earl had promised that he would take him out of Scotland and so he was taken to Berwick under guard; the Earl kept his promise. But his guards were told not to free him and so he returned that evening to Edinburgh. There he was hanged at the Mercat Cross, with one of his associates on either side, but MacGregor was hanged the distance of his own height above his friends. In February, nine other MacGregors were hanged, and in March seven MacGregors and Armstrongs were hanged at the Mercat Cross. (*Diarey of Robert Birrel*)

———◆———

1871: A curious letter was printed in *The Scotsman* on this day:

> Sir, — I sent a lad today to pay my account for servants' beer, and he brought back 5 per cent discount, with a message that it was for the butler. I sent back the money so returned, saying that I knew nothing of the butler being so considered, and he was then told that he might keep the money to himself, as he had paid the account. I am, &c. 'A Householder'.

January 10th

1666: John Baptist Quarentino (aka Querento), an Italian mountebank (a 'quack' doctor, from the Italian *montimbanco* – to get up on a bench), was given a Royal warrant by the Privy Council to practice in Edinburgh, as long as he did not come into conflict with the work of the surgeons, and the town council extended his permission until 1 February, allowing him to set up his stage and sell drugs and cures until that date. On 10 October this was further extended; on 25 October when Quarentino (who described himself as a physician) again applied for a licence to erect a stage on the High Street for the sale of his medicines and for practising his methods of surgery. He was given permission to put up his stage at any part of the south side of the High Street between the top of Niddrie's Wynd and the Netherbow. The council asked the Dean of Gild to supply a diagram showing the location where the stage was to be erected until 1 January 1677. On 15 December 1676 the council again granted a warrant to Quarantino to continue putting up his stage until 2 February, but declared that they would not allow him any further permission after that. (*ERBE*)

January 11th

1455: A bond by the provost, bailies, council, and community of Edinburgh was made to William Prestoun, son and heir to the then deceased William Prestoun of Goirtoun, whereby, on the narrative that the deceased had at great cost and trouble procured the arm bone of St Giles, and had left the same without condition to the Kirk of St Giles of Edinburgh, they undertook within six or seven years to build an aisle outside of Our Lady's aisle where the deceased was buried, with a monument and altar; that whensoever the relic should be borne, the nearest in blood to the deceased should bear it before all others; and that a chaplain should be appointed for five years to sing for him. (*ERBE*)

———— •◆• ————

1870: On this day an alluring advertisement appeared in *The Scotsman*:

> Beautiful Hair for 1870.— Renew your youth with the New Year. Get a bottle of Mrs S. A. Allen's World's Hair Restorer. See how surely and quickly it does its work. Grey hair restored (not dyed) to its original colour, gloss and beauty; the thin hair thickened, and new growth promoted. No pomade or oil required with it. Sold by chemists and perfumers, only in large bottles, 6s. Depot: 566 High Holborn, London.

January 12th

1450: Led appropriately by William Skinner, representatives of the craftsmen Skinners signed a statute for the upkeep of the altar of St Christopher in the parish Kirk of St Giles and confirmed this by oath. For the rest of their lives, according to their means, they promised to support a chaplain and to pay for repairs and for adornments to the altar. Five shillings would be contributed for repairs to the altar whenever an apprentice was taken on. This agreement was signed by a notary public at the Church of St Mary in the Field, at the third hour of the afternoon, in the presence of three chaplains, a merchant of good repute and other specially invited witnesses. (*ERBE*)

———— ◆ ————

1596: A proclamation was made declaring that the King had appointed eight Lords to examine the Exchequer Accounts, and impose regulation on the irregularities and disorders in Scotland. These Lords were known collectively as Octavians – Alexander Seton of Pluscartie, Walter Stewart of Blantyre, Mr John Lindsay, Mr Thomas Hamilton, Mr James Elphinston, Mr John Skene, Mr James Craigie of Killatie and Mr Peter Young of Seton. (*Diarey of Robert Birrel*)

January 13th

1567: On this day, Mary Queen of Scots and her son Prince James came to Edinburgh. King Henry Darney was lying sick in Glasgow with the smallpox. On the last day of January, the King and Queen came to Edinburgh; the King travelled in a chariot and took his lodging in the Kirk o' Field. On 9 February, the King was murdered in his lodging at the Kirk o' Field at around midnight. The house belonged to Sir James Balfour, provost of that kirk. The house was lifted into the air with gunpowder and the King's chamberman, John Tailor, was found alongside him, lying in a yard under a tree. The King, if he had not been cruelly wyrriet (strangled) with his own garters after he fell to earth, would have lived. On 15 February, King Henry was secretly buried during the night at Holyroodhouse. On 17 June, Captain William Blacketer was arrested under suspicion of being involved in the King's murder. On 24 June he was carried facing backwards in a cart from the Tolbooth to the Mercat Cross and then hanged for the murder of the King. In 1574, Black Ormistoune was hanged at the Mercat Cross for being present at the murder of the King. (*Diarey of Robert Birrel*)

January 14th

1586: From his contract of marriage with the daughter of a merchant in Edinburgh, it appears that the provision settled on George Heriot, a goldsmith and founder of Heriot's Hospital, joined to the dowry he got with his wife, amounted to £214 11s 8d. In 1597, Heriot was appointed goldsmith to Anne of Denmark, James VI's Queen and, soon after, was appointed goldsmith and jeweller to the King. Upon his Majesty's accession to the throne of England, Heriot followed his master to London. Becoming a widower, he came to Edinburgh and, in 1608, took a second wife, with whom he got a dowry of about £333. He returned to London, survived his second wife also, and died there on 12 February 1624, without leaving any lawful children. What wealth Heriot possessed is uncertain, but probably it was not under £50,000. He left legacies to two natural daughters and to his other relations and friends, to a great amount. The residue of his estate he left to the town council, and to the ministers of Edinburgh, in trust, for building and endowing a hospital for the maintenance and education of indigent children, the sons of burgesses of that city. (Arnot, *The History of Edinburgh*)

January 15th

1880: On this day *The Scotsman* printed several news stories:

Sudden Illness in the Street.— A well-dressed young man, who used crutches, being lame in one leg, fell down insensible in St Andrew Street, Edinburgh, between twelve and one o'clock this morning. He had just asked a policeman to show him the way to Elder Street. The constable, who saw him fall, obtained assistance, and had him conveyed on a stretcher to the Infirmary, where up to about two o'clock he was still insensible. He is supposed to be a medical student.

Edinburgh Police Court.— There were thirteen new cases at this Court yesterday—namely, six charges of drunk and incapable, three of theft, and one each of assault, breach of peace, loitering, and suspected theft.

Edinburgh Photographic Society.— The first popular meeting for the season under the auspices of this Society was held last night in Queen Street Hall, when a series of 'instantaneous studies from Nature' were shown by Mr William H. Davies, honorary lecturer of the Society, by means of the oxy-hydrogen light. Mr Davies, in the course of some introductory remarks, pointed out the great disadvantages under which the photographer laboured in attempting to attain the successful representation of any animal or object in motion.

January 16th

1913: This story featured in *The Scotsman* on this day:

A Scottish Marriage Dissolved. In the Divorce Court yesterday, before Mr Justice Bucknill, Mrs Katherine Scott W. Holland, Mid-Lothian, petitioned for the dissolution of her marriage with Harry R. H. Holland, her husband. Counsel for the petitioner stated that the parties were married at the Caledonian Station Hotel, Edinburgh, on 3 September 1908. The marriage was by banns and the form of the Church of Scotland. After the marriage the parties lived at different places. In June 1911, the petitioner was under the necessity to institute proceedings for restitution of conjugal rights of the marriage, as then proved by a Scottish lawyer named Campbell. On 13 November of the same year a decree was pronounced in the petitioner's favour, which was not complied with by the respondent. The petitioner had made an unsuccessful effort to get her husband to return to her and make a home for her. On 3 September the respondent wrote stating that he had stayed with a lady who was not his wife at an hotel at Brighton. Inquiries were made, and as this was found to be correct, the present proceedings were instituted. After evidence bearing out counsel's statement, his Lordship pronounced a *decree nisi* with costs.

January 17th

1513: King James IV issued regulations to deal with the pestilence and ordered the provost, bailies and council to put them into effect. Accordingly, the burgh was divided into three parts. The first, east of Forresters' Wynd on both sides of the street and under the town wall to Castlehill. This was to be controlled by Thomas Wardlaw. The second part ran from the stair of the Tolbooth where Walter Young lived, in the north part of the High Street to the Loupin' Stane. This was to be controlled by Walter Young. The third part ran from the Loupin' Stane to Forresters' Wynd in the south part of the High Street, with part of the Cowgate. This was to be controlled by George Dickson. (*ERBE*)

———— •◆• ————

1861: 'Reconnoiterer Glass, 9 pence. Very portable, light, and Achromatic and so strong that the Houses, &c., in Fife, Ten Miles off, are plainly seen from Messrs Salom's Windows. The *marvellous* Cheapness of this "Tourists' Favourite", to whom it is a *never ending* delight, arises from the economy of labour and profit permissible through *immense* Sales. Most valuable to Riflemen. Posted free, 10 shillings. An *Extraordinary* Favourite with Farmers, Keepers, &c. Salom & Co., 25 South Hanover Street.' (*The Scotsman*)

January 18th

1823: 'We understand that the late Miss Stair Primrose of Hermitage, Leith, has left legacies to two of the charitable institutions of that place. One of fifty pounds to the Female Charity School of Industry, and another of twenty pounds to the Society for Relief of Indigent Old Women. We observe, with pleasure, that the work of ornamental improvement is still proceeded in upon the North Loch and the grounds contiguous. Within these few days, a number of full sized trees have been planted upon the north side of the Castlehill, at irregular distances; and though the appearance of them, at present, from their being pruned of their luxuriances, is rather grotesque, their effect, in the course of a year or two, must be very delightful. Last week, upwards of a dozen bakers' apprentices were fined by the Police Court in a small sum each, for carrying their bake-boards upon the pavement. When it is recollected that about four years ago, a lady lost her life in consequence of having been struck by one of these boards, the master bakers owe it as a duty to the public to discourage, as much as possible, this dangerous practice on the part of their servants.' (*The Scotsman*)

January 19th

1815: 'Theatre-Royal. Will be presented, the grand *Tragedy of Pizarro*, to which will be added, 14th time, The new Pantomime of Harlequin & Nostrodamus, Or, Mirth And Magic. A New Medley Overture, Composed and Arranged by Mr W. Penson. Scenery. The magic Study of the Sorcerer Nostrodamus, an Apothecary's Shop and Sylvan Bower. The Temple Of Concord, as Exhibited in the Park in London at the Jubilee in August. After numerous Incidents, Tricks, and Escapes, the Pantomime ends with the Superb Palace of Clouds, and Revolving Sun. Yesterday The State Lottery began Drawing in London, and the First Drawn Prize above £25 may prove Thirty Thousand Pounds. Whole Tickets and Shares, in the greatest variety in the kingdom, will continue on Sale at the Fortunate Office of Andrew Sievewright, 102 South Bridge, Edinburgh, till Friday Evening. Currant Wines, &c. E. Wilson, Newbattle, begs leave to acquaint her friends and the public, that she has always on hand a Stock of Currant and Gooseberry Wines. For the accommodation of her friends in Edinburgh and the neighbourhood, she has prevailed with Mr Thomas Arrol, 27 Prince's Street, to sell it on her account, who will always have a quantity on hand, and who will receive orders for her.' (*Caledonian Mercury*)

January 20th

1671: The council received a petition from a teacher from Poland, Mr John Alexander, who asked permission to establish a school for learning German and Polish. Permission was granted to him to advertise publicly to teach those languages until otherwise informed. A year later (17 April 1672) a Frenchman, William Destinbrue, was given permission to open a public school, either in the town or the suburbs, for teaching French, a language considered to be very useful. On 22 November 1672, the council reaffirmed its support for his French school, allowing him to charge six pounds Scots quarterly to city burgesses and their children, and whatever sum should be agreeable to both parties. In order to encourage him, the council granted him the sum of one hundred Scots merks. On 26 March 1675, the council received a request from Louis Defrance, saying that he was a highly proficient musician and produced his certificates to prove his knowledge of French and Italian music. His music school was approved. Defrance applied for a grant of house rent, but the council reserved consideration of his request. His prospectus promised instruction in Italian and French tunes, such as were sung at the French court. *(ERBE)*

January 21st

1802: These cautionary stories appeared in the *Caledonian Mercury*:

On Friday, a young man took lodgings in the Cowgate, Edinburgh, and, next morning, in the absence of the landlady, entered the apartment of a fellow-lodger, and took away a dark duffle half-wide coat, and several other articles of wearing apparel — He pretended he was a watchmaker; is about five feet three inches high, dark complexion; wore a dark blue coat, white waistcoat, and white stockings. Between Saturday night and Sunday morning an attempt was made to force off the window of a grocer's shop in the High Street. One of the panes was broken, but it is probable the depredator had been scared, before he had fully accomplished his purpose.

Assault. On Wednesday evening, about nine o'clock, high words and a scuffle ensued between a shoemaker and a soldier in a house in Ponton Street, when the shoemaker took one of his working knives and stabbed the soldier in the belly, in so dreadful a manner, that part of his entrails came out. Medical assistance was procured, and the wound sowed up, but little hopes are entertained of his recovery. The shoemaker was committed to jail.

January 22nd

1810: 'Fourth, and Positively the last Subscription Concert, in which Madame Catalani will perform. Friday, the 26th January 1810. Mr Corri has the honour of informing the Subscribers and the Public, that Madame Catalani being now perfectly recovered of her late disposition, the Concert will be in the Assembly Rooms, George Street. Plan of the Concert: ACT I Haydn's Grand Overture, in which is introduced the celebrated Indian march. Song, 'Lochinvar', Miss Davenport. New Duet, Harp and Piano-Forte, Mr and Miss Dale. Canadian Boat Song for three voices, Miss Davenport, Mr Jones and Mr Kent. Grand Bravura Song, Madame Catalani. ACT II Pleyel's New Overture, for Violin, Oboe, Tenor, Flute and Violoncello. Song, 'Angels ever Bright' Madame Catalani, the first time of her performing it in this City. — *Handel.* Concerto Organ, Mr Alexander.— *Handel.* New Air, with variations, 'O momento di contento', Madame Catalani. — *Pucitta.* Finale — *Gyrewetz.* Leader of the Band, Mr Girolamo Stabilini. Mr Corri to direct at the Piano-Forte. Principal Oboe, Mr W. Catalani. To begin precisely at Eight o'clock. Tickets, seven shillings, to be had at Mr Corri's Music Shop, front of the Theatre-Royal (late Corri's Rooms), and at the Assembly Rooms, on the night of the performance.' (*Caledonian Mercury*)

January 23rd

1800: 'To Be Sold By Public Roup, Upon Wednesday the 12th of February 1800, within the Royal Exchange Coffeehouse, Edinburgh. The House, No 36, on the south side of George's Square, with the Offices and Plot thereto belonging, presently occupied by Mrs Robertson, at the yearly rent of £90 Sterling. The house contains a dining-room, drawing-room, ten other rooms, kitchen, servants hall, excellent cellars, besides closets, &c. There is a water-pipe lately brought into the house, and a pump-well belonging to it. Without the house there is a laundry, water closet, coal cellar, and ashes house. The offices belonging to the house are a coach-house, and a stable for four horses, with hay-loft above them. The house to be seen on Thursdays, from one to three o'clock and particulars as to the price, &c. may be learned on application to Archibald Dunbar, W.S., who will show the title-deeds. To Be Sold by public roup, within John's Coffeehouse, Edinburgh, on Wednesday the 29th day of January curt, that Lodging in Wilson's Court, Canongate, belonging to the late Alexander Gordon of Campbelton. The premises may be seen every lawful day from one to three o'clock.' (*Caledonian Mercury*)

January 24th

1644: On this day the comptroller of accounts advanced funds for the equipment of the Town's Regiment for service in England under the command of Colonel James Rae and for an expedition to Stirling. Colonel Rea submitted accounts of £1,227 17s 4d, which he had sent in procuring regimental colours, partisans (a pole weapon) for the under officers, drums, axes, marking irons for horses and other miscellaneous materials. Merchant John Tweidie and surgeon John Scot were recompensed for buying baggage horses at £3,838 11s 4d. John Kniblo and John Livingstoun, merchants, bought canvas and cotton cloth to make tents and sacks, as well as ladles, cups, dishes, spoons, pots, pans (£1,078 2s 6d). John Kniblo was paid £6,141 6s 8d for arms he supplied for the use of the Regiment. Colonel Rea also received the cost of a surgeon's chest (£210). The provost, Sir John Smith, was recompensed for the £20 he paid for a horse for the minister of the Regiment. The goldsmith Robert Gibsoun was paid £53, 12 d for making a large gilt bowl for Lieutenant Colonel Mill and £44 for two pieces of gold given to Colonel Rae. (*ERBE*)

January 25th

1815: On this day, highway robbers Kelly and O'Neill were executed on Morningside Road, near the place where they committed the robbery.

———•◆•———

1816: In MacEwan's Rooms, one hundred gentlemen dined as part of the first public celebration of the birthday of the poet Robert Burns. Mr Walter Scott was in the company and it was resolved to have a public celebration of the poet's birthday in Edinburgh every three years.

———•◆•———

1817: The first edition of *The Scotsman* newspaper was published, consisting of four pages. The Editor wrote: 'Before proceeding to the ordinary business of our paper, we beg to observe, that we have not chosen the name of SCOTSMAN to preserve an invidious distinction, but with the view of rescuing it from the odium of servility. With that stain removed, a Scotsman may well claim brotherhood with an Englishman, and there ought now to be no rivalry between them, but in the cause of regulated freedom. In that cause it is our ambition to labour; but we must remind our more sanguine friends, that it is impossible in a first number to develop all our principles. Time and change of circumstances afford the only sure tests of human conduct.' (*The Scotsman*)

January 26th

1510: At three o'clock in the afternoon, provost Alexander Lauder, dean of guild William Fowler and the burgh council, assembled at the tenement of Christina Lamb on the south side of the Cowgate, along with James Aikman and the town councillor and surveyor Walter Chepman, to resolve a boundary dispute between Mrs Lamb and Bartholomew Wawane. The lawyers established from the old bound charter belonging to Mrs Lamb that a boundary line running from the adjoining stone wall in Walter Chapman's yard to the Wawane croft enclosed two and a half roods in a plot of waste land 5ft wide running up to the vennel going west from the Kirk of Field. The judgment arrived that Mrs Lamb should be allowed to maintain that distance in her plot from Bartholomew Wawane's land as marked out by the wooden fence fixed into the ground. *(ERBE).*

Three years earlier, Walter Chepman, with his business partner Andrew Myllar (who had served his time as a printer in France), were given permission by King James IV to set up a printing-press. Their earliest printed volume is John Lydgate's *The making and disport of Chaucer*, 4 April 1508. (http://www.nls.uk/firstscottishbooks/)

January 27th

1526: From Edinburgh, under the great seal, King James V wrote to Abbot George Crichton of Holyrood, councillor and keeper of the privy seal, expressing his appreciation of the 'good, faithful and gratuitous service' provided by the provost, bailies, council and community of Edinburgh since the death of his father, King James IV, at the Battle of Flodden. He valued especially the hardships they endured through the 'great injury, trouble and wrath of the nobility'. Accordingly, the King put away his anger and any thought of revenge for the burgh's treasonable rebellion against the late Great Chamberlain John Lord Fleming. He forgave their plotting against the Chancellor and Lords of his Privy Council and their resistance against his cousin, James Earl of Arran, Lord Hamilton by closing the gates of the Netherbow Port and beating him back, although he was the King's Lieutenant and provost of the burgh. The King also forgave the provost, bailies, council and community of all other treasonable actions, transgressions, crimes and offences, with the exception of any murder, fire-raising, rape of women and common theft. This pragmatic remission was communicated to James Beaton, Archbishop of St Andrews and Lord Chancellor of Scotland. (*ERBE*)

January 28th

1830: 'To the Editor. Sir— May I beg through your useful paper to call the notice of those whose business it is to superintend the repairs of the Lothian Road, to state of its footpath, from Bread Street to the West Church Gate. From there being no wall betwixt it and the adjoining field, which in some parts is six feet higher than the footpath, the earth has crumbled down, so that about one half of it is at an angle of 45 degrees in mud; whilst on the other the action of puddling is carried on by every passer-by.' (*Caledonian Mercury*)

———•◆•———

1830: 'Society of Antiquaries of Scotland. The third evening meeting of his Society, for this session, was held on Monday last the 25th, in the apartments on the Mound. The Curator noticed the following Donations, which had been presented to the Society:—A Cap found lately behind the wood lining of one of the rooms in Holyroodhouse, called Queen Mary's apartments—by James Ritchie, Esq. architect. The conclusion of Colonel Miller's *Essay on the Site of the Battle of Mons Grampius* was read, together with extracts from a Dissertation on the same subject, by the Rev. Mr Small.' (*Caledonian Mercury*)

January 29th

1820: These advertisements appeared in the *Caledonian Mercury*:

Honduras and St Domingo Mahogany for Sale. To be sold by auction, in Messrs J. and W. Gowans' Yard, Leith Walk, upon Tuesday the 1st February, at twelve o'clock. Logs Honduras Mahogany, and St Domingo ditto. The very best quality, and many of them Table Size. W. Grinly, Broker, St James' Square, Edinburgh.

To the Shoemakers to be disposed of: A Shoemaker's Stock of Boots and Shoes, Shop Furniture, &c. The Shop is in one of the most eligible situations, and presents a favourable opportunity to a person wishing to commence business, so the purchaser may have immediate possession. Apply to William Peddie, 435 Lawnmarket.

Rowland's Macassar Oil, freshly supplied. This Oil is the original and genuine, composed of the most salubrious properties, and is warranted to afford the greatest nourishment to the human hair: removes the scurf, harshness and dryness, makes it soft and glossy; prevents it falling off, or turning grey; creates a thick growth on the baldest place.

January 30th

1607: It was agreed between the bailies, the council and John Orley, an Englishman, that he should serve the town as a musician with his shawms (double-reeded wind instrument, with a piercing sound, from the Middle East) and hautbois (like the shawm, a fore-runner of the oboe), assisted by four other proficient musicians, who would walk along the Cowgate and through High Street playing their instruments and singing early every morning. They would then play again at midday for a given time from St Giles' steeple. In the evening, they would all blow and play for a period between six and seven o'clock. For this the council would pay him one hundred merks a year. They also authorised the town treasurer to have made and supply him and his musicians with five silver badges showing the town's coat of arms, each badge weighing two ounces. This commission was accepted by John Orley (who was present at the council meeting). Although George Heriot was asked to make a mould for the badge, it appears that the installation of the musicians did not go ahead – although it is possible that the arrangement was trialled. *(ERBE)*

January 3-1st

1818: 'Corporation Gossip.—It was pleasant to observe the unanimous way in which the Incorporation of this City expressed their sentiments on Burgh Reform. We say unanimous, because we consider the small minority, which the utmost exertion and influence of the junto have been able to command, is but the lees of the Corporations. This minority is composed of—The Weavers—in number about 8, whose Deacon is the present Convener. They appear as tenacious of the antiquated set of the Burgh, as if they had woven the Blue Blanket. The Fleshers, in number about 12, have been lately taking a cup of plotey *alias* mulled-wine with the descendants of Henry the 9th, and certain other great whippers-in of administration. The Furriers and Skinners, in number about 9. With these gentlemen 'Robes and Furred Gowns' cover a multitude of errors. They would as life be flayed alive, as depart from their volatory mode of election. We hope the Bakers' next batch will be better leavened,—the last was most indigestible; and we really expect that the honest and independent members of the Corporation will not think that the staff of life depends upon the shake of a baton, or the wink of a representative of the Club.' (*The Scotsman*)

February 1st

1800: 'Militia Substitutes Wanted. A Handsome Bounty will be given to Young Men, who are willing to serve as Substitutes in the Militia, by applying to Sievewright and Greig, No. 12, Nicholson's Street, Edinburgh; or their Agents in the country formerly advertised. NB Besides the Bounty they will be entitled to a number of privileges and advantages in consequence of their service.' (*Caledonian Mercury*)

1800: 'A Capital Tavern and Hotel in the City of Edinburgh to be Let, for such number of years as can be agreed upon, and entered to at Whitsunday next. That Large, Elegant and Well-frequented TAVERN in the New Assembly Close, known by the name of the *King's Arms*; containing ten good rooms, one of which is 35 feet by 30 feet, with two kitchens, several cellars, water-pipe, and every other conveniency adapted to a large tavern.—As also, the Ball-room adjoining, which was formerly the Edinburgh Assembly Hall, and is much frequented as a place of exhibition and dancing-room, all belonging to the Incorporation of St Mary's Chapel, and presently possessed by Mr John Reid. For particulars, apply to Alexander Gardner, Exchequer; or John Ross, painter, Castlehill, present treasurer to the said Incorporations.' (*Caledonian Mercury*)

February 2nd

1860: On this day the *Caledonian Mercury* reported on a suspicious case:

> Yesterday morning, shortly after seven o'clock, the grave-digger employed in the Canongate Burial-ground observed a parcel lying close to the wall of the ground, which, on being opened, was found to contain the body of a child, with the head cut off and rolled up in the same parcel. The body was evidently that of a still-born child, and had the appearance of having been kept for some time. The only clue … is a statement by the grave-digger that on Monday he was accosted by an Irish labourer, who asked him how much he would charge for burying a still-born child. The individual in question had also put the same question to the Recorder, but the burial never took place.

News of an 'Important Railway Case' also featured in the newspaper:

> A case … arose out of an action brought [in the Small Debt Court] against the North British Railway Company by a gentleman named Anderson, who complained that while travelling in a first-class carriage from Musselburgh to Edinburgh on the 17th of December last with his wife and daughter the carriage was entered by a gentleman in a state of intoxication, who, as was alleged, had spoiled one of the ladies' dresses by vomiting upon it.

February 3rd

1820: 'The Proclaiming of King George IV.—Major-General Sir Thomas Bradford, Commander in Chief of the Forces in Scotland, ordered a detachment of the 10th Hussars (his present Majesty's own regiment), to be in readiness to march into the city. Meanwhile the Castle flag was hoisted half-mast high, and at eleven o'clock the firing of minute guns began, which continued till 60 guns were fired, being one for every year of his late Majesty's reign. The 10th Hussars lined the streets from the Cross to the Castlehill, where the ground was kept by the 4th veteran battalion. At twelve o'clock the procession moved from the Parliament House to the Royal Exchange. When it reached the Mercat Cross, the Heralds Pursuivant, Lord Provost, &c. ascended the balcony in front of the Exchange, when the proclamation was read by the Lord Provost and Heralds. Then the Heralds proclaimed the style and title of his Majesty King George the Fourth three times, each time accompanied by a flourish of trumpets and loud acclamations, with a royal salute from the guns in the Castle ... the day was very unfavourable, as a dense fog hung over the city, notwithstanding which, the whole had a grand and imposing appearance.' (*Caledonian Mercury*)

February 4th

1510: The leaders and masters of the Cordiners (shoemakers), including the kirkmaster John Davidson, appeared before the burgh council and presented a request that their statutes, articles and regulations should be approved and granted by the council in a seal of cause, being in conformity with the love of Almighty God, the honour of the realm, the reputation and benefit of the burgh and the profit of the King's subjects (and others who entered the burgh) and for the increase of divine service at the altar of St Crispin in St Giles' Kirk. This measure was aimed at harmonising the many conflicting regulations that had been handed down over the ages and also to avoid ambiguity or the dangers caused by lack of direction. These regulations included a mandatory seven-year apprenticeship; a 6s 8d payment to be made by every new apprentice to support divine service at the craft altar; no apprentice would be permitted to open a shoemaker's business in the burgh without having been assessed as sufficiently technically skilled and experienced, and being admitted into the craft by the masters, and created a freeman and burgess of Edinburgh, and having paid an entry fee. (*ERBE*)

February 5th

1523: Sir William Sinclair of Roslin, Knight, praying for the eternal happiness of his soul, his family's and for anyone from whom he or his predecessors had taken properties unlawfully for which proper satisfaction had not been made, and for the eternal happiness of all the faithful departed and all the benefactors of Rosslyn Chapel, gave and granted to the four collegiate canons and perpetually confirmed land beside Rosslyn Chapel as an endowment for the construction of four houses with gardens for four priests, each a plot measuring 112ft by 180ft. The duties of the priests were to offer up prayers and intercessions for everyone mentioned above. Sir William guaranteed this arrangement to the canons who would sing the Holy Office day and night and offer Mass for the souls of the departed. Sir William signed and attached his seal to the charter in Edinburgh in the presence of Robert Dickson, James Maxwell, James Mossman and John Davidson, with public notary William Stevenson and a large crowd of others. The seal showed a ragged cross in red and white wax. (Father Richard Augustine Hay, *Genealogie of the Sainteclaires of Rosslyn,* published 1835)

February 6th

1875: On this day *The Scotsman* printed an article about the burning of the Theatre-Royal, Broughton Street:

The conflagration was sudden in its outbreak, and over-poweringly rapid in its progress. From the first alarm, about two o'clock, hardly half-an-hour elapsed before the whole theatre was a mass of raging flame, which there was no hope of subduing, and by four o'clock nothing remained but the four walls enclosing a mass of smouldering ruins. Between one and two o'clock in the afternoon the various members of the theatrical company had repaired, as was their wont, to an office adjoining the stage, known as the 'Treasury', where Mr Nevin, the treasurer, attended weekly for the payment of salaries and settlement of accounts. On the left of the stage, as seen from the auditorium, the principal apartments were the Treasury, wardrobe room, and manager's room; on the opposite side were the various dressing-rooms occupied by the company, as also the gas-room, containing the oxygen and hydrogen tanks used in connection with the lime-light, which was under the level of the stage … an ominous cloud of dense black smoke was seen by the passers-by to start from the roof over the part of the theatre occupied by the stage.

February 7th

1700: The council examined the sad and deplorable state of the city occasioned by the late terrible fire on the previous Saturday night about ten o'clock. It broke out of the north-east corner of the Meal Market and consumed the whole market to ashes, along with all the stately buildings that belonged to the late Bailie Thomas Robertson on both sides of the Kirkheugh (the slope beside St Giles), parts of the Royal Exchange and whole Parliament Close, except the Treasury Room, which by great providence had been well preserved. The council recommended that a list of all the families affected by the fire should be made, so that the council would know which persons were able to absorb their losses and which could not afford to do so, so that speedy remedy might be taken to relieve them. The bailie was also to summon the collectors of the property taxes and get an exact record of the valuation of all the burnt buildings. Similarly, the council recommended the bailies of the town and suburbs to ask the constable in each of their areas to search carefully for all looted goods so that they could be secured for their rightful owners. (*ERBE*)

February 8th

1626: The council, the extraordinary deacons with nineteen merchants and nine craftsmen, saw that there was turmoil abroad, with wars and rumours of wars, uncertain when a foreign army might invade. They considered the fact that many of the inhabitants of the burgh were not properly prepared for military service both in equipment and training. They noted that it was usually not superiority in numbers that won a battle but knowledge and experience of warfare that gave confidence in time of war. Therefore the council decided that it was vital that every inhabitant should be taught and instructed in the rules of war and exercised and strengthened by military discipline such as might be practised by an enemy on the battlefield. All the inhabitants of the burgh would be divided into eight separate companies, each company containing two hundred persons or more. (*ERBE*)

These military preparations followed closely on King Charles' decision to send an expedition to assist the Huguenot Protestants in La Rochelle. By the end of 1626, Great Britain was at war with both France and Spain.

February 9th

1850: In *The Scotsman,* an article concerning the urban heart of Midlothian was printed on this day:

Frost prevailed over the greater part of last month, and more snow fell than in any January since 1838. Towards the close of the month fresh open rainy weather set in, and the land is now thoroughly soaked, so much so, that even the furrows of well-drained fields are carrying little rivulets, and the drains are pouring forth a full stream of not very limpid water. On light naturally dry land ploughing of lea or stubble can be proceeded with without injury; but, where clay exists, or upon partially drained fields, it has not been advisable to prosecute the working falling into arrear from the continuance of frost. Much manure has been laid out, and this practice seems increasing—the labour during spring being lightened, and the green crops earlier sown. The wheat has come from under the snow strong and vigorous, as well as the young grass; while the snow-drops, the harbinger of spring, is now visible. Turnips have not suffered from frost, and afford the usual amount of food. Sheep feeding on them in fields have not improved much of late, and deaths have been numerous. Cattle, when fed from the store, have thriven well.

February 10th

1800: On this day, these property advertisements appeared in the *Caledonian Mercury*:

House in Princes Street for Sale by Private Bargain. No 34, very centrically and advantageously situated. It consists of three storeys besides the attic and sunk ones, with back ground, excellent coach-house, stables, and hay loft; hen-house, garde mange, water pipe, cellars, catacombs, and many other conveniences. The sunk and first floors are well adapted for, and may be easily converted into convenient shops, without materially injuring the remainder, which will still make a genteel and commodious house. To be seen on Mondays and Thursdays, from 12 to 3 o'clock, and particulars may be learned of Mr Maclean, Antigua Street.

Villa to be Let, and entered to at Whitsunday next. The Villa of Newington, situated within a mile of Edinburgh, entering from the Dalkeith Road. The house is large and commodious, containing dining-room, 25 feet by 20; drawing-room, 31 feet by 21; with fifteen other fire-rooms, besides light closets, and every kind of convenience in the kitchen storey. There are two gardens, with a hot-house, and gardener's house. The offices consist of a coach-house, and stable for five horses — the gardener will show the house and garden. For further particulars enquire at Alexander Wood, Writer to the Signet, York Place.

February 11th

1890: 'Sir,—With reference to the movement now being made to get a ride or gallop in the new Inverleith Park, I would like to point out that the Town Council can very easily cause such a ride to be made without almost any alteration on the plan for laying out the park. The plan for laying out the park shows a carriage road running near the side of the park, and going completely round it. In addition, two other roads cross it — the first from the Arboretum gate to the road which runs in front of Fettes College; the second bisecting the first, and running from the farm steading northwards. At the point of intersection of these two roads a bandstand is to be placed. No one will have a word to say against these two roads, but what is the use of the road inside the park skirting its borders? On three sides the park is bounded by three as fine roads as ever were made. Who will go off these to drive along the road inside the park? All that is wanted is a carriage road on the south side of the ground.' (*The Scotsman*)

February 12th

1829: 'On Thursday, betwixt the hours of two and three o'clock, a number of young men assembled on the Calton-hill and proceeded to equip a large effigy of an Anatomist, who has been rendered very obnoxious to the public by recent events. The figure was dressed in a black coat, raised aloft on a pole, and had a label attached to its back, naming the person intended to be represented [Dr Robert Knox]. About 3 o'clock the procession left the Calton-hill, and proceeded along the Bridges ... On arriving at Newington, the mob halted at the gentleman's door, and a number of lads deliberately proceeded to 'Burke' the effigy, amid loud huzzas. Having squeezed and throttled the figure for some time, they tied a rope about its neck, and suspended it from a small tree, but the branches giving way, the effigy was thrown on the top of the tree preparatory to immolation. A lighted torch was then procured, but before ignition could be effected, a strong body of police arrived, and took several of the ringleaders into custody. The road being newly metalled in that neighbourhood, the mob took advantage of the freely available ammunition and the doctor's windows were smashed.' (*The Scotsman*)

February 13th

1826: On this day *The Scotsman* printed an article on the Inauguration of the Royal Institution:

On Monday, the Directors, with the artists, and a number of amateurs and gentlemen belonging to the city, dined in the new Hall. The Earl of Elgin was in the chair, supported by the Lord Provost and the Earl of Leven … After the routine toasts were disposed of, the Chairman gave, 'The Institution for the encouragement of the Fine Arts in Scotland' and explained its objectives, and the advantages which it was expected to produce to the country … The healths of Mr Skene, the secretary, Mr Allan, Mr H. W. Williams and the Reverend Mr Thomson, and the memory of Sir Henry Raeburn, were severally drunk. When 'The health of the amateur contributors' to the Exhibition was given, Mr Scrope replied in a speech which was much admired for good taste, and knowledge of the history and principles of the art which it displayed. The party broke up between eight and nine o'clock. The Institution … is founded on the model of the British Institution in London. 'Its aims embrace whatever may at any time appear calculated to promote the improvement of the Fine Arts, by exciting a more lively interest in their successful progress.'

February 14th

1659: The council received a paper sent by the ministers and Kirk Sessions which listed a number of scandalous profanations of the Sabbath day. These included many both young and old persons, who walked or sat and played on the Castlehill and upon the streets and other places after the sermons, so that it was made perfectly clear for all to see that family worship was neglected, leading to a number of harmful consequences. Therefore, the council ordered several pairs of wooden stocks, so that anyone walking without good reason or sitting idly on the streets, should either pay a penalty of eighteen pence sterling or be put into the stocks. (*ERBE*)

———•◆•———

1666: Andrew Cheyn, treasurer of the College (university) informed the council that the janitor had broken through two stone walls of the building in order to set up an apparatus for brewing beer. He had also repaired a number of items in the College and submitted inflated accounts for the same. He had not handed in the rent money from the students, although he had collected it. He had taken part in smuggling goods over the town walls, involving the students in betting and lotteries. (*ERBE*)

February 15th

1699: The council discussed the various lotteries organised within the houses and upon the streets of the city and suburbs, which harmed children and servants in the houses by persuading them to idles and vice, besides losing their money. Accordingly, the council placed a ban on every kind of lottery – the Wheel of Fortune, Jobbing lotteries, Royal Oak, Fair Chance and others. If the council discovered any such lottery being organised within houses or on the streets in the city and its suburbs, then the lottery and its equipment would be confiscated. The owners of houses where lotteries were played might be fined or imprisoned by the magistrates each time they were caught. Thirty years before, on 8 December 1669, it was all so different. Then, the council had granted a warrant to Robert Clerk to keep and organise a play or game within the city, called the Pricking Book Lottery, which used plates, rings, glasses, cabinets, hoods and whistles as prizes. However, on 7 October 1674, the council received a petition from an Englishman, Henry Debrie, who stated that Captain William Fraser of Beltie held the Royal patent for the game for life. The council granted his petition. *(ERBE)*

February 16th

1801: 'The Persons following, balloted to serve in the militia of this City and Districts, having failed to attend, or provide substitutes, at a general court of Lieutenancy, held in this Office on the 11th day of February instant, notwithstanding of the intimations made to them in terms of the Militia Acts to that effect, viz. District of Edinburgh: John Kerr, spirit-dealer, Niddry Street; Robert Waugh, journeyman baker at Cleghorn's and Sceale's, bakers in Leith. District of Canongate: Joseph Cooper, shoemaker, McKell's Land, Fleshmarket Close. Therefore, the absentees before named, being now liable to be apprehended and punished as deserters, and in case of not being taken within two calendar months from the foresaid date, then the parishes to which such deserters shall belong, shall, within one calendar month after notice given, procure a fit and able person to serve instead of such deserters, and in default, the Deputy Lieutenants and Justices of the Peace shall proceed to ballot for others from the original ballot boxes … it is earnestly recommended to parishes in general, and particularly to such persons on whom the ballot has not yet fallen, to … give the necessary information … where one or all of the above absentees may be found.' (*Caledonian Mercury*)

February 17th

1598: King James was in the Great Kirk of Edinburgh at the sermon. Mr Patrick Gallaway read out the method of dividing the four kirks of Edinburgh: a quarter of the town for each kirk. Between nine and ten in the morning, a great darkness came because of an eclipse. Such darkness had not been seen in living memory. The population of Edinburgh did not know what it was and thought it was Domesday. Merchants and others who were confused, shut their inner and outer doors and ran to the kirk to pray, as if it was the end of the world. (*Diarey of Robert Birrel*)

------◆------

1812: On this day, a shocking accident was reported in the *Caledonian Mercury*:

Yesterday, during the time of worship in the forenoon, an elderly woman at Portsburgh, put a period to her life, by hanging herself. Friday evening, an accident occurred in Leith Walk, by the starting of a spirited horse, which was yoked in a cart, and with which he ran off with such rapidity, that the nails which join the body of the cart to the axle, jumped out and left the wheels; and one of the shafts struck Andrew Kerr, a servant of Mr Learmonth's, with such violence, that he died a short time after in his house.

February 18th

1473: In the chamber of the Tolbooth the provost, bailies and council of the burgh of Edinburgh recorded that they had agreed to the request of the master-craftsmen Hatmakers present to choose a deacon from among them who would preserve the standards and regulations of the craft. The Hatmakers' regulations stipulated that those wishing to be masters of the craft had to produce two examples of their work and insisted that they should not take on apprentices for less than five years. So as to show the strength and high standards of their craft, they received from the council a seal of cause (symbol of institution) to testify to the commercial standards that Hatmakers needed to achieve. (*ERBE*)

———•◆•———

1842: After three years of construction, at a cost of £1.25m, the Edinburgh & Glasgow Railway opened. In the late morning, directors and their friends travelled from Glasgow to Edinburgh and, in the afternoon, fifty-two carriages went from Edinburgh to Glasgow, where the dignitaries were given a lavish banquet. The euphoria of the Edinburgh to Glasgow return was somewhat dampened, however, by the fact that a mindless vandal cut the Cowlairs rope! Once the railways were up and running, great disputes took place on the subject of Sunday trains.

February 19th

1801: 'Sale of Nursery stock, and subset of Nursery Gardens, at Leith Walk, Edinburgh. To be sold by public voluntary roup upon Friday the 28th day of February inst. within John's Coffee-house, at six o'clock in the evening, by the Trustees of David Richmond, seed merchant, West Bow, and his creditors. Lot 1st, being Quarryholes Nursery Park, situated nearly in the middle of the Walk, east side, and consisting of about four acres, properly fenced and enclosed, together with a delightful commodious dwelling house, of two storeys, and stable, cellar, cart-house, and house for a servant thereto belonging. There is a hot-house and greenhouse on this Nursery, containing a considerable collection of Green-house plants &c. Also the materials of these houses, of wood, glass, hewn stone and stone pavement. Lot 2nd, being a Nursery Park of five acres or thereby, situated upon the north-west side of that line of road, leading from the west side of the Walk towards Bonnyton Toll-Bar. Possession to the Gardens may be had immediately after the sale, and to the houses at Whitsunday next. For other particulars apply to Mr Sinclair, merchant at the West Bow, one of the trustees, or to Peter Halkerston, solicitor, New Street, Edinburgh.' (*Caledonian Mercury*)

February 20th

1598: Thomas Dobie drowned himself in the Quarry Holes beside Holyrood Abbey. The following morning his body was taken, facing backwards on a cart, through the town and then hanged on a gallows for having committed suicide. (*Diarey of Robert Birrel*)

———•◆•———

1809: 'Capital coal in the Neighbourhood of Edinburgh to be let. The extensive and valuable seams of coal on the Marquess of Abercorn's estates of Duddingston and Brunstain, in the county of Mid-Lothian, are to be let separately or together, for such terms of years as shall be agreed upon. The coal is of the best quality, and this field possesses the double advantage of being the nearest, in point of situation, to Edinburgh and Leith, and (it is believed) the only one to which a wagon road or iron railway can be made, which may be done easily, and at a comparatively small expense.—When the quality, extent, and local advantages of this coal, as well as the high price and unlimited market in this neighbourhood are considered, it may be fairly said, that to a person or company of enterprise and capital, few better or more promising speculations have ever been offered.' (*Caledonian Mercury*)

February 21st

1839: On this day, the *Caledonian Mercury* featured an article about Old Greyfriars Soup Kitchen:

The parish of Old Greyfriars is one of the poorest in Edinburgh; and while there is much suffering from poverty at all times, that suffering in this Winter peculiarly and painfully aggravated by the present high price of provisions for the poor — potatoes being double their usual price, while oatmeal is one-fourth higher than ordinary. The Kirk Session taking this into consideration, resolved to establish a Soup Kitchen. They divided the parish into small districts, and along with a large number of gentlemen belonging to the Congregation, carefully visited these districts: while some were found who did not require the charity, and while there were others who could pay a little, they met with a large number on the borders of actual destitution, to whom the supply must be given gratis. After the most careful enquiries on the part of the visitors, so as to prevent impositions and abuse, and with the most prudent management, yet the expenses (exclusive of what is received for the soup and bread) amount to £3 per day, as there are about 420 families, or 1,280 individuals supplied daily.

February 22nd

1467: Having been given a charter by King James III consenting to a request from the provost, bailies, councillors and the community of Edinburgh for the erection of St Giles into a Collegiate Kirk, the same officials asked Pope Paul II to change the Kirk of St Giles from a parish church under the bishop into 'collegiate' status – staffed by a small community of canons (priests) who could more cheaply and effectively provide some of the spiritual and secular benefits of much larger monasteries. The Pope duly consented and asked the Bishop of Galloway and the Abbot of Holyrood (itself a collegiate church) to erect St Giles' Collegiate Kirk. Over forty such collegiate churches existed around this period in Scotland but these religious establishments became less attractive propositions by the following century, and many collegiate churches, such as Rosslyn Chapel in Midlothian, were never finished, with little more than their east-facing choirs being completed. (*ERBE*)

1854: Several people were killed in Leith Wynd, a narrow street bounded by high tenements on one side and the city wall on the other. A large section of the wall collapsed into the street, burying all who happened to be in the street at the time.

February 23rd

1573: The miseries of civil discord led the nation to wish ardently for peace. A treaty to that effect was agreed on between the leaders of the opposite factions, but Sir William Kirkcaldy would not be included in it. The Regent solicited Queen Elizabeth's assistance to reduce the castle and Sir William Dury, who before this had left Scotland, returned with 1,500 foot soldiers and a train of artillery. He summoned Kirkcaldy to surrender but he, in token of defiance, unfurled his ensign from the top of the garrison. The English general and the Regent opened the trenches and pushed the siege vigorously. The fortress was defended with great gallantry but a great part of the fortifications being demolished, the water-well being choked with rubbish, every supply of water cut off and the garrison, though resolute, not animated with the undaunted and unconquerable spirit of their commander, after a siege of thirty-three days, the castle was surrendered. The English general had promised in the name of Queen Elizabeth that the Governor would receive favourable treatment but she handed him over to the Earl of Morton, who hanged him. (Arnot, *The History of Edinburgh*)

February 24th

1687: Writing from Roslin Castle in Midlothian, close to Rosslyn Chapel, Father Richard Augustine Hay (1661-1735) described to his fellow Augustinian priests in France the liturgy in King James VII's new Roman Catholic Chapel Royal at Holyrood Abbey:

The Chapel was open on St Andrew's Day with ceremonies that were so-so. On Christmas Eve they sang a High Mass ... Father Abercrombie, a Benedictine priest, celebrated the Mass. He is in personality very open and fair but since Nature did not bless him with a good singing voice and he has been away from his monastery for a long time — in which I suspect that plainchant was little used — the poor priest carried out his duties at the altar very badly ... The Choir at the Chapel Royal is made up of: a gentleman who passes here as a musician (although he has no voice nor any understanding of plainchant); Mademoiselle Alexandre and two young French girls whom she had brought over from France, with another girl from the same country who is married here to a saddle-maker. Today Vespers was chanted after dinner and the other feast days — all pitiably poor in execution. (*Scottish Catholic Archives* BL 1/101/18)

February 25th

1657: By Act of Council, the surgeons and apothecaries were united into one community, ratified by Parliament. From the time that the arts of surgery and pharmacy were united, the corporation laid aside entirely their business as barbers. This occasioned an Act of Council of 26 July 1682, recommending to the corporation to supply the town with a sufficient number of persons qualified to shave and cut hair, who should continue dependent upon the surgeons. But, in the year 1722, the surgeons and barbers were separated from each other, except that the barbers were still obliged to enter their apprentices in the register kept by the surgeons. (Arnot, *The History of Edinburgh*)

—•—

1843: 'To Ladies. The only genuine Widow Welch's Pills are those prepared by Mrs Smithers (grand-daughter to the Widow Welch), from the real Family Recipe, without the least variation whatever. This medicine is justly celebrated for all Female Complaints, Nervous disorders, Weakness of the Solids, Loss of Appetite, Sick Headache, Lowness of Spirits, and particularly for irregularities of the Female System. Mrs Smithers recommends Mothers, Guardians, Managers of Schools, and all those who have the care of Females at an early age never to be without this useful medicine.' (*Caledonian Mercury*)

February 26th

1816: 'Corri's Rooms. Friday, the 1st March 1816. Grand Promenade and Ball, Catches & Glees, Scotch Music, &c., &c. Under the patronage of the Countess of Moray, Countess of Glasgow, Lady Ashburton and Lady Drummond. The Nobility and Gentry are respectfully informed, that on the above Evening the whole suite of Rooms will be open for a Grand Promenade and Ball. During the Promenade, Catches and Glees will be performed; interspersed with Scottish music, conducted by Mr Gow. The Side Rooms will be laid out for Cards, and the whole set on the plan which met universal approbation on former occasions. Doors to open at nine o'clock. Tickets, Five Shillings; to be had at Mr Corri's Music Shop, and at the Rooms on the Night of the Promenade.' (*Caledonian Mercury*)

1816: The *Caledonian Mercury* printed an advertisement for an exciting evening of entertainment:

> Olympic Circus, North College Street. Second night of Monsieur Godeau's engagement. The performance will commence with Horsemanship. Oriental Procession of Men and Horses, to conclude the Horse Ballet with a colillion danced by six horses. Various extraordinary equestrian feats by Mr Carter; Slack Rope Vaulting by Monsieur Hengler; Miss Bannister, intrepid female equestrian, will go through her celebrated performance on a single horse; Grand Pyramids on Three Horses, forming, in various postures, several ingenious pyramidical devices.

February 27th

1510: Around the twelfth hour of the day, Master Gavin Douglas, provost of the Collegiate Kirk of St Giles of Edinburgh, the senior cleric, along with all the canons, meeting together admitted their failure to celebrate the mass of the Most Holy Blood of our Lord Jesus Christ with the dignity it merited. In reparation, the priests collectively promised to celebrate and sing the same mass every Wednesday. If this was not carried out then the clergy would each pay one merk to the common fund of the Confraternity of the Holy Blood. Master Douglas protested that if this were to happen, and if the money which might have accumulated for the Confraternity was a large sum, that the priests should have a little of it for their own refreshment, provided the service had been first performed with the necessary dignity. These decisions were taken while the canons were meeting in chapter. (*ERBE*).

Bishop of Dunkeld, Douglas (*c.* 1474-1522) was a notable Scottish poet. Embroidered in 1520 for the Confraternity of the Holy Blood at St Giles, the Fetternear Banner is the only Scottish, medieval and religous banner known to have survived.

February 28th

1818: 'Regent's Bridge — From what we have heard, we have no doubt that an attempt will be made to complete the building on the north-west corner of Regent's Bridge, fronting Prince's Street, already founded, and projecting twelve feet into Shakespeare Square. Now we can conceive no proceeding that could indicate a greater want of taste, and a more total disregard for the ornament and conveniency of the city. It is needless to dwell on the absolute certainty of accidents very frequently occurring from carriages coming into contact with each other; inasmuch as drivers coming along the bridge, with an intention of turning down Leith Street, cannot possibly be aware of the approach of those who may be coming up Leith Street, with an intention of driving eastward along the bridge. No person, indeed, can look at the junction of the Regent Bridge, Prince's Street, and Leith Street, without being convinced that the road, even as it formerly stood, and when there could be no danger from carriages coming unperceived on each other, was much too narrow. This, we believe, has never been denied; and yet, notwithstanding that a new thoroughfare is to debouche on the same spot, it is now proposed to narrow it twelve feet.' (*The Scotsman*)

February 29th

1808: On the final day of February, the *Caledonian Mercury* printed this caution:

> The only Genuine Dr Walker's Jesuits Drops by Joseph Wessels. Caution.— A black stamp encloses the genuine medicine, and the following Names are engraven thereon, to secure the Proprietors from piracy (by order of his Majesty's Commissioners of Stamp Duties), 'Shaw and Edwards, successors to Joseph Wessels, 66, St Paul's Church Yard.' The many depredations made by envious and malicious Wholesale Medicine Vendors, on the property of the Proprietors, compels them to give the above Caution, and again to inform the Public, that no one bottle will be sent out of their house without a black stamp fixed. For Dropsy, Stranguary, Gleets, Weakness of the Kidneys, Ureters, or bladder, the Jesuit Drops are an absolute specific; and when taken on the first attack of Venereal Infection, they will infallibly accomplish a Cure. Should the disease be far advanced, it will be necessary to take the Specific Remedy with the Jesuits Drops; and from the first stage of infection to a confirmed Lues, the patient will find these two medicines a perfect antidote. Sold wholesale and retail and may be had of J. Baxter & Co. Italian Warehouse, South Bridge, Edinburgh;— and Messrs Smith, Raeburn, Moncrieff, Manderstone and Gardiner, Edinburgh.

March 1st

1869: The month began with an announcement of the new Waverly Markets in *The Scotsman*:

The formal delivery to the city by the North British Railway Company of the new vegetable markets in Princes' Street, which are to be called by the name of the Waverley Markets, took place at one o'clock ... Mr Walker [secretary of the NBRC], on the part of the railway company, handed the keys of the markets to Bailie Miller, acting Chief Magistrate ... The simple ceremony of the opening was witnessed by a large number of spectators outside the enclosure, both along Princes' Street and the Waverley Bridge ... Mr William Macgregor [a contractor] mentioned ... that on one occasion when there was a danger of some earth giving way, 100 tons of material were built into the wall within two and a half hours. The works, completed within ten months, included 38,000 loads of earth, 24,000 feet of foundations; 40,000 loads of rubble; 1,700 loads of lime; 6,500 loads of sand; 333,000 bricks; 2,000 loads of causeway; 10,000 feet of hewn stone; 15,500 feet of pavement; 40 tons of iron; 300 loads of timber, slates, plaster, &c; 19,000 tons of excavation; making a total of about 112,000 tons of materials that had been used in completing the contract.

March 2nd

1625: Following the death of King James I and VI, the council was presented by new King Charles I with a series of Articles concerning the burgh church. In view of what he referred to as 'the old confusion', the King asked the burgh council to organise the people into several congregations, each of a reasonably equivalent size, with distinct geographical boundaries. There should be four parishes with two ministers in each. Each minister should be provided with a church house in his parish and be given stipend of not less than 2,000 Scots merks. The funds for this would come from an annual levy imposed on every house and tenement in the parish. Every parish should be governed by its Kirk Session, a body annually elected. The King asked that where a place was vacant, ministers would be chosen by the patrons — the provost, bailies and council, and their names forwarded to the Archbishop of St Andrews, in order to avoid 'the confusion and trouble of popular election'. The King required the provost, bailies and council to attend St Giles at least in the fore-noon, their families attending their own parish church. (*ERBE*)

March 3rd

1596: George Christie, son of Andrew Christie, burgess of Dysart, was called before the town council, a suspect because of his recent arrival in the town and for describing himself as a Jesuit priest. He was warned to leave the country of his own free will as soon as possible and not to return without the special permission of the King and the Kirk of Edinburgh, under pain of being hanged. Eduard Nesbett and John Christie, a brother of the self-declared Jesuit, promised to see he left Scotland in Michael Thomesoun's ship at Dysart and land him in France (or in Flanders) and to obtain a legal statement to that effect from the town where he disembarked. In the meantime, he was not to say Mass nor attempt to convert any of the King's lieges from their own religion. Born in Edinburgh in 1562, Christie was educated in Paris. He was ordained a priest in Rome (1591). In 1595 he was sent to Scotland and returned there in 1608 and again in 1621 and 1627. He died in Scotland on 14 April 1629. (*ERBE* and T.M. McCoog, 'Pray to the Lord of the Harvest'; *Innes Review*, 2002)

March 4th

1846: 'In the course of yesterday morning this city was visited by a gale of wind, from the south-west, surpassing in violence any which has been experienced here for many a day, and, we are sorry to add, attended not only with some destruction to property, but also in one case with loss of life. The heaviest casualty took place in a house, No. 16, Hope Street, the residence of Captain Christie, R.N. whose family generally had left for London only the day before. A chimney-stalk on the back part of the house, fell about eight o'clock in the morning, upon the roof, which it penetrated, and carried down to the area floor part of the attic and three other floors. Stewart Robertson, servant to Captain Christie, who it appears had been left in charge of the house, was either killed or suffocated by the falling ruins, his body being only got out about mid-day. A very extraordinary escape was made here. Catherine Morrison, servant in a family which occupied the upper and attic stories, was carried down by the debris through three floors, and was taken out with some severe bruises, none of them dangerous. She was conveyed to the Royal Infirmary.' (*Caledonian Mercury*)

March 5th

1662: The gardener, John Thomson, agreed to work, labour and manure the grounds in the south side and east end of the Parliament House with the brae (slope) all along, between the great stone dyke (wall) of the Meal Market on the south of the Parliament House and the timber fence at the head of the brae upon the north, the dykes upon the east and west, high and low, and to make walks and plant herbaceous plants, trees and flowers of the best sort – no kail, cabbage or other common green vegetable to be sown or planted there. The east end of the yard was to be fenced with a hedge between the Smiths' house and the end of the Goldsmiths' shops up along the head of the dyke of the kirk heuch [sloping path]. The yard was to be keep in good condition, pleasant and fruitful and delectable for the pleasure of the council for all the days, years and terms of nineteen years. The council therefore assigned the yard and brae to John Thomson and his heirs, together with the tall house above the Customs House in the Meal Market to be his dwelling-house. *(ERBE)*

March 6th

1462: Bishop Andrew Muirhead of Glasgow promulgated a bulla (bull) of Pope Pius II dated 23 October 1460, authorising the annexation of the Poor Hospital of Soltray (modern Soutra) to the Collegiate Church and Hospital of the Holy Trinity in Edinburgh. In future, three men would be maintained at Soutra on condition that they offered daily prayers to God for the repose of the souls of the founder and the community in general, along with special intentions. Soutra Hospital, close to Dere Street, the Roman road running from Hadrian's Wall to Cramond in Edinburgh, is believed to have been founded by Malcolm IV in 1164, but is probably older. The Hospital had the privilege of sanctuary, marked by a chain and a cross. At Soutra, a community of Augustinian canons practised medicine, using surgical techniques and a variety of botanical treatments, traces of which have been found in extensive blood-pits. Since 1986, the Soutra Hospital Archaeoethno Pharmacological Research Project (SHARP) has carried out investigations at Soutra under Dr Brian Moffat, revealing evidence of blood-letting, amputation and the use of plant-based medicines made from water-cress, bilberries, opium and digitalis. All that remains today of the medieval hospital is the Soutra Aisle, the family burial vault of the Pringle family.

March 7th

1848: On this day the *Caledonian Mercury* reported on a violent riot in the city:

On Tuesday evening the peace of our city was for several hours disturbed by a riotous mob, which consisted chiefly of young blackguards, well-known thieves, a sprinkling of navvies, accompanied by numbers of loose women, and neglected children. The aims of the rioters were evidently sheer mischief, and plunder. There was nothing of a political character in the outbreak, which commenced at half-past eight o'clock. About that hour, a band, led on by one or two men, who were armed with formidable-looking sticks, and who appeared to belong to the mechanic class, took up their position in Prince's Street, between St David and Hanover Streets. The crowd, which was composed of several hundred persons, proceeded westward to the Mound. In their progress, the ringleaders, with their bludgeons, smashed every lamp that came in their way, amid the cheers of the mob that accompanied them. Their destructive propensities were not, however, confined to breaking lamps; for in a spirit of wanton maliciousness they destroyed several windows in the Royal Institution and in the Royal Hotel, and attempted to destroy with stones the clock of Messrs Bryson, watchmakers, but from the height at which it was placed, they fortunately missed their aim.

March 8th

1800: 'We [the editors] mentioned formerly that several women were apprehended here on suspicion of picking some gentlemen's pockets in the Fish Market. The magistrates have bestowed every attention in order to discover their concern in these depredations; in this, however, they have not been successful, but it appears to be a very fortunate circumstance that they were apprehended, for it has been discovered, that the whole of them came to this city on Thursday last from Glasgow, and all lie under accusations of one kind or another. Two of them had formerly been tried at different Circuit Courts, and one is under sentence of banishment. Their visit to this city was no doubt with a view to obtain plunder, and the inhabitants would in all probability have smarted pretty severely had they not fortunately been detected on the very day of their arrival. On Thursday a person was detected selling unwholesome salmon [caught in the River Tweed] in the Grassmarket of this city. He was immediately summoned before the magistrates, who, after due investigation, ordered the fish to be buried, and sentenced the salesman to pay a fine.' (*Caledonian Mercury*)

March 9th

1566: David Rizzio, the Italian secretary to Mary Queen of Scots, as well as a singer and confidant, was killed in front of the Queen by Lord Ruthven. He and the Earl of Morton and Lord Lindsay were banished in January 1567. The diarist Robert Birrel quotes a passage from Patrick Anderson's *History of Scotland*: 'These Lords entered, rushing together into the Queen's dining room at supper time. She was sitting at the table with the Countess of Argyle. Before her eyes, they attacked Rizzio with their swords beside the cupboard where he was eating meat from the Queen's table – as servants of the Privy Chamber normally did. The Queen was heavily pregnant, trembling with fear. They pointed a pistol at her breast and she was in danger of imminent miscarriage. They pulled Rizzio out of her hands and dragged him into the outer chamber. All the time he screamed pitifully to the Queen, "Justice, justice, Madame! Save my life, save my life!" but they most cruelly and without pity killed him.' Henry Zaire was hanged at the Cross of Edinburgh and then quartered for being at the slaughter of David Rizzio. (*Diarey of Robert Birrel*)

March 10th

1597: On this day, Robert Birrel recorded information about several duels. He wrote that William Gluffer and James Hepburn killed each other on the hill known as St Leonard's Craigs and the two were buried the next day. More fighting followed on 15 March, a single combat between Adam Bruntfield and James Carmichael. Bruntfield challenged Carmichael because he had murdered his late uncle, Stephen Bruntfield. Adam Bruntfield bought a licence from the King and fought Carmichael at Barnbogle Links near Cramond, in front of 5,000 gentlemen. They fought on a small promontory by the sea, with a number of men of substance acting as judges. Being young and of average stature, Bruntfield killed Carmichael despite his being as good a fencer as any man alive. (*Diarey of Robert Birrel*)

———◆———

1823: 'The sloop *Gibraltar*, sailing from Easdale to Leith, with slates, in running for Kirkwall harbour, in a gale of wind ... struck on a sunk rock; but soon came off, and went down in shallow water. The crew took to the rigging, where they remained about fifteen hours, and were with difficulty saved, with the exception of the Master, who had previously fallen down, being exhausted with cold and fatigue, and was thus drowned, leaving a wife and six children to lament his melancholy fate.' (*Caledonian Mercury*)

March 11th

1889: On this day *The Scotsman* broke a shocking story with the headline 'Execution of the Stockbridge Murderess':

At eight o'clock yesterday morning, Jessie Kean or King was executed within the Calton Jail, Edinburgh, for murdering two children which, as a 'baby farmer', she had adopted for a money consideration. Her trial took place on the 18th February last in the High Court, before Lord Kingsburgh and a jury, and a unanimous verdict was followed by sentence of death. An agitation for a reprieve, started by people in the Stockbridge district, did not excite much sympathy. At the same time the Secretary for Scotland gave due heed to the respectful representations which were made to him; and a Medical Commission, at his insistence, reported as to her sanity. But after full enquiry, the advisers of the Queen could not see their way to recommend the exercise of the Royal prerogative of mercy, and the law was accordingly allowed to take its course. The magistrates and other official persons, remembering what occurred in the High Court when a sentence of death was passed, were fearful of a scene at the scaffold; and this apprehension was probably due to the fact that the representatives of the Press had intimation made to them that they could not be allowed to witness the actual execution.

March 12th

1848: On this day there was more crime to report in the *Caledonian Mercury*:

Peter Fraser, James Burns and Andrew Weir, all labourers, pleaded guilty to breaking into a hen house at Hailes House, Colinton, and stealing six turkeys, eight hens, and six other fowls, and were sentenced to be imprisoned for six months. James W. Smith, spirit dealer, Seafield, was found guilty of resetting the above, and was sentenced to four months' imprisonment. Janet Shaw was found guilty of breaking into a house at Advocate's Close, and stealing several articles of wearing apparel from lockfast places, aggravated by previous conviction, and was sentenced to be imprisoned for fifteen months. Andrew Scott, baker, was found guilty of stealing 25 volumes, being the works of Dr Thomas Chalmers, from a bookseller's boy, to whom the prisoner represented himself as the party who had bought them from his employer. Having been previously convicted of theft, he was sentenced to fifteen months' imprisonment. Elizabeth Lamont pleaded guilty of stealing six one pound notes from the house of a shoemaker in Dalkeith, and was sentenced to six months' imprisonment. George Cowan (previously convicted), was accused of breaking into a house in Stafford Street, by a false key, and stealing two top coats and a pair of gloves.

March 13th

1650: Bailie John Binnie presented his report to the council on the offers made by him at the order of the council to Bessie Hutchison, widow of the late John Davidson, tailor, for supplying Trinity Hospital at the foot of Leith Wynd (just below the Netherbow Gate) upon the following terms: the said Bessie would receive forty pounds for each resident to cover their meat, drink and washing of clothes. There should be twelve persons in the Hospital to start with. There should be coal and candles. The beds and bed-clothes should be brought in by the residents. She should have one hundred merks per annum for entertaining and maintaining three servants – a cook and two serving-women, one to wash the clothes and another to make beds. She should have the yard to grow vegetables and fruits for the kitchen. The cook and the gardener should be one man. Kitchen utensils should be provided – pots, pans, spits, racks, plates, dishes, and other necessities, all of which should be kept in good condition for inspection by the Governors. These requirements were to remain in force as long as the council thought necessary. When she became frail she herself should become one of the inmates. (*ERBE*)

March 14th

1689: None was more forward than the council of Edinburgh in offering their services to the Prince of Orange. Those men who so lately declared to King James that they 'would stand by his sacred person upon all occasions' and who prayed the continuance of his princely goodness and care, were now the first in offering their services to the Prince of Orange. A convention of estates was held in Edinburgh. It declared that King James, having assumed royal power without taking the oath required by law and altered the constitution by an exertion of arbitrary power, had forfeited his right to the Crown, which was now settled on William and Mary. A new election of magistrates and the ordinary council of Edinburgh was called for, to be held in St Giles' Church and administered by a poll of the burgesses. They deprived several ministers of Edinburgh of their churches, because they had declined to pray for the newly-appointed Sovereign. A meeting of the estates was converted into a Parliament; prelacy was abolished and the Presbyterian form of church government was established in its place. (Arnot, *The History of Edinburgh*)

March 15th

1596: King James prayed in front of the General Assembly, with many good promises and conditions. The diarist adds: 'I pray God he may keep them, be content to accept criticism, be pious along with his whole household and lay aside his own royal authority and be a brother among them and see all the kirks in Scotland well staffed with ministers.' There were in Scotland 900 kirks, of which 400 were without ministers or even lay readers. (*Diarey of Robert Birrel*)

———◆———

1800: On this day, the *Caledonian Mercury* printed an advertisement for a medicine that was professed to ease problems in marital life:

When conscious ineligibility is the secret but insurmountable bar to Wedlock, the unhappy sufferer pines in silence, and, despairing of relief, sinks into despondency.— To relieve those melancholy infirmities which occasion Impotency in Men, and Barrenness in Women, for Nervous Complaints, Diseases peculiar to females, and all disorders occasioned by Debility or Relaxation, *Les Pastilles Martilles de Montpelier,* or Aromatic Lozenges of Steel, are proved by experience, to be the most certain, safe … The genuine Lozenges of Steel are prepared only by Dr Senate, late of Soho Square, and sold wholesale and retail, at his warehouse, No 28, Tavistock Street, Covent Garden, London; and by Mr Baxter, Italian Warehouse, Edinburgh, price 7 shillings per Box, duty included.

March 16th

1655: Upon suspicion of a revolution in England, there passed from this town of Edinburgh, and other parts to England, a number of companies of English soldiers, sent for by order of the Protector (Oliver Cromwell). They marched upon the 16th and 17th days of March. Their march was 20 miles a day. Other companies, also English, both horse and foot, went to the North, to consolidate their power there. The reason for this revolt, as was reliably reported, was the dissatisfaction of the people of all the three nations by the government of his Highness Oliver, Lord Protector, reduced into that of a single person and also of a report given out by the Duke of York to some friends here in Scotland and England, to make themselves ready to go to England to meet his brother, the titular Scottish King, who was there at the head of an army. In this cause there were 5,000 foot soldiers and 200 horsemen raised in London at the Protector's direction; and all the horses in and around London, and many weapons were seized by his Highness the Protector and his Council, to prevent any uprising. (Nicoll's *Diary*)

March 17th

1863: 'Last night, the cabmen of Edinburgh were entertained to supper in the Freemasons' Hall by a number of friends, who forwarded subscriptions to Mr Gray, the missionary to the cabmen. The object was to give the cabmen an entertainment in honour of the Prince of Wales' marriage … It was originally intended to confine the entertainment to the members of the Cabmen's Temperance Society, which was formed in October last by Dr Guthrie and others, but the subscriptions flowed so liberally, that the whole of the cabmen were ultimately invited —the remainder as the guests of the society. Supper was laid out on a table reaching all along the hall, and about 500 persons, including the cabmen and their wives, sat down … In the gallery opposite the platform, [the author] Miss Catherine Sinclair and a party of ladies were accommodated, and watched the proceedings with great interest. The Very Rev. Dean Ramsay addressed the meeting. He had often wished that there was a guildry of cabmen, as there are corporations of bakers, fishmongers, and other trades, for he wished to see them raised in the social scale.' (*The Scotsman*)

March 18th

1826: 'Police Court. An old man who sells coals in the Castlehill, brought a complaint against a person who occupied the flat above him, for being in the constant practice of deluging his house with water through a hole in the floor, and several other species of annoyance. The only witness he had to support the charge was an old blind man, who stated, that though he could not see, his hearing was good, and what he had heard he would swear to. He declared that the defender had 'ane o' the warst tongues that ever stack in a head' … The magistrate, conceiving the evidence of one witness insufficient, dismissed the case. Yesterday a case was decided about the watchman on Northumberland Street, who, while going his rounds at three o'clock on the morning, observing three gas lamps to go out in regular succession, directed his steps to the scene of darkness, where he saw two young men busily engaged in turning the gas cocks. Seeing the watchmen approach, they made a hasty retreat. Both pleaded not guilty, but having failed to produce any proof, the magistrate ordained them to be fined a guinea each.' (*The Scotsman*)

March 19th

1808: On this day, this advertisement featured in the 'To be Sold or Let' section of the *Caledonian Mercury*:

Black Bull Inn, Edinburgh. These large, commodious, and centrical Buildings, occupied under the denomination of the Black Bull Inn, situated in Katharine Street, near the head of Leith Walk. The Tavern, part of these premises, consists of large kitchens, completely fitted up, and complete cellarage, &c. in the sunk storey; a detached house for the tenant, communicating with the premises; a large public room, and four small parlours, bar room, and waiter's room, on the first floor; three other large public rooms and a sufficient to carry on an extensive business in the Hotel or Lodging line; all in compete repair, and free of impost and town's taxes; and a range of excellent stabling, &c. in the court behind. The whole hath, ever since its erection, been occupied as an Inn, Tavern, and Hotel, and from whence the stage coaches running from Edinburgh north, south, east, and west, have been in use to start, and in returning to set down, and wherein the late proprietor is known to have made a genteel competency for his family during his short possession ...

March 20th

1601: Alexander Hunter was about to be sent by the burgh to England and to the Low Countries to bring back Flemish people and others for the manufacture of broad cloth and coarse cloth for furnishing, and other materials such as are made in Flanders out of Scots wool. His first objective was to bring back persons who could process Scottish wool by sorting, refining, combing, spinning, weaving – enough persons to produce six woven lengths at one time in the manufacturing hall, but not more than twenty. He was also to bring back enough working looms as were needed and one example of each type of loom so that they could be reproduced. One person who could make cloth with a mixture of colours was needed, a comb-maker, a dyer and a pressing machine. They should be workers who would make a profit for the enterprise and not be a drain on the country's finances. They would be brought over at no cost to themselves but would have to agree to a reasonable contract with the burgh or be sent back home (free of charge). They would be offered craft privileges, Scottish naturalisation and the freedom of the burgh. (*ERBE*)

March 21st

1805: A story of a prison break alarmed readers of the *Caledonian Mercury* on this day:

Broke Prison. William Grindlay, accused of Robbery, born in the parish of Falkirk, about five feet eight or nine inches high, short curled red hair and red whiskers, pitted with the smallpox, high browed, marked on the fleshy part of one of his arms 'W.G.', under which the figure of a woman, and at her feet 'A.S.'; bred a moulder at Carron; broke the Prison of Lanark, upon Sunday 17th current, during Divine service; had on when he made his escape a short blue coat, black velvet neck, and blue wide trousers, and a slouch hat. A Reward of Ten Guineas is hereby offered to any person who will apprehend him, and lodge him in Lanark jail, to be paid by applying to the Treasurer of the Burgh of Lanark.

March 22nd

1877: Reports of domestic violence in *The Scotsman* revealed the unpleasant details of several offenders:

Wife-Beating.— Sheriff Hallard had several wife-beaters before him yesterday. At the Summary Court he sentenced a coal-porter named John Johnston to two months' imprisonment with hard labour for having, in his house at Kellie Brae, West Port, on the 17th last, struck his wife on the head and face with his fists, thrown her down, kicked her, and beat her with a stick. The prisoner had been previously convicted of assault. Robert Ward, labourer, residing at Kirkgate, Leith, who had also been previously convicted, was sent to prison for one month with hard labour for ill-using his wife on the 19th— throwing her down, kicking and endeavouring to strangle her. Daniel Talbot, miner, residing at Campbell Street, Addiewell, was likewise sent to jail for a month with hard labour for striking and kicking his wife to the effusion of blood. At the Police Court, a blind man named Patrick Clark was charged with assaulting his wife in his house, Barnet's Close, on Monday night. Mrs Clark said the prisoner knocked her down, kicked her and beat her on the head with a pair of tongs, to the effusion of blood: but she admitted being drunk and attacking him first with a poker.

March 23rd

1597: King James VI was drinking in the council house with the bailies, the council and the deacons. While he was drinking in the council house, the bells in the steeple were rung to express joy at the amity between King and council. The trumpets sounded and drums and whistles played, with as many other musical instruments as there were players. Afterwards, they all accompanied the King to the West Port. The price of this happy agreement was that the town of Edinburgh was ordered to pay 30,000 Scots merks to the King as compensation for the public disorder on the previous 17 December. (*Diarey of Robert Birrel*)

———◆———

1801: 'Sailings. At Leith—for London, The Union Shipping Company's armed Smack, *Berwickshire Packet*, James Laws (master) — and Hazard (hired vessel), Alexander Clechorn (master). Will take goods, the former till Wednesday morning at 10 o'clock, and the latter till Friday mid-day, when they will sail. Union Shipping Co's. Office, Leith. At Leith for New-York, The *Agnes*, William Stewart (master). To sail 23d curt. She is a fine new Brig, sails fast, and has good accommodation for passengers. Apply to James Cathcart, merchant in Leith; or the Captain on board.' (*Caledonian Mercury*)

March 24th

1603: On the death of Queen Elizabeth I, the King of Scotland, James VI, was proclaimed King of England, Scotland, France and Ireland. On 27 March, the son of the gate-keeper of Berwick came to the King at Holyroodhouse and presented him with the keys of his town. On 31 March, many of the nobility of Scotland came to the Mercat Cross of Edinburgh where the secretary, Sir James Elphinston, read and Sir David Lindsay proclaimed King James VI King of England, France and Ireland, Defender of the Faith. On 3 April, a Sunday, the King came to the Great Kirk of Edinburgh where he made a prayer and a speech to the people. The King made a firm promise: to defend the Faith and that he would come North to visit his people of Scotland every three years. On 5 April, the King travelled to Berwick. There was great sorrow and mourning among the people of Scotland for the loss of the daily sight of their good Prince. People were speaking about the prophecy of the thirteenth-century Scottish poet Thomas the Rhymer. In fact, King James VI would not come back to Scotland until 1617. (*Diarey of Robert Birrel*)

March 25th

1843: 'Unemployed Poor. — In reference to a statement which has appeared in the newspapers relative to fraudulent persons collecting money as if for this fund, we are authorised to state, for the information of the public, that every collector who is employed by the Committee has a book, on which is marked the number of the book, number of the ward, and name of the collector; and this is also signed by Mr Miller, the secretary. In addition, each collector has a written authority empowering him to collect subscriptions within the ward, signed by the secretary. The public should in every case see the book and authority before subscribing.' (*Caledonian Mercury*)

'Examinations, &c. John Lunn, Builder in Edinburgh — to be examined in the Sheriff's Office there, 8th April, eleven o'clock. Creditors of William Wilkie, paper stainer, &c., George Street, Edinburgh, meet in the writing-chambers of Robert Webster, Prince's Street there, 8th April, twelve o'clock. Creditors of Falkner & Cuningham, wine merchants in Edinburgh, meet in the writing chambers of Alexander Low, Hanover Street there, 17th May, two o'clock. Creditors of the Leith Banking Company will receive a dividend from James Brown, accountant, George Street, Edinburgh, 8th May.' (*Caledonian Mercury*)

March 26th

1832: On this day, the *Caledonian Mercury* reported on the outbreak of cholera:

> Edinburgh: March 24.— New Case, 1. This was a woman in quarantine at Queensberry House. March 25.— New Cases, 3; Died, 3; Remaining, 1. The three new cases were a woman in Causewayside, a man in the Grassmarket, and a woman in quarantine. Total cases, 45; Deaths, 25; Cures, 19. Water of Leith: March 24.— One new case, which remains. March 25.— No new case. Total cases, 49; Deaths, 26; Recovered, 23. Canonmills: March 24.— New cases, 2; Died, 1. March 25.— Died, 1 . These were a man and his wife, named Kilpatrick, who were both decent persons and in comfortable circumstances, but living in a very ill-ventilated house near the river. Total cases, 10; Deaths, 8; Cures, 2.

Also in the newspaper was this report:

> Fire. Last night, about eight o'clock, flames were observed issuing from the roof of a house in Oakfield Court, Pleasance, the family inhabiting which were absent at the time. The whole of the fire establishment were very quickly on the spot, and succeeded in extinguishing the flames in the course of three-quarters of an hour. The premises where the fire broke out was used as a bookbinder's shop, and the roof was stuffed with paper shavings.

March 27th

1841: The newspaper, *The True Scotsman*, struggled to stay alive for two years, but finally succumbed on this day.

———•◆•———

1498: Speaking in the name of the King, the provost, bailies and council, having learned that outlying villages such as Swanston, Currie, Under Cramond and Hailes were infected with contagious pestilence, ordered that no one from those areas was to come to Edinburgh under the pain of execution and that no resident of the burgh should harbour anyone from these areas, under the pain of having all their moveable property burnt and being banished for life. (*ERBE*)

———•◆•———

1806: 'A raffle of Sundry elegant and valuable articles of jewellry and plate, belonging to Mrs Justine Tremamondo, relict [widow] of the deceased Mr Angelo Tremamondo, late Master of the Royal Academy, Edinburgh, is to take place in the Fencing Room at the Royal Academy ... The late Mr Angelo having instructed the Emperor Paul of Russia ... in the Arts of riding and fencing, his father, the Emperor Peter, sent to Mr Angelo ... a valuable and elegant Gold Snuff Box, with his Majesty's initials set in Diamonds ... Mrs Angelo is also possessed of some valuable jewels.' (*Caledonian Mercury*)

March 28th

1831: 'On Monday evening this city was pretty generally illuminated, in celebration of the second reading of the Reform Bill; and on that occasion the Edinburgh mobocracy fully sustained its character, as the most recklessly, mischievous, and wantonly wicked of all mobs in all countries or cities on the face of the earth. The illumination commenced between seven and eight o'clock in the evening; and about an hour after, several small corps of young blackguards, who had previously filled their pockets with stones, from road-metal easily procured in the vicinity, paraded the principal streets, chiefly in the New Town, dealing destruction as they went, to all windows not lighted up, and to many which were lighted, but which did not display a number of candles sufficient to satisfy the mobocracy that their proprietors were heart in the cause ... They began with parading an effigy of the City Member along the bridges, and up to the Cross, where fire being set to it, it was carried blazing down the High Street, amid the shouts and laughter of the multitude. The perambulators then perambulated the New Town, breaking glass as they went.' (*Caledonian Mercury*)

March 29th

1873: 'The election of a School Board for the city of Edinburgh took place on Saturday, and passed off, under the salutary operation of the Ballot Act, in the most quiet and orderly way. Besides two candidates who stood, so to speak, on their own basis, and two lady candidates, there were submitted to the arbitrament of the poll one or more representatives of six distinct parties, discriminated from one another mainly by their views in regard to religious teaching. Of the 38,000 and odd electors qualified under the Education Act, only 16,103 went to the poll, of whom it was reckoned that barely a twelfth were ladies. The enumeration of the votes was commenced at the Literary Institute on Saturday night, and is to be resumed this morning, the expectation being that the results will be declared this afternoon ... In the course of the day, too, several hundred persons, eager to exercise what they believed to be their right, were turned away disappointed, on the ground that their names did not appear on the valuation roll which had been placed in the hands of the polling Sheriffs.' (*The Scotsman*)

March 30th

1815: 'On Saturday last, a gentleman's servant was summoned before the Police Court, on a charge of having propagated a report that a house in Jamaica Street was haunted by a ghost, and thereby preventing the house from being let, to the damage of the proprietor, &c. Upon being called to plead to this heinous offence, the defender positively averred that he had seen the ghost upon several occasions; that he had conversed with it; that it was of a copper colour, dressed in a red night cap; but what the nature of the conversation was, the defender refused to reveal, having been enjoined to secrecy— The sitting Magistrate ordained the defender to find security to keep the peace for a year, under the penalty of five pounds! Before leaving the bar, the defender begged leave to ask the Magistrate, if he was at liberty to converse with the ghost in future, as he had promised to see him again, and to partake of his hospitality. Query— Is the defender bound over to keep the peace so that he shall not propagate such reports in time coming, or that he shall not again speak to the ghost? Or does this offence come under the cognizance of the Police Court? We, for our part, are of the opinion, that the ghost ought to have been called into Court for its interest.' (*Caledonian Mercury*)

March 3-1st

1689: Having just attended Sunday afternoon service, the eminent judge, George Lockhart, Lord President of the Court of Session, was leisurely walking home down the High Street and into Old Bank Close, when an enraged husband suddenly appeared behind, pistol in hand, and shot him through the back. The ball passed through his body and out the other side of his upper chest. The Lord President staggered and then fell onto the pavement. He was quickly brought into his house, but died almost immediately. Meanwhile, his assailant was seized by passers-by. He was John Chiesly of Dalry. The Lord President had recently ordered him to provide his wife and children with an annual income of £93. This reasonable judgement had infuriated Chiesly and he had sworn to kill the judge. Chiesly was imprisoned, tortured and sentenced to be taken through the streets and hanged. His pistol was to be tied round his neck, his body suspended in chains and his right hand nailed up at the West Port. However, his body was spirited away from where it hung. More than a century afterwards, when a hearthstone was being taken out in a cottage at Dalry Park, a skeleton was discovered, with a pistol wrapped round its neck.

April 1st

1820: 'A Literary Curiosity. There is a small white cottage standing in one of the parks at Bruntsfield Links, which most persons pass without being aware of the classical interest that attaches to it. It is situated at the top or south side of the Links, on the road leading to Canaan, and is immediately contiguous to the road on the east side. In this cottage John Home wrote his drama of *Douglas*, Dr Hugh Blair his *Lectures*, and Dr Robertson his *History of Charles the Fifth*. We give this interesting information on the authority of a very near relation of Dr Blair, to whom these particulars were often related by the Doctor with great interest.' (*Caledonian Mercury*)

1809: 'An audacious theft was committed on Tuesday last, in the back court of a house in Hopepark. The waste pipe of a cistern for rain water, 44 inches long by 2 inches bore, was taken away, in high day, while two carts were emptying coals in the court, and two young lads that were seen hovering about got off undiscovered.

April 2nd

1916: In the 1980s, an article appeared in a local newspaper describing a bombing that happened on this day in 1916:

> At 10 minutes to midnight, on a calm and clear night, a German Zeppelin airship dropped a bomb on a bonded warehouse in Leith. Five minutes later more rained around Leith as the airship made its way into the centre of Edinburgh. At midnight a bomb fell in East Claremont Street, shattering windows and injuring civilians with splintered glass. In the dark the low-pitched throbbing of the Zeppelin engine was clearly audible high over the city. Another bomb fell in Lauriston Place, along with some incendiaries. Many windows in the Royal Infirmary were broken. A direct hit devastated parts of George Watson's College. Five people were killed and many wounded in Marshall Street. Two people died at St Leonard's near the Pleasance. Then Edinburgh Castle was targeted but the bombs narrowly missed and instead caused extensive damage in the Grassmarket. Just after 12.30 the Zeppelin abandoned its attack. Its bombs had all been dropped. Then, on 2 May came the sudden threat of another Zeppelin raid. However, the attack did not materialise as the airship had jettisoned its bombs in fields south of the city.
> (J.C. Alexander, *Edinburgh Evening News,* 2 May 1987)

April 3rd

1800: 'Newhaven Navigation. On Sunday last two gentlemen from Edinburgh went early in the morning to Leith, with the intention of going over to Fife on a pleasure jaunt. On their arrival at Leith, they found that, owing to the calmness of the morning no large boat was to cross. They agreed to walk to Newhaven along with two other gentlemen, who wished likewise to cross to the other side, and there hire a fishing boat. Having accordingly procured one at Newhaven, the four gentlemen embarked along with two experienced seamen, as rowers ... They then put off, and rowed past the different ships in Leith Roads, and, as was thought, in the direct passage to Fife. The weather continued still hazy, and after being more than two hours on the water in a pretty cold morning, the passengers now became impatient to reach *terra firma*. After rowing for some time longer, the land was at last discovered, which was thought at first to be Burntisland or thereabouts, but upon coming a little nearer, to the surprise of everyone on board, the discovered land turned out to be Wardie, scarcely half a mile west of Newhaven.' (*Caledonian Mercury*)

April 4th

1801: 'Manufactures. That the present state of the muslin and cotton manufactures in and about Glasgow and Paisley, is truly lamentable and distressing, must be acknowledged by every intelligent person. Within these few weeks, it is said, about 2,000 looms have been laid aside in those parts. It afforded some consolation to look into the export lists from Leith for three weeks past. By them it appears exports have been made to Hamburg and Bremen, viz. 113,750 yards, and 91 pieces muslin; 8,580 yards printed cotton; 380 dozen muslin handkerchiefs; 176,387 yards cotton goods ... it is with some concern that in the same period are seen exported to the same parts, viz. 112,580 pounds of cotton yarn; 1 box of bleaching instruments and 2 hundredweight of bleaching salts. Hence it may be concluded, that by a connection formed between persons here, with those in foreign parts, our manufactures are gradually declining, while at the same time the weaving, bleaching, and finishing of muslins and cottons are gaining ground abroad, to the injury of our Imperial United Kingdom. It is likewise to be feared, that some of our most expert tradesmen have been sent over to the Continent to manage this business, and instruct foreigners in it.' (*Caledonian Mercury*)

April 5th

1845: On this day *The Scotsman* printed a news story with the title 'Horrible Murder in St Giles':

The neighbourhood of St Giles was throughout the whole of Tuesday the scene of great excitement, a consequence of an atrocious murder which had been committed on the body of a woman in a brothel in George Street, at about eleven o'clock on the preceding evening. It appears that the woman, accompanied by a man, went to the house in question, which is kept by a person of the name of Hall, shortly after ten o'clock on Monday evening; and passing through an outer room or lobby, entered a room on the ground-floor, in which there was a bed but scarcely any other article of furniture … The parties had not remained in the house much longer than ten minutes, when a noise was heard by the landlady, which induced her to leave her apartment for the purpose of making enquiries as to its cause. In the passage she met the man who had been in company with the woman, and attempted to stop his progress, but he burst away from her grasp, and succeeded in making good his exit. She then entered the lobby, and the sight which met her eyes caused her to give utterance to shrieks of 'murder'.

April 6th

1928: 'Princes Street: Scottish Granite Setts — a section to be laid. At yesterday's meeting of Edinburgh Town Council a recommendation with regard to the material to be used in the repair of Princes Street arose on the report of the Streets and Buildings Committee. The Committee visited Glasgow, where they inspected West George Street, which is laid with fine dressed Norwegian granite setts, and having in view the estimated costs for the repair of Princes Street by British granite setts and Norwegian granite setts — namely, £40,000 and £25,000 — recommended the use of Norwegian setts. Mr Gumley, who moved the Committee's recommendation, said that several methods had been discussed. Rubber, he said, had been tried round the London Cenotaph, and it had to be removed for two reasons — it began to rise up and people began to fall. A roadway must be safe, efficient, and economical. For appearance and amenity he did not think there was anything that could stand up to granite setts. There was a little more sound with them but it was rare that one found iron tyres in Princes Street ... They had not had granite blocks in Princes Street before. The Committee were ... not satisfied with simply taking what other people had found good.' (*The Scotsman*)

April 7th

1896: *The Scotsman* painted a fairly bleak picture of the health of Edinburgh:

The report of the medical Officer on the health of Edinburgh during March, submitted to the Public Health Committee of Edinburgh Town Council, showed that the total number of deaths during the month was 380, giving a rate of 16.49 per 1,000 of the population. The average death-rate in the same month for the past five years was 22.08; 32.63 per cent. were registered as under five years, 16.05 per cent. between five and thirty, 25.26 per cent. between thirty and sixty, and 26.05 per cent. above sixty. The deaths from diseases of the chest were 33.42 per cent. of the whole. Zymotic diseases proved fatal in 27 cases, or 7.10 per cent. of the total mortality. There were 694 births, giving a rate of 30.11 per 1,000. Of these 66 were illegitimate. The report for the quarter shows that the total deaths numbered 1,103 — a rate of 15.95 — the lowest for many years. Births numbered 1,838, giving a rate of 26.58 per 1,000, and there were 178 of the total illegitimate. The cases of infectious diseases reported during the month numbered 498, and for the quarter 1,258.

April 8th

1847: 'Edinburgh Water Company. A special general meeting of the proprietors of the Water Company were held on Monday in Gibb's Royal Hotel. John Learmonth, Esq. of Dean presided. Mr. Cameron, clerk to the company, read the draft of a bill introduced into Parliament by the directors to consider which, in compliance with the standing orders of the House of Lords, the meeting was called. The main features of this bill, which are already well known, require to be only briefly recapitulated. It is proposed to increase the capacity of the Glencorse reservoir, by raising its embankments four feet; to construct a new reservoir on the Logan Burn, and two additional store reservoirs on the north side of the Pentland Hills. It is contemplated by these means to have such a supply as will keep the pipes in constant service. It is also intended to extend a supply to Portobello. Further, the company propose to raise £80,000 additional stock ... the company had acquired property on the Castlehill, by which they would be enabled, at a moderate expense, to construct cisterns to contain two-thirds of each day's supply; a quantity amply sufficient to afford constant service to the highest tenements in the city.' (*Caledonian Mercury*)

April 9th

1670: On trial was the tall, dark-featured Major Thomas Weir (b. 1599, Lanarkshire) who had served as a Covenanting soldier in Ireland. In later life he had developed a reputation for extraordinary holiness and lived with his sister in the West Bow (just off the Lawnmarket) where he could often be seen striding over the cobbles with his black stick and black cloak. He was known as 'Angelical Thomas'. As the years passed, however, his true nature gradually emerged. He fell into a sickness where his mind, till then strictly controlled, was so disturbed that his secret imaginations welled to the surface. He began to confess to sexual depravity and financial corruption. He had never married but now he revealed an incestuous relationship with his elderly sister. Gossips in the street spoke of him as a wizard and claimed to have seen his black walking-stick running in front of him at night. He was taken into custody by the magistrates and when urged to pray, screamed out: 'Torment me no more!' He was found guilty and sentenced to be strangled and burnt. Major Weir was executed on 14 April, his last words being 'Let me alone ... I have lived as a beast, and I must die as a beast!' (Chambers, *Traditions of Edinburgh*)

April 10th

1809: 'Prize Ships and Cargoes for Sale. To be sold by public auction, at Younghusband's Coffeehouse, Leith, on Thursday the 29oth day of April current, at twelve o'clock noon, the Danish Brig *Wenskabet*, measuring about 103 tons, and the Danish Galliot *Fortuna*, measuring about 127 tons, both captured by his Majesty's ship *Ariadne*, Arthur Farquhar, Esq. Commander, also, the entire Cargoes of these vessels, consisting of the following goods, viz. *for home consumption*: 2,085 deals; 1,210 battens; 77 paling boards; 762 users or small trees; 31 hand-spokes; 760 hazel rungs; 30 tar barrels; 8 quarter tar barrels; 667 bars of iron; 29 casks of salt; a quantity of firewood. *Also, for home consumption or exportation.* 45 tons of dried cod and ling fish; 40 small kegs of sardines; 197 casks of fish oil; 74 barrels of pepper; 11 barrels of sugar; 779 pieces of cast iron. Apply to Ramsay, Williamson & Co., Leith. The Edinburgh & Leith Shipping Company's armed Smack, *Friendsburry*, William Martin (master), to sail on Tuesday the 11th current, at ten o'clock forenoon. R. Liddell, Manager, Edinburgh & Leith Shipping Co.'s Office, Leith. At Leith—for Pictou, *Nova Scotia*, the Brig *Helen*, Robert Kirk (master), will sail in fourteen days. For freight or passage apply to the master on board.' (*The Caledonian Mercury*)

April 11th

1705: The discontent which the Scots felt at the loss of their settlement in Darien (which they imputed in good measure to the ill offices of the English) inflamed their national animosity. A ship belonging to the Company of Scotland, trading to Africa and the Indies, was seized in the Thames. They solicited restitution in vain from the English ministry, but, upon making application at home, they obtained authority from the government to seize, by way of reprisal, a vessel commanded by Captain Green, belonging to the English East India Company, which had put into the River Forth. The unguarded speeches of the crew, in their cups or their quarrels, made them be suspected, accused and, after a full and legal trial, convicted of piracy, aggravated by murder and that committed upon the master and crew of a Scots vessel in the East Indies. Still, however, the evidence upon which they were condemned, was by many thought slight, and intercessions for Royal mercy were used in their behalf. But the populace were enraged that the blood of a Scotsman should be spilt unrevenged – Captain Green and two of his crew were hanged at Leith Sands. (Arnot, *The History of Edinburgh*)

April 12th

1821: These articles were printed in the *Caledonian Mercury*:

A very melancholy accident happened in Giles Street, Leith, on Saturday night. As a painter was incautiously boiling some oil in his house, it accidentally caught fire, and scorched a young boy, his son, in so shocking a manner that he died the same evening. The man and wife, in endeavouring to smother the flames, were also very severely burnt, and were brought up the same night to the Royal Infirmary, where the man died yesterday. A young girl, their daughter, was likewise burnt in her face and arms by the flames, but not severely. Yesterday morning, a man of the name of Charles Johnston, a labourer, employed at some new buildings in Drummond Place, was killed almost instantaneously by a fall from a scaffold, a large stone falling at the same time upon his head.

Deaths at Edinburgh, on the 2nd of April, Mr John Little, merchant, Lawnmarket. At Raeburn Place, Edinburgh, on the 5th of April. George, third son of Captain Williamson. Died at his father's house, 13 Union Place, Peter Elder, jun., after a long illness. A few days ago a new-born infant was found drowned at Leith Mills.

April 13th

1848: 'The professed Chartists of this city, attended by a large crowd of boys and thoughtless lads, congregated on the Calton Hill on Monday evening, to make a demonstration in sympathy with that in London. The multitude were addressed by several speakers, the majority thinking it necessary to season their orations with certain of those treasonable denunciations which were originated in Ireland, adopted in London, and are now transferred to our northern hemisphere. This violence was, however, deprecated by others. In conclusion a memorial was adopted to be laid before the Town Council on the following day. Bailie Stott, while discountenancing the violent and treasonable sentiments uttered at the meeting, thought proper to propose a series of resolutions in the Council, containing a list of grievances under which the country was alleged to labour, and only stopping short of an explicit demand for the Charter. These were met by counter resolutions moved by the Lord Provost, in which the People's Charter was unequivocally condemned ... On a division the resolutions of the Lord Provost were carried by 22 to 8. We think it would be more prudent for a Magistrate of Edinburgh ... to avoid this *quasi* fraternity with those who could utter such seditious language as that used on the Calton Hill on Monday evening.' (*Caledonian Mercury*)

April 14th

1828: On this day, these announcements appeared in the *Caledonian Mercury*:

Weather. Within these few days the weather has become milder; and yesterday we had a great deal of rain, with some thunder in the south-west. Accident. On Saturday afternoon one of the men employed in building the Tron Church steeple, while at work on a scaffold, fell down in a fit of apoplexy, and instantly expired.

Attempted Theft. A fellow tendering base coin in Leith threatened to stab a little girl in a public house there who had refused to give him change for a bad half-crown. The girl, on seeing the knife fainted, and some person coming in, he escaped, but was soon after apprehended by the police, and on Saturday was sent to Bridewell for sixty days, to be fed on bread and water.

March of Intellect. A gentleman the other day, visiting Mr Wood's school in Edinburgh, had a book put into his hand for the purpose of examining a class. The word *inheritance* occurring in the verse, the inspector interrogated the youngster as follows: — 'What is inheritance?' A. 'Patrimony.' 'What is Patrimony?' A. 'Something left by a father.' 'What would you call it if left by a mother?' A. 'Matrimony.'

April 15th

1819: On this day, the *Caledonian Mercury* informed of various performances at the Theatre Royal:

Mr Edmund Kean is engaged for a few nights and will make his last appearance here but two this Season. This present evening, Thursday, April 15 1819, will be performed, the first time these ten years, the Tragedy of 'The Distress'd Mother'. Orestes played by Mr Kean, Pyrrhus by Mr Calcraft, from the Theatre-Royal, Newcastle, being his second appearance here, Pylades by Mr Alexander, Hermione by Mrs H. Siddons, Andromache by Mrs Renaud. After the Tragedy, the junior Miss Worgman will recite, with appropriate music, Collins' 'Ode on the Passions'. To which will be added, fourth time here, a farce in one Act produced at the Theatre-Royal, Drury Lane, called Mr H., previous to which Mr Jones will speak the celebrated *'Alphabetical Prologue'*. Sir Wigsby Exquisite by Mr W. Murray, Mr H. by Mr Jones, Dr Gull'em by Mr Mackay. Tomorrow, the Comedy of 'The Merchant of Venice'; Shylock, Mr Kean; Portia, Mrs H. Siddons.— which, it being the birthday of Shakespeare, will be performed Garrick's Grand Jubilee, in honour of the Immortal Bard. Saturday, the Tragedy of 'Douglas'. Tickets and places for the Boxes to be had at the Box Office, from eleven to three o'clock.— The Play to commence at seven o'clock.

April 16th

1849: 'The Gold Regions of California. Mr. Marshall most respectfully intimates, that he has just opened a novel and interesting Panorama in his Rotunda on the Mound (newly enlarged and elegantly fitted up) of the Gold Regions of California, displaying the Towns of Monteray—San Francisco—The Valley and River Sacramento—The Sierra Nevada—Marshall's Saw Mill where the gold was first discovered—The Lower Mines, or Mormon Diggings; crowds of Mormons, Emigrants, Indians, Americans, &c. digging and washing for gold, exhibiting the entire process—Webber's Creek, &c.—Painted from Sketches made on the spot, by J. B. Folsom, Esq.; together with the highly finished Panorama of the City of Jerusalem, from David Roberts, Esq. R. A.'s Sketches, displaying the Mount of Olives—The Garden of Gethsemane—the Potter's Field—the Golden Gateway—the Dead Sea—the Brook Kedron—the Holy Sepulchre—the Village of Bethany—Mount Zion—Site of Herod's Palace—the Pool of Bethseda—Mount Nebo (where Moses was shown the Promised Land)—Gate of Stephen (where he was stoned to death)—House of Pontius Pilate—Numerous Groups of Turks, Arabs, Christians, Armenians, Pilgrims, and Jews ... Accompanied by Music, Description, &c. Day Exhibitions, from 12 till 4 — Evening ditto from 7 till 10. Admission, 1 shilling.— Gallery, 6 pence.— Children, half-price.' (*Caledonian Mercury*)

April 17th

1341: Edinburgh Castle was recovered by stratagem, by four gentlemen. One of them disguised himself as an English merchant. He went to the Governor of the castle and told him that he had a cargo of wine, strong beer and biscuit, exquisitely spiced, in his vessel just arrived, which provisions he wished the Governor would buy from him. He produced, as a specimen, a bottle of the wine and another of the beer. The Governor relished the liquors, they agreed about the price and this pretended merchant was to deliver the provisions next morning early, so that he would not be intercepted by the Scots. He came accordingly, attended by twelve armed followers disguised as sailors, and the gates were opened for them. Upon entering the castle, they overturned the carriage, upon which provisions were supposed to be heaped, and instantly killed the porter and sentries. Upon the sound of a horn, Douglas, with a band of armed men, rushed into the castle where the garrison, after a sharp conflict, were mostly put to the sword and the fortress recovered. (Arnot, *The History of Edinburgh*)

April 18th

1867: 'Edinburgh Police Court—This Day (before Bailie Russell). Isabella Davidson or Mill, Potterrow, was found guilty of illegally selling drink in her house, and this being her second offence, she was fined £15, with the alternative of three months' imprisonment.— Mary Menzies, Potterrow, was found guilty of a similar offence, and was fined £7, with the alternative of six weeks' imprisonment, this being her first offence.— Elizabeth Wilson or Sawers was fined £30, with the alternative of six months' imprisonment, for illegally selling drink in her house in Campbell's Close, Canongate. This was her third offence.' (*Caledonian Mercury*)

'Theft. John Smith was sent thirty days to prison for stealing a large quantity of block tin and solder from his employers in Abbeyhill. Leith Police Court—This Day (before Bailie Beveridge.' (*Caledonian Mercury*)

'Theft. John Leishman, a labourer residing in Queen Street, and his wife, were charged with stealing from a lodging-house where they were living, kept by Mrs Helen Paterson, a crinoline and a bonnet, the property of the said Mrs Paterson … Bailie Beveridge gave the male prisoner the benefit of his doubt and discharged him, sentencing the female prisoner to ten days' imprisonment.' (*Caledonian Mercury*)

April 19th

1802: On this day, a story titled 'The Rat's Nest' appeared in the *Caledonian Mercury*. It explained what had happened, within a few days, to Mr Kidd, an eminent horse dealer in this city. He had carefully deposited in a press a parcel of bank notes, to the amount of £80, for a payment he had to make. When the demand came, he went for his notes, but not one of them was to be seen, though they had been there shortly before. No person having been in the room except one man, suspicion naturally fell upon him, and of course gave him no small uneasiness. His protestations were of no avail, but on a minute examination of the closet, the corner of a bank note was perceived sticking through a small hole. This led to a further investigation, when the whole of the notes, perfectly entire, were found neatly piled up in the shape of a rat's nest, so that the property was safely recovered, much to the satisfaction of all concerned, except the unfortunate rat, who would now be under the necessity of returning to the straw!

April 20th

1822: This letter appeared in *The Scotsman*:

To the Editor of *The Scotsman*. Sir.— In your paper of Saturday last, the 6th inst., where you take notice of Mr Hume's remarks respecting the exorbitant salaries paid to some of the office-holders in Demerara, you state things prejudicial to that Colony, and which clearly show that your information regarding it is most lamentably defective. Believe me, when I assure you (and I trust you will give it publicity in your next paper) that Demerara contains upwards of 6,000 whites, 7,000 free people of colour, and nearly 80,000 slaves. And if to these respectable numbers you add that of the Indians (the original inhabitants) the total population will amount to upwards of 100,000 ... Were ... an additional 40 or 50,000 negroes permitted to be imported from the Bahamas and some of the West India Islands, where they are half-starved, Demerara, so far from being a 'petty colony,' would soon become one of the most valuable British possessions in the western world, and would outstrip, I have no doubt, even Jamaica itself. Having left the colony lately, after a residence of six years in it, I send you these remarks ... Yours respectfully, 'A Sugar Planter', East Coast, Fifeshire.

April 21st

1866: 'The High Constables' of Edinburgh Dinner. Mr Marwick [city clerk] proposed the toast of 'The Press.' He spoke of the great influence which the Press exerted, and said that, in its relation to political action, it was year by year establishing a more solid claim to the title which [Edmund] Burke gave it when he said it was the 'fourth estate.' Although the last it was assuredly the greatest power in the State, for it moulded and fashioned that public opinion which the greatest, the best, the wisest, and even the most Conservative of our statesmen admitted was ultimately irresistible. He hoped the Press would long be an institution which would teach everything that was good and great, and be the advocate of our rights and the protector of our liberties. He coupled with the toast the name of Mr. James Robie of the *Caledonian Mercury*. Mr Robie, in responding, said there was not in the world at large a Press more independent and earnest, or so altogether free from suspicion, as the Press of Scotland.' (*Caledonian Mercury*)

April 22nd

1614: On this day, it was decided that the children of the Latin and of the Vulgar (where Latin was not taught) schools, who were given a holiday on the Saturday before Palm Sunday every year (a practice disapproved of by the Kirk Session) would no longer get this holiday. The council decided to stop this practice completely and for all time. (*ERBE*)

———•◆•———

1850: 'Emigration to the United States. Mr Catlin, the well-known Historian of the American Indians, and Traveller of the Western Prairies, under the auspices of the United States Land Company, just formed and duly registered in London, is about to lead a numerous Colony of Settlers to one of the finest tracts of country in the Western States, familiarly known to him. Persons wishing to join in the formation of this Settlement, or to invest in the Shares of the Company (which are receivable for lands), should apply personally, or by letter, to George Catlin, Esq., at his Indian Collection, 6 Waterloo Place; or to William Prinsep, Esq., No. 9 Walbrook Cheapside, London; or to Robert Allan, Esq., Edinburgh, for the prospectus and accompanying documents, which will be forwarded to any part of the kingdom.' (*Caledonian Mercury*)

April 23rd

1669: Thomas Campbell, deacon of the Fleshers (butchers) of Edinburgh, had alerted the council to the fact that citizens coming to the burgh Flesh Market, and those who lived near it, made complaints every day that they hardly dare venture out to the Flesh Market or walk towards their own houses without being molested by the multitude of dogs kept at the market by the fleshers and their servants. There was no longer any reason for the fleshers to keep any other dogs than one or two strong dogs for herding cattle or sheep and a small dog for driving them. However, some fleshers kept as many as seven or eight dogs. The council considered Thomas Campbell's request very carefully and decided they had powers under the statute, ordering that all the fleshers in the middle market, along with their wives and servants, should keep no more than one or two strong dogs at the most and instructed them to keep such dogs inside a house or kennel and not permit the dogs to go out into the streets or to the market at night, at the risk of such penalties as the council should decide upon. (*ERBE*)

April 24th

1558: Mary Queen of Scots married François, Dauphin of France, at the Cathedral of Notre Dame in Paris. Centrepiece of the celebrations back in Edinburgh was a ceremonial procession (a 'Triumph'), along with a scripted play and a night illuminated by fireworks (known as fireballs). On the Nether Bow, the Butts (location of the archery targets) and the Tron were layers of clay into which branches of fir-trees were inserted, along with many yellow lilies. The Tron was surmounted by a large tree sprouting a hundred cherries, with twenty-four tennis balls wrapped in gold. At the Mercat Cross, twenty quarts of wine were placed so as to stream from thin lead pipes. A float built on a cart was pulled through the High Street by a horse. Upon it stood actors dressed as Cupid and the Seven Planets in brightly-coloured and gilded costumes. Others were dressed as Black Friars (Dominicans) and Grey Friars (Franciscans). There were also six dancers, with 370 small bells sewn into their costumes, who posed and tap-danced noisily on a wooden scaffolding. Along with the fireworks at night, nineteen artillery pieces, placed in the Fleshmarket, roared in salute. (*Accounts of the Burgh Treasurer, 1557-58*)

April 25th

1805: An advertisement for 'A Contractor Wanted' was printed in the *Caledonian Mercury*:

Persons willing to Contract for Excavating the whole inside of the Wet Dock, presently building at Leith, consisting of about sixty thousand cubic yards of clay, to be laid down behind the Quay walls of the Dock, will please give in proposals, sealed and marked on the back, 'Offers for Excavating a Wet Dock at Leith,' under cover, addressed to Mr Charles Cunninghame, Clerk to the Committee for constructing the Wet Docks at Leith, at the Dean of Guild's Office, Edinburgh, between this day and the 14th day of May next. They will receive what information they may require, concerning the nature and execution of the work, by applying to Mr John Paterson, resident engineer at Leith. As the whole excavation must be finished by the first day of November next, the most satisfactory security will be required for the punctual fulfilment of the contract.

April 26th

1855: 'Edinburgh Police. Estimates Wanted for supplying the Edinburgh Police Establishment with the following articles for One Year, from the 15th May next:— cast-iron lamp-posts; cast-iron bases; pillar bases of Craigleith stone, according to pattern; globes for gas-lamps—glass of first quality, and free from specks; stop-cocks and burners; glazing street lanterns; lion iron for cart wheels; low moor and common iron; tin plate; shovels and spades; hardwood (oak and British and American elm, cut for cartwright's purposes); whitewood plank; redwood plank and inch American deal; bells for dust-carts; white lead and Linseed oil; leather for hose; copper rivets; fire-cocks, fire-cock doors and fire-cock boxes; cast-iron ekes; branch pipes (the Estimate to state the price of the leather per Foot. Specifications and patterns may be seen by applying to Mr Mitchell, Master of Fire-Engines); best Greenland Whale oil; best Oxford woven tape Cotton; best Tow; household Coal (the Estimates to specify the quality of the Coals, and the price per Ton, including cartage and porterage); Skimmed Milk (the Milk to be of the best quality, and the Estimate to state the price per Imperial Gallon); Writing and Printing paper; books, quills, and other Stationery and the Printing required by the Establishment.' (*Caledonian Mercury*)

April 27th

1601: James Wood of Bonnington was beheaded at the Mercat Cross at six in the morning for destroying the buildings at Bonnington, which his father owned but which he believed should have been his. On the same day, Archibald Cornell, the town officer, was executed at the Mercat Cross. His body hung on the gallows for twenty-four hours. He was a pitiless, greedy creature. He seized and sold an honest man's house. He did the same to the King and Queen's pictures. When he came to the Mercat Cross to make a public valuation of the paintings, he hung them up on two iron nails driven into the wooden gallows. When people saw this, they sent word to the King and Queen. Cornell was arrested and then hanged. (*Diarey of Robert Birrel*)

April 28th

1472: King James III sent a letter under his privy seal, giving the burgesses and community of the burgh the power to construct defensive ditches, build bulwarks, walls, towers and turrets against another English invasion. The King further urged those who owned property to make a contribution to the costs of this operation. The burgh officers were instructed to force those who refused to co-operate in this work to do so and to demolish any houses built on the burgh walls where defences needed to be strengthened. Anyone who attempted to leave the burgh to avoid their responsibility would lose their privileges of the freedom of the burgh for themselves and their heirs. and have their goods confiscated to the value of the tax which they had failed to pay. (*ERBE*)

———•◆•———

1624: The council stated that many and varied complaints had been made by the merchant booth-keepers of the burgh against the portable stall-holders (kramers) over the frequent selling of all trimmings, lawn and cambric, and such decorative haberdashery that was offered for sale in the stalls, items that were licensed for sale only by the guild members in their booths. The Dean of Guild was ordered to go to the kramers and warn them to stop or be subject to serious consequences. (*ERBE*)

April 29th

1659: Steps were taken to remove houses of ill-repute from the vicinity of the College; earlier in 1659 the College Council forbade one Thomas Thomson from keeping a billiard board in his house at Bell's Wynd, as students were enticed away from their studies by the game. The regents agreed to reintroduce the minor penalties formerly in force at Edinburgh and in other universities and approved by the town council. For coming late into private classes after the bell had been rung, a fine of two pence would be imposed for each half hour late and four pence after that; a two pence fine each time a student spoke in the Scots language. Absences from private classes for a whole diet (session), two pence. All delinquencies at the time of public meetings, whether from lessons, disputations, or examinations to be charged double the fine for similar misdemeanours in the private classes. For breaking glass windows or damaging any part of the fabric of the College building the fine was at least half a crown. The regents asked the council to allow them the discretion to commute corporal punishment and replace it by a fine. (*ERBE*)

April 30th

1470: King James III, the provost, bailies, and community of Edinburgh, had petitioned Pope Paul II to free the Collegiate Kirk of St Giles and its clergy from the jurisdiction of the Bishop of St Andrews. The Pope accepted their formal request by issuing a bull (a charter authenticated with a lead seal known as a 'bulla'). Writing from Rome, the Pope informed the petitioners that he had decided to make St Giles directly responsible to Rome and not to the local bishop. This implied freedom from the constraints imposed by the Bishop of St Andrews and made St Giles answer only to a higher authority. (*ERBE*)

1717: On this day, a terrifying crime unfolded. Robert Irvine, tutor to John and Alexander, sons of Mr James Gordon of Ellon, had attempted on several occasions to seduce one of the family maidservants. The boys had seen him and told their father, so the tutor took them out on the pretext of going for a picnic on what is now the New Town. There he killed them both. His terrible savagery was watched from the Castlehill. Irvine was chased, captured and then hanged, after his two hands had first been hacked off. (Chambers, *Traditions of Edinburgh*)

May 1st

1644: The burgh council had in the past repeatedly forbidden the wearing of plaids around and over women's heads. Common strumpets, whores and other indecent women habitually covered their faces in this way to prevent them from being distinguished from honest women. These sorts of women had been banished from the burgh for their obscenity in pretending to be honest. On this day, proclamation was made renewing the council order that no one should wear a plaid over their head in churches, streets or vennels (passages) under pain of being declared infamous and of having their plaids confiscated by any citizen who could seize them. Any person who brought such a plaid to a magistrate would receive twelve shillings.

On 31 March 1645 the council, during a time of plague, condemned 'that indecent and strumpet-like habit of plaids so often forbidden, by which people so disguised can come not only onto the streets and public markets but also to the kirks, as a threat to all others.' Women who wore a plaid would be fined twenty pounds. This condemnation was repeated on 1 June 1648: ordinary officers and under-guards were ordered to take and apprehend such plaids and confiscate them under threat of themselves being put into prison. (*ERBE*)

May 2nd

1597: Bonfires lit up the night sky above Holyrood Palace on the arrival in Leith of James VI and Anne, daughter of the King of Denmark, his new Queen, for whose entry the damaged stonework of the Netherbow gate was repaired. The master of the Song School had prepared his pupils to act and sing in a costumed pageant. Romany violets, herbs and new-mown grasses were strewn on the floor of St Giles, in the lofts and seats. A large tapestry was hung in the aisle, the carpenters working through the night by the light of candles held by two pauper boys, sustained by ale and bread. Aromatic gum burned in the kirk and the pillar-heads were brightly painted; streamers flew from the steeple. Afterwards, their Majesties were entertained by Highland dancers and sword-dancers, the bells on their costumes tinkling rhythmically. On 2 June the Duke of Holstein, brother of Queen Anne, was given a banquet by the town at Bailie MacMorran's lodging on the south side of the Lawnmarket. The King and Queen were both present, entertained with great merriment. The Duke sailed away from Leith on 3 June. To wish him god-speed, the ordnance at Leith bulwark shot a 60-gun salute. (*ERBE*)

May 3rd

1823: 'Arable farms in the County of Edinburgh to Let, with entry at Whitsunday first, and separation of present crop:— Catcune, containing about 200 acres; Borthwick Mains, about 160 acres, making altogether 360 arable Scotch acres, or thereby, as presently possessed by Mr Francis Shirreff. The farms adjoin, and will be let together or separately, and on a grain or money rent, or part of each, as offerers incline. They are in a high state of cultivation, with a full proportion of fallow and grass; to which, as also to the dung on the farms; and the straw of the growing crop, the tenant will have free entry. The working of the fallow is in considerable forwardness, and immediate entry may be had to it. These farms are ten miles south-east of Edinburgh, by Fushie Bridge; and four from Dalkeith, and in the immediate vicinity of coal and lime. For further particulars apply to Hugh Watson, Esq. W.S., 1 Charlotte Square, Edinburgh; or to Alexander Innes at Vogrie, with either of whom offers may be lodged, betwixt today and the 29th May. Peter Wilson, servant at Borthwick Mains, will show the lands.' (*Caledonian Mercury*)

May 4th

1843: 'Thomas Cunningham begs to announce his return from London, where he has succeeded in obtaining the appointment for Bandonni's Patent *Combinaison* Hat. They are extremely light, elegant, and short in the pile. Velvet Parisian Hats, quite new style. Also, a choice selection of Gentlemen's Hussar and Forage Caps, new in design. Youths' and Infants' French Hair and Velvet Caps, latest fashions for Summer. Boys' Brazilian straw hats, &c. 61, New Buildings, Edinburgh.' (*Caledonian Mercury*)

'Ladies' Bonnets. The subscriber begs respectfully to intimate that he has just returned from London with a magnificent assortment of splendid Bonnets, and will be glad to be favoured with a visit from intending purchasers. A Lot of Boys' Leghorn hats; the newest Ribbons; Straw Cords, Tassels & Edgings. John Burnet, Manufacturer of Straw Bonnets, 15 South Bridge Street.' (*Caledonian Mercury*)

May 5th

1508: The provost, bailies and council ruled on this day that Fleshers should have their stalls and stands protected by stout canvas awning, and the meat on sale covered with proper wrapping. Those selling the meat should be appropriately dressed, with clean aprons. The meat should be sold in a well-organised covered location. Anyone who failed to meet these requirements should pay forty shillings to the kirk's community fund. (*ERBE*)

——— ◆ ———

1800: On this day, the *Caledonian Mercury* printed an article about the murderer Daniel Collins, who had killed John Wilson, Officer of Lanark, with a cutlass:

> Collins was born and bred at Laughgall, in the county of Armagh, Ireland; is of a long thin visage, about five feet seven inches high, brown complexion, brown eyes, about twenty-five years of age, broad-shouldered, bandy legged, commonly wears his hair queued; generally wore a long blue coat, with yellow buttons, a round hat, deep in the crown, leather or drab-coloured breeches; speaks the Irish dialect, and when pronouncing the word 'three', speaks it shortly as 'tree'; carries about with him a diploma from the Union and Crown Lodge of Glasgow. All persons are hereby required to be assisting in apprehending him … that he may be brought to justice. Sheriff-Clerk's Office, Lanark.

May 6th

1544: This extract is an edited version of a boastful letter sent to Lord Russell:

It was determined by the Lord Lieutenant, the Earl of Hertford, utterly to ruin and destroy Edinburgh with fire. This we did not fully achieve on that day, as the night was drawing on. However, we set fire to three or four parts of the town and then returned to our camp. Very early the next morning we began where we had left off and continued to burn all that day and the next two days, so that neither within the walls, nor in the suburbs, was left one house unburnt, besides the innumerable booty, spoil and pillage that our soldiers brought out, over and above the abundance which was consumed by fire. We also burnt the abbey known as Holyroodhouse and the Palace next to it … In the meantime, while we held the country thus occupied, there came unto us 4,000 of our light horsemen from the Borders by the King's appointment. They performed such exploits in devastating the country that within eight miles of Edinburgh in every direction, they left neither castle, village, nor house standing unburnt.

('The Late Expedition in Scotland', sent to Lord Russell, Lord Privy Seal, Imprinted at London, 1544)

May 7th

1674: Following an agreement with the town council, Mr Peter Braus, a Dutch engineer, began work on a project to bring water from Tod's Well at Comiston in a 3in-diameter lead pipe. He also agreed to build a fountainhead or reservoir and five cisterns. These were to be placed at the Weigh-House, at the head of Forrester's Wynd, at the Mercat Cross, at the head of Niddrie's Wynd and near the Netherbow. His remuneration for this work was £2,900 sterling, in three instalments. If the work was completed to the council's satisfaction, a gratuity of £100 sterling would be paid to his wife. Robert Milne was engaged by Braus to build the stonework for the fountains. Five additional fountains were ordered, one at the foot of the Bow, another at the head of the Canongate, and the others in the Fishmarket and at the foot of Niddrie's and Forrester's Wynds. On 5 March 1675 another pipe was laid into the Tolbooth, for the use of prisoners. By 28 April the water supply was working. The council, worried about the vandalism that 'malicious base vagabonds' or 'idle persons' might cause by tampering with the water-cocks, appointed overseers for a number of the fountains. (*ERBE*)

May 8th

1366: At Holyrood Abbey, a Council was held in which discussion over a peace with England took place. It was agreed that the assessment to raise money for the King's ransom should be voluntary. The Scottish Mint was also ordered to strike new coins for this purpose. (*ERBE*).

———————•◆•———————

1860: These events were written of in the *Caledonian Mercury*:

Newington Free Church. Revivals in Ireland and in the North of Scotland. The Rev. Mr Moore of Ballymena will address the Prayer Meeting in Newington Free Church, this evening, at seven o'clock, and will give details in regard to the Revivals in Ireland and the North of Scotland, from which he has just returned.

Church of Scotland, India Mission. A meeting of the General Committee will take place in the Schemes Office, No 22 Queen Street, Edinburgh, on Thursday next, the 10th last, at Two o'clock PM. James Craik, DD, Convener.

Temperance Lecture. Samuel Bowley, Esq., of Gloucester will deliver a lecture under the auspices of the Edinburgh Total Abstinence Society in Richmond Place Chapel on Thursday evening 10th inst. Chair to be taken at quarter-past eight o'clock. In consequence of the above there will be no Meeting this evening.

May 9th

1918: On this day, an article about a Scottish Bolshevist appeared in *The Scotsman*:

> In the High Court of Justiciary, Edinburgh, John Maclean, ex-teacher, who was recently appointed Russian Consul in Glasgow by the Bolsheviks, appeared for trial before the Lord Justice-General and a jury on a charge of sedition. The charge was that on certain dates and at various places, and in each case to an audience forming part of the civilian population, and consisting in part of persons engaged in the production, repair or transport of War material ... he made statements which were likely to prejudice the recruiting, training, discipline, and administration of His Majesty's Forces, and by which statements he attempted to cause mutiny, sedition, and disaffection among the civilian population and to impede, delay, and restrict the production, repair and transport of War material and other work necessary for the successful prosecution of the War.

———◆———

1957: A massive fire at Bell's Brae in the Dean Village destroyed the premises of one of Britain's largest theatrical costumiers: around 90,000 costumes were lost. Fraser Neal was a member of the Masque Theatre Company and in 1932 he bought the wig-making firm of William Mutrie, transforming it into the largest theatrical costumiers outside London.

May 10th

1506: King James IV issued letters ordering proclamations to be made at the Mercat Cross prohibiting the packing and parcelling of goods or merchandise in Leith and in the Canongate, or the shipment of goods until the same were examined in Edinburgh and Customs duty paid to the burgh. Also prohibited was the sale to strangers in Leith of cloth, hides, wool or other merchandise on which duty was liable. Such merchandise had to be taken to Edinburgh to be sold and not covertly exported. The punishment for breaking these regulations was confiscation. (*ERBE*)

———•◆•———

1859 'Edinburgh City Artillery.— A detachment, consisting of one officer and twenty-nine men, went by train to Glasgow at half-past six yesterday morning, en route to Fort Matilda, to be stationed there until further orders. This morning, a detachment, consisting of four officers, four sergeants, four corporals, two drummers and ninety gunners, will march from the Corn Exchange at half-past five, proceeding by rail to Glasgow, and thence to Dumbarton Castle, to be stationed there. The headquarters of the regiment are to march into the Castle, Edinburgh, on Thursday. Numerous applications are daily made by respectable young men to join the corps.' (*The Daily Scotsman*)

1660: A report was delivered to the council on St Paul's Work. The recommendations included that a seat was provided for the children in the community loft; that there should be five residents in the Work and that the children sent down should be divided among them. Beds should be provided for the children and other necessities; the boys should be apprentices for seven years and the girls for five; the supervisors of St Paul's Work should be obliged to teach the children all the stages of their trade – spinning, making fine woollen yarn, stocking-weaving and the manufacture of woollen serge cloth; a man should be appointed to test the proficiency of the children. At the same meeting, the council arranged for enough blue cloth to be provided to make thirty gowns for the celebration of King Charles II's thirtieth birthday. The King's Almsgiver was asked to inspect the blue gowns. The Mercat Cross was to be prepared with lead pipes so that wine could run out of the spouts and the Burgh Treasurer would provide wine glasses, with dry sweets. Eight trumpeters were to be engaged and thirty old crown coins in purses prepared for distribution to the poor. (*ERBE*)

May 12th

1838: The *Caledonian Mercury* printed this caution:

Two Englishmen are presently levying money from the humane and generous of this city upon false pretences. Sometimes they represent themselves to be weavers out of employment, in consequence of their master's bankruptcy, and they have artful certificates. Military and naval gentlemen have been imposed upon: one of them represented himself as an officer in the army, but having fought a duel in Gibraltar, he was obliged to abscond. Being asked by the gentleman where his commission was to prove his identity, he artfully answered that it was lost during the duel; and having mentioned a name answering to an affair of honour of the kind which had actually happened, the gentleman was credulous enough to believe him. One of the swindlers is a little man, and the other rather tall, above the ordinary size, and it would be well to hand them over to the police.

May 13th

1667: The council confirmed the court held at the Water of Leith on 21 March and approved its decisions: the firlot measure for taxing malt would be used by the millers for sacks coming to the mill; the grinders should be allowed to keep six pence on each bag of malt carried on their own horse to the mill; the grinders should not sweep up any malt-dust or pig-food within 16 ft of the hopper or trough and what they swept outside was to be placed in the farthest corner of the mill and none of it should be sold. In the case of theft, both buyer and seller would be punished according to the will of the magistrates. The court gave powers to the brewers or their servants to bring anyone found selling or carrying material away before the magistrates. The millers should be attentive night and day to provide good service to the grinders in loading their horses and grinding their malt. No boys were to be allowed into the malt mill except those who were authorised by the taxmen or grinders as being their servants. No horseman who carried for hire or the grinders' horsemen should be allowed to open the sacks and give malt to their horses. (*ERBE*)

May 14th

1849: This attempted suicide was reported in the *Caledonian Mercury* along with a cautionary warning:

> On Saturday forenoon, while a county police constable was passing over Corstorphine Hill, he observed a man striking his head forcibly against the wall, near the seat 'Rest and Be Thankful', and on being questioned, he admitted his purpose was to commit suicide. He had also a rope and knife in his possession, which he intended to use if the other novel and painful method failed. He was taken into custody, and turned out to be a poor German street minstrel. On being examined it was evident he was insane and his wife bore testimony to his lunacy. His head was carefully bandaged, and he was removed to the asylum at Morningside. Caution.— on Saturday, two criminal officers observed a young woman, a notorious thief, in a sale-room, Hanover Street, jostle a young lady among those present, and their suspicions being excited, she was apprehended and found to have abstracted a small note-book from the lady's pocket. There was, however, but little money in it, but those present at the sales, which are frequent at this time of the year, would do well to guard their pockets, as, when their attention is taken up otherwise, such thefts are very often successful.

May 15th

1928: 'Two deserters from the Foreign Legion, an Austrian and a German respectively, have been landed at Granton from a Leith steamer, which arrived with a cargo of esparto grass from Susa, Tunis in North Africa. The men, who were clad in the Legion uniform, lay concealed in the esparto grass for five days till hunger and thirst drove them out. Thereupon they threw themselves on the mercy of the captain of the ship. They were well treated, and on arrival at Granton their respective Consuls were informed. Their uniforms were changed for civilian clothes, and the men were placed on a vessel bound for Hamburg.' (*The Scotsman*)

——— • ◆ • ———

1800: 'A culprit escaped from Justice—and a Reward of Fifty Guineas offered for securing him. James Barton, late travelling Chapman in Newmilns, aged about 35 years ... dark complexion, dark hair, with ordinary sized whiskers ... appears to be an Irishman. From what has come out upon precognition, there is little doubt of Burton being actively concerned in the many depredations committed in Greenock within these thee weeks past.' (*Caledonian Mercury*)

May 16th

1402: At a Council-General held in Edinburgh, the King officially pardoned the Duke of Albany and the Earl of Douglas for the death of David Stuart, Duke of Rothesay (c. 1378-1402), son of King Robert II (1316-90) and the heir apparent. Rothesay had been made Lieutenant of Scotland by his father (who was elderly, physically weak and of a retiring disposition), replacing his uncle, the Duke of Albany, in that post. However, in 1402, Albany and the Earl of Douglas put him under arrest. While in prison and under their joint custody, the Duke of Rothesay died and it was suspected that they had deliberately put him to death. Since their guilt was not definitively proved, and since Scotland desperately needed firm government, Albany and Douglas were given the benefit of the doubt. (*ERBE*)

King Henry IV of England invaded Scotland in 1402 and captured Edinburgh Castle. The Kingdom of Scotland was once again placed in Albany's hands and he continued in that role even after Robert III died, as the new king, James I, was at that time a prisoner in England, having been captured at sea in 1406 by pirates.

May 17th

1617: King James VI returned to Edinburgh (the first time since 5 April 1603). The council had paid for a new effigy of the King to be placed on the Netherbow Gate. The portrait was painted on cloth that had been first undercoated and stretched on a wooden frame. Then the painting was carried out and completed with a great deal of gold leaf on the heraldic arms, with a sceptre, St Andrew, St George and the Order of the Thistle. This was then coated with wax, rosin and sulphur and the panel fixed into the stonework. The council provided a banquet, held in a banqueting-house specially constructed in the council-house yard. Among the many provisions were: six puncheons of French wine; a cask of sherry; two tuns (252 gallons) and eight puncheons (cask of eight gallons) of ale; venison; fowls and rabbits; ten hams; water from St Anthony's Well; six quarts of Rhenish wine; eight hundred oranges; milk; strawberries; egg; flour; twenty-seven dozen quails; veal from Berwick; seven turkeys; spices; drinks which the town officers took while keeping order as dancers performed through the town; fish; sweet meats; table-cloths; eight damask napkins; twenty-one towels. The total cost of the banquet was £6,333 17s 5d. (*ERBE*)

May 18th

1650: James Graham, Marquess of Montrose, landed in the North with about 500 foreigners, gallantly attempting to seat the King on his native throne. However, he suffered a total overthrow and, disguising himself as a peasant, he entrusted himself to a friend by whom he was perfidiously betrayed and was carried prisoner to Edinburgh. There he was treated with all the ignominy with which base spirits exult over the object of their fear, when reduced within their power, and with the severity natural to men inflamed against each other by a long train of civil wars, heightened by all the rancour of theological fervour. At the Watergate he was met by the magistrates, the city guard and the executioner, who conducted him along the streets in fatal pomp. The other prisoners, bound two and two, walked before him. Montrose followed on a new cart made for the purpose, with a high seat to which he was bound with cords so that he might be the more fully exposed to the rabble, the hangman riding before him in his livery coat and bonnet, while Montrose sat uncovered. (Arnot, *The History of Edinburgh*)

He was hanged on 27 May 1650.

May 19th

1851 'Attempted Suicide.— Early on Saturday morning, while some parties were taking a stroll in the Queen's Park, they suddenly stumbled, near the Hunter's Bog, on the body of a middle-aged woman, with a frightful gash in her throat, inflicted apparently by a razor, which was lying by her side. As she still, however, exhibited some signs of life, she was immediately removed to the Infirmary; and it was subsequently ascertained that she was the wife of a man residing in the Canongate.' (*Caledonian Mercury*)

'Dog Lost. Lost on Thursday last, a black Retriever dog, with white on the breast; answers to the name of 'Toozer'. Whoever has found him, will please return him to Mr Donald Urquhart, innkeeper, Davidsons Mains, by Blackhall, Edinburgh.' (*Caledonian Mercury*)

'Dog Found. Found at Blackhall, on Thursday last, a black Retriever dog. If not claimed within ten days, he will be sold to pay expenses. Apply to Alexander Bailie, smith, Blackhall.' (*Caledonian Mercury*)

May 20th

1806: 'Tuesday, the Lord Provost, magistrates and council of this city, and a numerous company of Ladies and Gentlemen, met at the Assembly Rooms, Leith, and about three o'clock moved in procession to the Ferry Boat Stars, preceded by a band of music where two very fine smacks, decorated with the colours of the different European nations, lay ready to receive them. The magistrates and company having gone on board, a gun was fired as a signal to unmoor, when the vessels proceeded towards the Dock, and at twenty minutes past three, the Fifeshire, belonging to the Union Shipping Company, entered, followed by the Buccleuch, belonging to the Edinburgh and Leith Shipping Company, amidst the reiterated acclamations of an immense number of spectators, and repeated discharges of artillery from the Fort at Leith, his Majesty's ships of war in Leith Roads, and guns stationed on the Quays of the Dock. This Dock, the first of the kind in North Britain, has been wholly executed within the high water mark ... The space occupied by the Dock is above five acres ... The sea-wall ... is wholly composed of large ashlar stones, from a quarry at Rosyth.' (*Caledonian Mercury*)

May 21st

1901: An article concerning the Edinburgh School Board featured in *The Scotsman*:

A meeting was held in the Board Offices, Castle Terrace, yesterday afternoon. Dr Mackay moved —'That measures be forthwith adopted to put the training of the pupil-teachers in the service of the Board on a satisfactory footing.' Speaking to his motion, he said that the present system was very unsatisfactory, and they ought to give the matter their best attention. It would be unfortunate if they had to discontinue the pupil-teacher system. Mrs Kerr seconded the motion. Mr Henderson moved as an amendment—'That it be remitted to the School Management Committee to consider and report as to whether it is desirable to alter the system of training the pupil-teachers under the Board, and, if so, what they would suggest.' Mr Mill seconded. The Chairman held that the present pupil-teacher system was not unsatisfactory. The amendment was adopted. With regard to the examination of pupil-teachers of the Board, held in December last, for admissions to a training college, it was reported that of the nine pupil-teachers examined, seven had been placed in the first class, one in the third, and one had failed; while of the fifty females, twenty-nine had been placed in the first class, sixteen in the second, and five in the third.

May 22nd

1691: Responding to a petition from a Dutchman, Mr Mathias Fase, which notified them that he had brought three Turkish people to the city – a man, a woman and a little boy, all of whom he proposed to exhibit in public – the council gave liberty to do so, having obtained a licence from the Master of the Revels to exhibit the three Turks in public at any location in the Canongate, not requiring him to go through the formalities of advertising the show by the sound of a trumpet through the whole town; instead requiring only to advertise it in front of the close or over the window where the exhibition was taking place.

However, exotic Turks, dressed in their native costume and jewellery, as well as exciting popular curiosity may have suggested danger. On 3 November 1693, the council announced that a voluntary contribution would be asked for at every church door in each division of all parishes within the city and suburbs for Archibald Bartholomew and James Kay, who were at that time prisoners of the Turks. (*ERBE*)

May 23rd

1677: The council, along with the extraordinary deacons, met to consider that the magistrates, fulfilling their responsibilities, had enlisted the help of two companies of soldiers under the command of Captains Murray and Stewart, and several horsemen under Major Cochrane, to suppress the trade apprentices who had been called together the previous Friday in Holyrood Abbey park. Bailie Dick had permitted them some time to hold their assembly, a gesture that the council believed to be fair and just. The council ordered the burgh treasurer to recompense Bailie Dick for the sums of money he had been required to spend on security. (*ERBE*)

The craft youths, with other disorderly persons from the country, were said to have numbered between 1,500 and 2,000 men. They held two bailies sent to negotiate with them, until the youth prisoners in the Tolbooth were set free and their conditions granted. Evidently, it was the provost, Town Clerk and several members of the Privy Council who ordered out Major William Cochrane of the King's troop. His men fired on the crowd and one or two persons, including a woman, were killed. This riot is not mentioned in the Privy Council minutes.

May 24th

1853: 'Destruction of the Adelphi Theatre by fire. On Tuesday afternoon the Adelphi Theatre, Broughton Street, was completely destroyed by a fire, the progress of which was so rapid, that in little more than an hour after it was first discovered, there was nothing left but the bare walls. The building comprised under one roof the theatre, a house occupied by Mr Wyndham (the lessee), and two shops — one let to a tobacconist and the other to a spirit-dealer. Its walls were close to a large block of houses on the south-west, and adjoining it on the north-west, stands St Mary's Catholic Chapel. About a quarter to five o'clock in the afternoon, shortly after the rehearsal, while Mr Wyndham was engaged in his own house, a carpenter rushed in from the theatre with the first intelligence of the fire. Mr Wyndham hastened to the spot, and observed flames rising into the private box on the left hand side of the stage, and apparently proceeding from the musicians' room underneath. He immediately despatched messengers to the Police-Office and the various insurance offices, and set about removing as much of his property as possible. His first care, however, was to get Mrs Wyndham, who had been confined on Saturday last, conveyed to a place of safety.' (*Caledonian Mercury*)

May 25th

1809: 'Trafalgar Light Post Coach. The public are respectfully informed, that the Trafalgar Coach for sometime running between Newcastle and London, is to be extended to Edinburgh, on Monday the first day of May, by Whittingham, Cornhill, Greenlaw, &c. These coaches will start every lawful day, from Mrs Atkinson's, Shakespeare Coffee-room, Newcastle, and the Crown Hotel, Edinburgh, at six o'clock morning, where Tickets will be given out, and Parcels received; and as the Proprietors intend to have a communication with the principal Manufacturing Towns, further particulars will be given in a future advertisement. The Coaches are new, and very commodious, and was built on purpose, in a superior style; and as the principal Innkeepers are all Proprietors, they cannot fail of being carried on so as to give satisfaction to the Public.' (*Caledonian Mercury*)

May 26th

1845: The *Caledonian Mercury* reported on a fire that caused havoc the previous day:

Yesterday morning about five o'clock, a fire broke out in the premises occupied by Mr Purves, tailor, North Bridge, which communicated to the premises below, belonging to and occupied by Messrs Millar & Son, watchmakers. Fortunately for the latter parties, the greater part of the valuable stock, together with the watches of their customers, were ... secured in an iron safe, and thereby escaped damage. The fire for a time seemed to threaten great destruction; but by the active exertions and judicious management of Mr Hardy and his fire brigade, it was confined to the premises where it originated and to the shop below. As it was, however, considerable damage was done. The premises and stock of the Messrs Millar were insured; Mr Purves was not, but happily for him the loss he sustained was comparatively trifling. The fire originated from the stove kept for heating irons, which had, it is supposed, been smouldering between the flooring and the roof of the shop all night ... it may be proper to mention, that the West Port engine was at the scene of the conflagration in a very short time after the one kept at the Police Office.

May 27th

1661: As head of his clan, Archibald Campbell was one of the richest and most powerful men in Scotland. Repeated conflicts with Charles I over the introduction into Scotland of Anglican forms of religion led to Argyll becoming leader of the Covenanting party. At the time of the Civil War, the King made him Marquess of Argyll in the hope of winning him over, but Argyll intensified his efforts to extend the influence of the Covenanters, particularly in an alliance with the English Parliamentary party and Oliver Cromwell, against his most effective military opponent, the Marquess of Montrose. After the execution of Charles I, his son and successor Charles II arrested Argyll, who was found guilty of treason and sentenced to death on this day. Standing on the platform before the 'Maiden' (a Scottish version of the guillotine), Argyll showed courage and cheerfulness as he faced death. By a piece of supreme irony, the body of his great adversary, Montrose, was being exhumed, embalmed and interred with honour in St Giles' High Kirk. Argyll was hanged eleven years to the day after Montrose. After his execution, Argyll's head was displayed on the very same spike that had until recently held the head of Montrose.

May 28th

1861: On this day, a letter appeared in *The Scotsman*:

Sir.— I was overjoyed to see our large hearted friend 'Randolph', who is ever foremost in defending our quaint old city against the ruthless hands of the destroyer or restorer, for they are one and the same, raising his voice against the desecrations now being committed in Rosslyn Chapel. I should know every stone of that glorious old building, having within the last eighteen months spent, at the least, six months within its walls … but no one who has done so then will ever forget the glorious coloured robe in which nature has decked it; and to think that that robe which has taken 300 years to perfect is to be destroyed at one fell swoop, is something barbarous. 'Randolph' hints at the possibility of the Earl of Rosslyn not being cognisant of the havoc that is going on, but I have been told that the Earl does know (I have seen him there myself), and is thoroughly pleased with what has been done, and also with the workman who has displayed his genius in restoring the canopies and brackets at the east end of the chapel. Quaint things they must have been originally, but look at them now, without one particle of originality, expression, or grotesqueness.

May 29th

1661: Thomas Murray, treasurer, drew up a bill for the entertainment of His Majesty's Commissioners at the College and repaid the bailies from the levy collected from the residents of the town. The expenses included payment for: a hogshead of vinegar; hams, lemons and glasses; a tun (252 gallons) of wine from Leith; a draft of sand; five trumpeters; the town officers; Thomas Johnston, viol player; cooks and spit-turners; ten bottles of Canary wine; eight gallons and a pint of Canary; seven pints of Malaga wine; four and three quarter pints of Rhenish wine; a hogshead of vinegar; half a pound of pepper; three ounces of Cochineal; nine and a half stone of butter; eighteen pounds of candles; silverware; three cases of knives; three bolts of ribbons; to Gideon Lithgow for printing verses; to James Cuthbertson, the gardener, for providing salads and straw. The total cost was £8,044 4s. Other costs included: the workmen for putting in the wine, changing it and carrying it; to James Boig for carrying 700 boards, thirty double trees, forty single trees and thirty small trees and six buckets of coal; to Peter Norie, sent with a letter to Lord Aboyne, asking for some venison. (*ERBE*)

May 30th

1831: The *Caledonian Mercury* reported on several incidents, including an artilleryman who was killed by an infuriated ox in Sandport Street, Leith, which was being driven to market. It said how the poor fellow was twice tossed, and dreadfully gored by the animal. Another incident happened on the previous Thursday: Philip Docherty, an Irish labourer, was killed at Orchardfield, by a loaded cart. While in a state of intoxication, he had attempted to leap upon the cart, but fell before it, and the wheel passed over his body. On the same Thursday, in the Police Court, three girls, the eldest not eleven years of age, were remitted for trial for breaking into a dwelling-house in the Cowgate and stealing from it a great quantity of table linen. Another incident in the news was a drowning; William Roberts, a mason, in crossing in a boat from North to South Queensferry, fell overboard and was drowned. There was a squall of wind at the time. An outbreak of fever was also reported: several cases of typhus had again appeared in Leith, but, with one or two exceptions, was of a mild and modified nature. However, an old man of the name of Stewart lost three full-grown daughters, in as many weeks.

May 31st

1878: On this day, Eugène Chantrelle was executed within the Calton Jail for poisoning his wife, Elizabeth. As a girl she was sent to the Newington Academy where she met Frenchman Eugène Chantrelle, a 43-year-old teacher. Romance blossomed between Chantrelle and his pupil. She discovered she was pregnant and, against his will, Chantrelle was forced to marry her. Then his free-spending lifestyle led him into debt. Chantrelle then began to work out an undetectable method of poisoning Elizabeth. On the morning of 2 January 1878, his maid found Mrs Chantrelle lying on her side near the edge of the bed. Mrs Chantrelle was taken to the Royal Infirmary but died at 4 o'clock that afternoon. Dr Henry Littlejohn's opinion was that Chantrelle had fractured the gas-pipe to draw attention away from the opium that he had placed in her food or drink. Dr Maclagan, Professor of Medical Jurisprudence at Edinburgh, was convinced this was a case of poisoning. After trial, Chantrelle was found guilty of poisoning. He was hanged on Friday 31 May. The large crowds who came to the Calton Hill to try and see over the wall of the jail were disappointed. The only sign of his execution they saw was the hoisting of the black flag.

June 1st

1801: 'Carron Stock. To be sold by public roup, or auction, in the Royal Exchange Coffeehouse, Edinburgh, on Thursday 9th July, 1801. Some shares of Stock in Carron Company, belonging to the sequestrated estates of Francis Garbett & Co., and Charles Gascoigne, both late of Carron Wharff. The Stock will be put up at the rate of one hundred and thirty-five per cent, and the purchaser will have right to the dividends after the 13th of April last. The Company are possessed of a large sum of undivided profits. They pay regularly a dividend of eight per cent and their affairs are conducted with such attention as to ensure, not only the continuation of such dividends, but to give well grounded hopes of an increase. For particulars apply to Walter Hog, at the British Linen Office, or to Mr Andrew Macwhinnie, writer, No 37, North Hanover Street, Edinburgh.' (*Caledonian Mercury*)

June 2nd

1941: 'Edinburgh Lady Provost's Comforts Flag Day.— It is estimated, though a number of collection boxes are still to be counted, that a sum of at least £1,200 was raised for the Fund by the flag day and its accompanying entertainments on Saturday. In the course of the week, house-to-house collecting has been done, and hundreds of flag sellers, including a number of uniformed nurses, were on the streets on Saturday. Over a ton of coppers was counted. A variety entertainment organised by the producers of the 'Sunday Night at Seven' Usher Hall concerts was given in the afternoon at the Ross Bandstand in Princes Street Gardens, and attracted a large crowd. The first half of the programme was provided by members of the King's Theatre 'Half-Past Eight' company, including Dave Willis ... and four of the Charles Ross Girls and the pipers from the show's Scots finale. The bright and rapid-moving performance, for which the Empire Theatre orchestra was conducted by Ellis Midgeley, the musical director of the King's Theatre, was exceedingly popular, and the orchestra under their own conductor, Harry Joseph, figured prominently in the remainder of the programme, sustained by members of the Reptiles Concert Party who have been regularly entertaining troops.' (*The Scotsman*)

June 3rd

1597: Robert Cathcart was relieving himself on the wall at the head of Peebles Wynd when he was killed by William Stewart, son of Sir William Stewart. Cathcart had been present at the murder of Sir William Stewart some time before, so the motto is, 'who kills, will in turn be killed'. When he was murdered, Sir William Stewart was one of the Earl of Bothwell's associates. (*Diarey of Robert Birrel*)

———◆———

1819: 'Sir.—As directed by Minutes of the Calder District, I have to request that you will call a General Meeting of the Trustees on the Roads in this County— 1st—for power to erect a Side Bar to prevent the evasions at Kiershill Toll Bar. 2nd—For reconsidering the plan of bringing down a Surveyor from England. To the Convener of the Trustees for High Roads in County of Edinburgh—George Fergusson, C.C.D. In consequence of the above Requisition, the Trustees for the High Roads in this County are hereby required to hold a General Meeting within the County Rooms, on Friday the 11th day of June instant, at one o'clock afternoon, for the above-mentioned purposes. By order of the Convener, Thomas Cranstoun, Principal Clerk.' (*Caledonian Mercury*)

June 4th

1647: The council considered a bill of complaint submitted to them by David Sinclair (blacksmith), Andro Gibson (baker), William Drummond (pistol-maker), John Lennox (pistol-maker), all residents of the Calton, speaking on their own behalf and on behalf of the other residents. They described how for three days (for what reason they did not know), a large number of apprentices and journeymen had come to their houses in Calton with swords, batons and other offensive weapons and mortally wounded George Watt (a weaver). William Drummond, Alexander Gray (shoemaker), James Miller (tailor) and certain other neighbours had their houses damaged, their doors and windows smashed, their belongings stolen, and suffered abuse and other outrages. The council decided to question its members to see if any of them knew any of the people the complaint was made about. Every deacon was ordered to convene his own craft and to see if any of their apprentices and journeymen were members of the mob. Lastly, the council sent for the bailies of the Canongate: Alexander Peiris, their leader, had called together a large number of the most respected inhabitants and ordered forty of them to assemble at William Forrester's house. If there was any disturbance they were to suppress it and notify him. (*ERBE*)

June 5th

1815: 'Dr Boerhaave's Red Pill. Famous throughout Europe for the cure of every stage and symptom of a Certain Complaint. It is a melancholy fact, that thousands fall victim to this horrid disease, owing to the unskilfulness of illiterate men, who by an improper treatment of this direful calamity, not infrequently cause those foul ulcerations and blotches which so often appear on the head, face, and body, with dimness in the sight, noise in the ears, deafness, strictures, obstinate gleets, nodes on the shin bones, ulcerated sore throat, diseased nose, nocturnal pains in the head and limbs (frequently mistaken for other disorders), till at length a general debility and decay of the constitution ensues, and a melancholy death puts a period to suffering mortality. With each box is given a copious bill of directions, by which all persons are enabled speedily to cure themselves with safety and secrecy, without the least confinement or hindrance of business. Its amazing sale within the last 50 years, though seldom advertised, is a certain criterion of its immense utility.— Price only 4s 6d per box. Another supply is just received from London, and for sale by most of the following Vendors of Dr Solomon's Medicines: A. Smith, Perfumer, 33 North Bridge; Mr Scott and Mr Baxter, North Bridge; Isaac Baxter, Italian Warehouse.' (*Caledonian Mercury*)

June 6th

1825: 'The first Stated Annual Meeting of the Partners of the Wine Company of Scotland was held on the 2nd instant, in the Waterloo Hotel, John Craig, Esq. of Great King Street, in the chair. The Meeting was numerously attended, and the statements of the Company's affairs, submitted to it by the Directors, in terms of the contract of co-partnery, were highly satisfactory to the proprietary, as they exhibited greater success during the first year of such an establishment, than even the most sanguine of its promoters had ventured to anticipate. All the actings of the Directors were approved of, and the cordial thanks of the Meeting were voted to them for their great and successful exertions in behalf of the Company Agriculture. The fields around Dalkeith have a most beautiful appearance. The potatoes are all rowed, and the grass is of great length … In the neighbourhood of Tranent, there is a very fine field of early white peases for the Edinburgh market. It contains them at three different stages of advancement; one portion of them being in bloom, another about a fortnight later, and the third about four inches above the ground. Besides there is a large field of strawberries in bloom.' (*Caledonian Mercury*)

June 7th

1690: The council, considering several serious questions, declared the post of Lieutenant of the Town's Company Militia, held by Thomas Lendall, to be vacant, stating that he was not eligible to serve in that capacity in the future. The council went on to discuss the major public disorder caused by the recent riots in Edinburgh. The Town's Company were dismissed from office by the magistrates and told to go to their own homes. The regular Town Guard was ordered to replace them. There had been great difficulty for the Trained Bands in maintaining watch through the day and night, and their loss of income by having constantly to abandon their civil employment. However, the King's High Commissioner and the Privy Council complained daily about their short-comings. They threatened that if there was not enough of the militia guard appointed, they would order the army to come and be quartered in the town. If that happened then the privileges enjoyed by the town would be put into jeopardy. For these reasons the council reluctantly re-appointed the former company of militia, consisting of the standard number of men, to be brought back to duty and mount the guard as before. (*ERBE*)

June 8th

1508: William Goldsmith, water-ballie of the Town and Port of Leith, sat in judgement in Leith on the dispute between William Kerr and Thomas Winter, the latter of whom claimed that William Kerr had unjustly withheld ten consignments of salt imported from Tralsound (modern Stralsound) on the Baltic coast of North Germany. Each consignment of pure salt, delivered in Scotland free of all transport and other costs, consisted of twelve barrels. For each barrel, Thomas Winter was to pay twelve shillings in Scots money. He began by handing over one French crown in part-payment, this having a value of fourteen shillings Scots. William Kerr was unhappy with this part-payment and the two men agreed that their course of action should be to submit to the judgement of judges and lawyers in the town of Tralsound. Witness to this was Mr Robert Pringle, rector of Morham in East Lothian and Mr Thomas Strachan, vicar of Boncle in Berwick. (*ERBE*)

June 9th

1648: Alexander Denholm, a baker, was imprisoned in the Tolbooth for a second time for his reckless behaviour and actions in making some rash comments to the Duke of Hamilton in the High Street of Edinburgh sometime after eleven o'clock at night. Denholm was armed with a sword and a pair of pistols without the permission of the magistrates. However, when he was brought in front of the council, he acknowledged his mistake. He was sorry for the wrong he had committed and presented a humble signed plea to the council. The council reviewed his misdemeanour but considered it to be so great a fault, and so odious, that they could not let it pass without censure as an example of their dislike of any seditious disorder. In order to put fear into anyone who was thinking of imitating him, the council sent him back to jail, to remain there during the council's pleasure. After his release, should he commit a similar misdemeanour he would lose his liberty within the burgh. He was also dismissed from his office as lieutenant. (*ERBE*)

June 10th

1872: 'In view of the restoration of St Giles' Church, the operations in connection with which commence today, special services took place within the old building yesterday … At the end of the forenoon discourse, Dr Wallace said—Before I close, permit me to explain why it has been sought to impress a special character upon the services of this day. You are aware that arrangements have been made for removing the interior furnishings of this church, and replacing them … with fittings and decorations more in keeping with the architectural character of the edifice, and the sacred use to which it is devoted … These seats which you occupy for the last time today, have … gathered round them associations of their own, derived not only from personal but from public recollections—from the presences, royal, magisterial, judicial, and ecclesiastical that have occupied them in succession; and as you leave them I can readily believe that it will be with something of the sadness that dwells in every form of farewell … These arches have shaken to the voices, or looked down upon the forms of those prophets and kings and statesmen who have made us what we are.' (*The Scotsman*)

June 11th

1931: On this day, gambling habits were exposed in *The Scotsman*:

Gambling and Betting were denounced by Bailie Andrew Young, at Edinburgh Burgh Court yesterday, when seven youths appeared before him and admitted having assembled in a stair in Gorgie Road for the purpose of gambling. Bailie Young said:—'You have cost the country hundreds of pounds in educating you, and this is how you waste your time, sitting in a stair and throwing down cards like a lot of fools. It is idiotic. All those people who come before me charged with betting and gambling are a lot of parasites. They don't do a single iota for the good of the country.' He imposed a fine of 2 shillings and sixpence, with the alternative of five days' imprisonment, on each.

Street Betting Offences. At Edinburgh Burgh Court yesterday, James Campbell, 6 Simpson's Court, Greenside, admitted having loitered in Greenside Row for betting purposes, and was fined £20. He had three previous convictions. Thomas Wynne, 52 Ravenshaugh Road, Levenhall, Musselburgh, admitted having loitered in Potterrow for betting purposes. He had two previous convictions, and was fined £15.

June 12th

1567: The Queen (Mary of Scots) and the Duke of Orkney rode to Dunbar in East Lothian. They sent proclamations through the country to call men to arms because of the threat of war, and to help her against those who pursued her. Two days later, the Queen came to Seton Castle with four companies of soldiers and several Earls, Lords and Barons. The Lords in Edinburgh, hearing of this, gave an immediate alarm and marched to Restalrig Links where they rested till the morning. On 15 June (a Sunday), the armies came face to face. One stood on the Carberry Hills with four regiments of soldiers and six brass field cannon. The other army stood opposite, with messengers going between them day and night. During this parley, the Duke fled secretly to Dunbar. Then the Queen came and handed herself over as a prisoner to the Lords. They took her to Edinburgh, to the house of the provost, Sir Simon Preston. (*Diarey of Robert Birrel*)

———— • ◆ • ————

1806: In the House of Lords on this day, Henry Dundas, Lord Melville, was acquitted of charges of the misappropriation of navy funds, a verdict that was received with widespread satisfaction in Edinburgh, the town council and many other public bodies voting him congratulatory addresses.

June 13th

1805: 'Positively the Last Night. At the King's Arms Assembly Room, High Street. For the Benefit of Mr Wilkinson. Saturday Evening, 15th June, Mr Bell, late of the Theatre-Royal here, will perform the celebrated Collins' Evening Brush. In addition to the usual Entertainments, there will be exhibited, many wonderful Magical Deceptions, by the Celebrated Herman Boaz, who, on this occasion, very generously goes through his unparalleled and astonishing performances gratis, with a view of serving Mr Wilkinson. Between the Parts, Mr Wilkinson will perform several Select Airs on his improved and much admired Musical Glasses; and Miss Wilkinson, a child of six years of age, will speak a Prologue and an Epilogue.—Previous to the Brush, several Surprising Feats will be performed by Mr Wilkinson's Wonderful British Dog. For particulars see the hand-bills.—Doors open at seven, and the Performance begins at eight o'clock.—Tickets to the Rooms 2 shillings; to the Gallery 1 shilling each—To be had at the shops of J. Weddell & Co., North Bridge, and of Messrs Montgomery and Steele, Prince's Street.' (*Caledonian Mercury*)

June 14th

1849: 'Estimates Wanted. The Governors of George Heriot's Hospital wish to contract for the following Articles to be delivered such times and in such quantities as may be required. All offers to be made at the lowest cash prices, and every article to be delivered at the Hospital free of all expenses whatever. The Contracts to commence 10th July next, and terminate 10th January 1850, except as after provided:— Brown Broad Cloth for boys' Clothes—about 400 yards, of the same quality, width, substance, shade, and finish, as the sample piece which may be seen at the Treasurer's Chambers. One half to be delivered by the middle of September next, and the other on the 15th March 1850. Bread of the best quality—20,000 Loaves, less or more, of 20 ounces in weight each, at so much the four pound loaf. Butcher Meat of the best quality—consisting of Rounds of Beef free from the great bone, Runners, Nineholes and Sirloins, all of ox Beef. Also Hind Quarters of Wedder Mutton and Lamb after the middle of July. The quantity may be 600 stones or less or more—the Steward to have the choice of the pieces … Treasurer's Chambers, 11 Royal Exchange.' (*Caledonian Mercury*)

June 15th

1698: The council authorised the Town Treasurer, Samuel McClellan, to arrange with stonemasons and carpenters for the construction of a Bedlam (short for Bethlehem) house or hospital, following a design already committed to paper. The cost of construction would be £8,000 Scots for all the stonemason, carpentry, slate roofing, plumbing, glazing and blacksmith work. The contract for this building was to be formally drawn up and elaborated and signed the following Friday. On 17 June, the council met with the committee appointed to oversee the Bedlam project. They had met with a number of tradesmen and come to an agreement with them for the construction for the sum of 12,000 merks. The contract was read over before the council. This Bedlam, or hospital, was built in the New or South Greyfriars yard. In 1740, it and the adjoining grass-yard were used for the Edinburgh Charity Workhouse. *(ERBE)*.

The Edinburgh Bedlam is best known as the place where the poet Robert Fergusson (1750-74) died. The effects of a serious fall down a flight of steps led to him being committed to the Bedlam. After two months, he died in his cell on a bed of straw, in the terrors of the night.

June 16th

1939: 'Danzig Question Discussed by Pole in Edinburgh. Poland's determination to fight if Danzig were threatened was stressed by Mr F.E. Boniakowski, member of the Rotary Club of Katowice, Poland, when he addressed the members of the Edinburgh Rotary Club in the North British Station Hotel yesterday on 'The Past and Present of Poland' ... Mr Boniakowski described Danzig as 'the vast hinterland of our exports.' Eighty per cent. of the commerce of Poland was carried on through Danzig and Gdynia. They all understood what it meant to lose this. If they lost Danzig, they lost Gdynia, and they would never give up Danzig without fighting. If Poland lost Danzig to Germany, Poland would become a vassal to Germany, and would become a second or third class nation, instead of being a first class nation as she was. That is why Poland had said 'Stop!' They had done the same in 1920 with the Bolshevists. Speaking of the collections made in Poland for the strengthening of their Air Force, the speaker remarked that even the minority people were giving contributions, because they knew that if Poland lost her independence it would be much worse for them because Poland today was a liberal country.' (*The Scotsman*)

June 17th

1605: A tulzie (battle) was fought in the High Street at the Salt Tron between the Laird of Ogle in Perthshire, the younger and his associates and Wishart, the young Laird of Pitarrow in the Mearns. The fight lasted for two hours, from nine o'clock at night to eleven o'clock. A number were hurt on both sides and a very handsome man called Guthrie, a follower of Pitarrow. The following day they were taken before the council and imprisoned. On that day also, William Thomson, a dagger-maker in the West Bow, was killed by John Waterstone, a cutler who was beheaded a day later on the Castlehill. (*Diarey of Robert Birrel*)

———◆———

1883: 'The ladies of Brighton Street congregation have presented their pastor, the Rev. James Turnbull, with a very splendid pulpit gown, as a mark of their respect for his character, as an able , faithful and enlightened minister of the Gospel.' (*Caledonian Mercury*)

June 18th

1660: As the following day had been appointed a public Day of Solemn Thanksgiving for King Charles II's happy return to government of the whole kingdom, all inhabitants of the burgh were required to go to their parish churches to hear divine service in the forenoon. Public markets, open booths, shops or taverns would remain closed until noon. The entire city was required to build bonfires of joy at four o'clock in the afternoon until nine o'clock at night, at a reasonable distance to keep the front stairs of the houses free from any danger or risk of fire – considering the hot weather. A banquet was to be provided at the Mercat Cross. However, muskets, pistols, squibs or fireworks should not be let off on the High Street or aimed out of shot-holes or windows. Every citizen was required to behave correctly and discreetly as all good Christians should, without excessive drinking or other misdemeanours, because His Majesty had recently issued a proclamation forbidding riotous behaviour. In St Giles' Kirk the King's loft was to be rebuilt, and painted and gilded in the richest colours, with the royal arms: crown, sceptre, lion, thistle, as in good King James VI's day. (*ERBE*)

June 19th

1893: 'Church of Scotland Day of Humiliation and Prayer. The Rev. Dr MacGregor, of St Cuthbert's, preaching to that congregation in the Synod Hall, Castle Terrace, yesterday afternoon, said—All over Scotland the members of the Church of Scotland were that day having a day of humiliation and prayer in connection with a threatened danger to the nation and the Church. That day the whole Church of Scotland was prostrate in prayer before the God of their fathers, beseeching Him in His mercy to save the nation from a great danger and from a great crime. To say, as they heard it said, that there was nothing in the principle of the Establishment was to cast aspersion on the struggles of our great forefathers and the history of our dear native land. When the Union which had existed in the National Church so long between the civil and ecclesiastical powers was broken, then the State—the nation in its corporate capacity—ceased to have a God. The principle of a national religion and the duty of the State to be loyal to God and to his Christ ... was the very thing for which our Covenanting forefathers struggled and bled and died.' (*The Scotsman*)

June 20th

1942: On this day, changes to marriage laws were printed in *The Scotsman*:

Important changes have been made in the law affecting preliminaries to marriage in Scotland by an Act of Parliament amending the Marriage Notice Act of 1878, and a corresponding amending Act of the General Assembly of the Church of Scotland on proclamation of banns ... Under the special war-time provisions, any person desiring to be married in Scotland, whether at present residing in Scotland or not, may have notice of marriage published, or alternatively banns proclaimed in the registration district in Scotland in which he or she had usual residence on 3 September 1939 ... Explaining the new procedure at a Press conference at St Andrew's House, Edinburgh, yesterday, Mr James Gray Kyd, Registrar-General for Scotland, said that since the war started they had had quite a number of inquiries from Scottish people who had left Scotland either to join the Forces or to engage in some form of war work ... Asked whether there had been any difficulty in connection with the marriage of British subjects to nationals of another nation, Mr Kyd said that if a foreigner were marrying a Scottish girl, the advice was generally given that contact should be made with the Consul of the country to which the prospective bridegroom belonged.

June 21st

1700: In a letter from Murray of Philiphaugh to William Carstares, a description of what he called 'the Rabble at Edinburgh' on the previous day was described. This is a translation into modern English of what he wrote: 'We had, last night, one of the most numerous and most insolent rabbles that has been here of a long time. The pretended occasion was that news had come of the Spaniards making a descent and an attack upon our colony of Darien, and that our people had routed and defeated them. Upon this, it was resolved by the meeting at the Cross Keys (as I hear) that all true Caledonians (as they call them) should have illuminations in their windows. This resolution was handed about and, without ever taking notice of commissioner, Privy Councillor or magistrate, there were in the evening lights put up in many windows, and some bonfires set on. The mob gathered to huge crowds from all corners, and began breaking the windows that were not illuminated, without distinction of the indwellers' quality or character — or if they made any distinction it was to do much mischief and insolence to those in the government ... I am told they destroyed above five thousand pounds Sterling worth of glass.' (*ERBE*)

June 22nd

1801: 'To be sold by public roup, in John's Coffeehouse, on Wednesday the 15th day of July next, betwixt the hours of two and three o'clock afternoon I.— An excellent lodging in Shakespeare Square, being the third flat of that land lately built by Mr Hill, architect, consisting of dining room, drawing room, two bed chambers, a dark room, two bed closets, a staged kitchen, with other conveniencies, and two cellars under the street. II.— A large Land in St John's Hill, lately built for a factory house, consisting of a ground floor 60 feet long, 22 broad and 11 high, within the walls, having 8 chimney vents, and divided into two weaving houses, the one 20 and the other 40 feet long; the first floor above is divided into six dwelling houses, and the garret floor is divided into one dwelling house, and an excellent loft fitted up for holding corn. This Land is possessed by sundry tenants. Persons wishing to purchase any of the above houses by private bargain, may apply either to Mr Charles Livingston, writer, Alison's Square, or to Mr Thomas Scotland, Writer to the Signet, Queen Street; the articles of roup and title-deeds may be seen in the hands of Mr Scotland.' (*Caledonian Mercury*)

June 23rd

1829: 'On Tuesday the noble edifice which the liberality of the Corporation of the City of Edinburgh and the classical genius of Mr Hamilton has provided for the accommodation of this ancient and distinguished Seminary was opened ... the procession moved from the Old High School [with the] Janitor, in his gown, and bearing his Baton ... [then, the High School classes, then] Noblemen and Gentlemen who had attended the High School ... Deacon Lorimer, the contractor ... delivered to the Lord Provost the keys of the building ... after which the Lord Provost ... [spoke]:— 'Early in the 16th century, certain immunities and privileges were granted to it ... it appears that from about the middle of that century, the magistrates paid the rent of a house for the accommodation of the school in Blackfriars Wynd, where it continued to be held till the year 1578, when a school-house was built by the Town Council in the churchyard of the Blackfriars Convent ... In 1566 the magistrates obtained from Queen Mary a gift of the patronages and endowments belonging to the monasteries in Edinburgh, including, of course, that of the Grammar School, which had till then been vested in the Abbot of Holyrood.' (*Caledonian Mercury*)

June 24th

1562: The provost, bailies and council ordered that the idol, St Giles, was to be cut out of the town's flag and a thistle put in its place and that the burgh treasurer should provide taffeta for the replacement, the cost of which would be entered in the burgh accounts. (*ERBE*)

The heraldic arms of Edinburgh today no longer features St Giles. In his place stands the figure of a woman. King David I is said to have been unable to resist his passion for hunting on a day when his confessor warned him to devote himself to prayer. His punishment was to be attacked by a giant stag between whose antlers the King saw the Cross of Christ. He fell to the ground and then came to his senses. In reparation for his selfishness and cruelty, he founded the Abbey of the Holy Cross (Holyrood) and the badge of the Canongate (where the Augustinian canons later walked) became a stag with a cross between its antlers. It is more likely that the Abbey was named after the fragment of the True Cross which David's mother, Queen Margaret, had brought to Scotland. This was contained in a cross of gold which opened to reveal the relic. (*See* September 14th)

June 25th

1935: The headline 'Catholic Congress Ends' appeared in *The Scotsman* with this story:

Exciting scenes marked the close of the Eucharistic Congress in Edinburgh last night. Buses containing Catholics were stoned, and batons were drawn by the police. Four men were arrested, and two men were treated at the Infirmary for head injuries. There were other minor injuries also in the course of the evening. The centre of the disturbance was on the south side of the city, in the Morningside and Bruntsfield districts, where large crowds had gathered to view the holding of a Solemn procession of the Blessed Sacrament in the grounds of St Andrew's Priory in Canaan Lane. The police cleared the lane and guarded all approaches to it, but for three or four hours Morningside Road was thronged from the station to Bruntsfield Place. This meant that the police had to control a crowd which stretched for about three-quarters of a mile, in addition to watching various points in other districts where sympathisers with the Protestant Action organisation had gathered ... As the hour of the gathering approached, tramcar after tramcar brought Protestant extremists and others to the scene and there was a regular trek of demonstrators who made their way along Morningside Road on foot.

June 26th

1809: The *Caledonian Mercury* printed these notices:

Notice. Having learnt, that a respectable House in Leith, in the Wine Trade, has lately assumed as a Partner a Young Gentleman named William Henderson, and has circulated Letters to that effect, some of which have fallen in to the hands of my Friends, and they have conceived that I am the William Henderson assumed, I feel that it is a duty I owe to myself and family, to announce, that I have no connection with any House or Company whatever, and that I continue to do Business in the Wine Trade, as formerly, as well as in all the other branches, on my own account solely, at the Warehouse, No. 106, South Bridge Street. William Henderson, Ginger and White Spruce Beer, of superior quality, up in bottles.

Notice. Thomas Henderson ... has now resigned his business at the Russia Warehouse [Linen Drapery] in favour of his two sons, Thomas and William, who, with his nephew, Mr John Weir (long in his employment), will in future carry it on under the firm of Thomas and William Henderson & Co. and he trusts will conduct it in such a manner as to deserve that generous friendship and support which he has so long experienced.

June 27th

1844: 'Fatal Colliery Accident.— About seven o'clock on Monday morning, two colliers were ascending a shaft at Sheriffhall Colliery in a basket, when one of them named William Bennet, having leant too much on one side, was caught by another basket which was being lowered at the same time, and fell about 21 fathoms to the bottom of the pit and was killed on the spot. Bennet was a married man about 27 years of age, and has left a widow and one child. Fatal Accident. On Sunday forenoon, as a coach was proceeding towards the village of Greenend, a boy about 12 years of age leapt up on the back part, and by the force of the spring he made his head got jammed between the hind wheel and the body of the coach. The coachman was quite unconscious of the accident, and had proceeded about 500 yards from the place where the boy leapt up, when he was called to by some persons on the road. On the boy being taken down, he was found to be quite dead. The front of his head was much cut, and the road was tracked with blood for a considerable distance.' (*Caledonian Mercury*)

June 28th

1571 The Earl of Morton conducted a body of Scots, who adhered to the King, from Leith to Restalrig, where they drew up in order of battle. The Queen's forces marched from Edinburgh to encounter them. The armies separated, agreeing to retire to their respective quarters. But this amicable accommodation became the means of the Queen Mary's forces being ensnared by Morton's treachery. Making a circuit with his troops, they made an unexpected attack upon the Queen's soldiers when they were entering the Water Gate and killed about fifty of them, while of Morton's followers only two were slain. In the course of the siege, the King's party marched from Leith and, in order to provoke the Queen's forces to an engagement, they approached unwarily too near the castle. To strike terror into the country people, they hanged two men for carrying sheep to the market and scourged five women with great severity for similar practices. The violence of the party spirit, heightened by mutual injuries, had now exasperated them to such a pitch of rancour, that the prisoners on each side, without respect to their quality or condition, were led to immediate execution upon gibbets erected within sight of their friends. It is said that the unhappy prisoners, by fifties at a time, fell victim to such shocking barbarity. (Arnot, *The History of Edinburgh*)

June 29th

1610: Thirty-six pirates were brought to Edinburgh from Orkney, of whom twenty-seven were hanged in Leith within the sea-mark. A month to the day later, the council ordered that the pirates' goods, munitions and equipment should be stored in a secure location in Leith to allow an inventory to be made so that it could be sold at the most favourable price. On 8 September 1610, the money obtained for the pirate ship and goods seized in her for the council were declared as £13,094 15 shillings and 3 pence. The compensation was distributed as follows: £500 to Thomas Nicolson in Orkney for goods seized by the pirates; £530 for wine, arms and ammunition provided; 6,000 merks to the captains for the sailors and soldiers and the heirs of the men killed; 5,500 merks to the captains and masters for the ships' part; the balance, amounting to 6,500 merks, to the town for expenses and to satisfy Captain Thomas Geddes, George Todrig the younger, and William Mawer, mariner, wounded on the voyage. (*ERBE*)

June 30th

1916: On the final day in June, *The Scotsman* announced a landmark ruling for war-time women:

Women and Medical Classes—Important Decision by Edinburgh University Senatus. The Senatus Academicus of Edinburgh University decided at their meeting yesterday, to recommend to the University Court that the classes in the Faculty of Medicine should be open in future to women. The meeting, which was presided over by the new Principal, Sir James A. Ewing ... was attended by the majority of the members, nearly forty being present ... and it is understood that the decision was arrived at by a substantial majority. The question of introducing women to the medical classes in the University was brought before the Senatus on a direct representation by the women students themselves. The case they presented was strengthened by circumstances arising out of the war. Its main point is that as the University qualifies the women it should also be responsible for their education, which at present has to be obtained in an extra-mural institution. The war, it is pointed out, has brought out the fact of the important place qualified women medicals can take and are taking in the country and that the shortage of men, owing to the war, had given a tremendous impetus to the study of medicine by women.

July 1st

1505: The kirkmaster and brethren of the surgeons and barbers presented a formal request to the provost, bailies and council that, to promote the love of God, the honour of the King, the respect and administration of the burgh, the future good order and regulation of the two crafts, they should be granted suitable privileges, rules and statutes. Using their weekly dues, the craftsmen had supported an altar in the College Kirk in honour of God and their patron, St Mungo. They now asked for the authority to appoint a kirkmaster (president) whose decisions would be obeyed by all the brethren. They required that no one who was not a freeman and burgess of Edinburgh should be allowed to practise as a surgeon or barber. Before they were admitted to the craft, candidates should also have passed an examination in anatomy and know the location of all the veins in the body for blood-letting. Also they should understand the effect of planetary movements on the different parts of the body. They asked to be given one dead body of a criminal annually for the instruction of anatomy. (*ERBE*)

July 2nd

1801: The *Caledonian Mercury* printed these advertisements for medical remedies:

To the Faculty, and those who take Opium, and its preparations, is recommended, The genuine Black Drop, which many of the most eminent physicians and Surgeons in the United Kingdom of Great Britain and Ireland employ and prescribe in preference to any other preparation of Opium ... this preparation, which is highly concentrated, one drop being nearly equal to four of common Laudanum, is applicable to all cases in which Opium or its preparations are employed. It is prepared by J.A. Braithwaite, Member of the Royal College of Surgeons in London, and surgeon in Lancaster; and by appointment sold by Mr R. Scott, Druggist, South Bridge.

Mr A. Smith, Perfumer, North Bridge, begs leave to inform the Public that he has received a fresh parcel of Anti-Impetigines, which is the best and only medicine now extant, for the radical cure of the Scurvy, Gout, Rheumatism, King's Evil, Leprosy, Ulcers, Pimpled Faces, Humours after Smallpox and the Measles, &c. The Anti-Impetigines is only to be had as above at 10 shillings and sixpence a bottle, with folio bills of direction. The Anti-Impetigines may also be had of Mr A. Smith, Perfumer, No 38 North Bridge Street, Messrs. Davidson and Gladwin, Confectioners, No 5, St Andrew Street.

July 3rd

1855: 'Scottish Curative Mesmeric Association.— The friends of curative mesmerism held a social meeting last evening, in the Calton Convening Hall. In the absence of Professor Gregory from indisposition, Andrew Stein, Esq., W.S., occupied the chair. After tea, the chairman congratulated the association on the encouraging hopes which the present position of curative mesmerism was calculated to inspire. Mr Jackson followed, and remarked that this was the first time that mesmerism appeared to be in a fair way of leaving the recesses of learned castes, and becoming the possession of the people at large. Messrs Davey and Jackson then instituted a number of experiments on various persons in the mesmeric condition. Mr Alex. John Ellis, B.A., made some observations on the practical character of the association, and contended that it would be as absurd to reject the electric telegraph because we were ignorant of the fundamental laws of its operation, as to reject curative mesmerism because we had not yet discovered the laws which regulate it. A variety of musical pieces were sung during the evening by a party under the direction of Mr George Dowie, and the meeting separated shortly after ten o'clock.' (*Caledonian Mercury*)

July 4th

1505: The provost, bailies and council announced that they had given Thomas Glendunwyne the post of burgh Bellman, with the task of ensuring that the High Street was kept clean in summer and winter. He was obliged to supply a horse with a covered cart and two assistants whose duties were to clear and clean the High Street (between the Castlehill and the close-heads at St Mary's Wynd and Leith Wynd) from every kind of muck, remnants of meat and fish, wet or dry manure, gravel or other debris and remove it to a suitable refuse pit and use it for his own profit. The council also ordered that any muck or manure lying more than twenty-four hours in the street would become his property. The latter would have the right to collect a penny per quarter from every booth, vault, cellar or dwelling-room in the burgh, from every market-stall or huckster. Where any horse bringing food or other loads came into the market and was not in a stable but tethered on the High Street, eating and dropping manure, the Bellman would be permitted to ask for a halfpence in cash or kind at the market. (*ERBE*)

July 5th

1904: On this day *The Scotsman* printed an account of the frightening fire in Edinburgh Royal Infirmary:

An alarming outbreak of fire was discovered yesterday forenoon in the Pathological Department of Edinburgh Royal Infirmary. At the time the fire was observed a post-mortem examination was going on and during its progress Dr Shennan, who is in charge of the specimen room, and some students noticed that molten lead was oozing through the ceiling. The alarm was quickly given, and the Infirmary Fire Brigade, which consists of thirty men, had four lines of hose directed towards the scene of the fire. It was then found, however, that the supply of water was inadequate, and the pressure consequently was insufficient. The City Fire Brigade were afterwards summoned, and on their arrival the roof of the building was in flames. Several lines of hose leading from street hydrants were soon in use, and by a fairly good supply of water the firemen were successful in confining the outbreak to a very limited area. The flames, however, had got such a hold of the roof before the fire brigade were at the building that the rafters and other supports were almost completely destroyed ... the plaster work of the ceiling in falling rendered useless many valuable specimens.

July 6th

1833: 'We recommend to Strangers a visit to the Splendid Saloon of the Turkish Divan, decorated with five Oil Paintings, 23 feet long by 11 high, representing the principal Views of Paris, such as have never been exhibited in Scotland before. London, Glasgow and Edinburgh Papers, Café à la Française, Cigars, Spirits and Wines. Hotel and Café de l'Europe—Table d'Hôte every day at half-past five o'clock. Dinner, 2 shillings and sixpence. Saloon for private parties to the number of 80. 8, South St David Street, three doors of Prince's Street.' (*Caledonian Mercury*)

'The Subscribers have just received a large supply of Italian goods, viz. Finest Honey Comb, Parmesan Cheese, Macaroni, Anchovies and Salad Oil. On hand Gruyère, Stilton, Cheshire, Wiltshire, Double Gloucester and Dunlop Cheese; also Wiltshire Bacon, Yorkshire, Cumberland and Dumfries Hams, Smoked Ox Tongues, German Sausages and Tongues, all of first quality. W. & R. Hill. 45, Frederick Street.' (*Caledonian Mercury*)

July 7th

1675: On this day, the council granted to Mr James Sutherland, a herbalist, a nineteen-year tack (tenancy) of the yard and gardener's house at Trinity College, with the obligation that he keep the roof and the yard dykes (walls) in repair. On 8 September, the council considered the benefit to be derived from the study of botany and the culture of medicinal herbs, and its usefulness to the university curriculum. The council noted that this was much desired by the nobility and gentry, by both physicians and surgeons. They granted a salary of £20 sterling to Sutherland, to be paid by the College treasurer, who was also asked to find premises in the university suitable for storing seeds and books. Sutherland's salary was confirmed to him and his successors for the instruction of students in the history of plants as part of the Natural Philosophy course. A committee was appointed to inspect the garden, consisting of the provost, a bailie, the dean of gild, two surgeons and three physicians – Drs Archibald Stevenson, Andrew Balfour and Robert Sibbald. On 22 June 1677, in the garden, Andrew Cassie, an apprentice apothecary, was examined on the art of pharmacy and his knowledge of plants. (*ERBE*)

July 8th

1823: The *Caledonian Mercury* reported on the death of Sir Henry Raeburn and other matters:

It is with sincere regret we announce the death of that eminent artist, Sir Henry Raeburn, who has for a long period occupied the first place among the portrait painters of his country. Sir Henry died at his house at St Bernard's, Stockbridge.

Early on Tuesday a very distressing case was heard in the Police Court. A Jew of respectable appearance charged the daughter of his landlady, a very decent woman, with having robbed him of a number of articles of jewellery, the value of which, altogether, might amount to £15. She confessed to having disposed of his two rings; and a pawnbroker proved her of having pawned with him a valuable seal belonging to the complainer. Questions were repeatedly put to the girl, but her agitation was so extreme that she could reply to none of them; indeed, she could scarcely support herself at the bar. She was convicted of the theft to the extent of the rings and seal, and sentenced to ten days' confinement in the Lock-up-house, and to find caution for her good behaviour.

The eclipse on Tuesday morning was not observed here, the sun being obscured by clouds.

July 9th

1887: *The Scotsman* featured an account of an eminent philanthropist's philosophical speech:

Yesterday, Mr Andrew Carnegie, who also laid the foundation stone of a Free Library to which he donated £50,000, received the Freedom of the City with the words: 'It has been my duty during the past few years to consider the most difficult problem — How best can a man use surplus wealth which is not required for his modest and unostentatious wants? To bestow wealth, so that it will not produce evil, is in itself something of a problem. A penny given to the beggar will work more misery than any pound will cure ... I am often tempted to exclaim 'Oh, Charity! What crimes are committed in thy name.' The only true good which can be done is where you can stimulate others to well-doing—where you can act as force to create co-operation on the part of those you help. One day, walking the streets of Edinburgh, when I was not so well known as I am now, I saw the return in which the citizens declared that they would not support a Free Library in the city. I said to myself, with a little bite of the lip, I will make this city reverse that vote.'

July 10th

1802: This article was printed in the *Caledonian Mercury*:

The anniversary sermon for the Orphan Hospital is to be preached in St Andrew's Church, New Town, on Tuesday the 13th curt by the Rev. Mr Balfour, one of the Ministers of Glasgow. The bell is to ring at 12 o'clock. The Orphan Hospital of Edinburgh is an institution of which the utility has been long known and acknowledged. Into it are received orphan children, or children deprived of the support of their parents, from all parts of the country, who are thereby rescued from situations in which they are useless or baneful, and their industry and talents are brought forward to be of benefit to themselves and to society. The distresses of the poorer classes of the people for the two last years, arising from the immoderately high price of every necessary of life, made a strong call for increased support and assistance from their charity … In making these exertions, the Managers relied on the blessing of Providence, and the aid and support of the humane and generous. There are in the Hospital at present 90 girls and 76 boys; and the number in the house, including teachers and servants, are 176.

July 11th

1940: An article in *Edinburgh Evening News* on 2 September 1989 revealed the alarming outcome of the bombings on this day, and the following days, in 1940:

After the first major air-raid on Edinburgh began with five 250 lb bombs and six incendiaries falling near Craigmillar Castle, a 1,000 lb bomb fell beside Albert Dock, Newhaven on 11 July; three bombs fell on railway lines at Leith and 48 incendiaries at Seafield Road: 38 civilians were injured and eight died. On 18 July 1940 bombs fell on Leith and Newhaven. More followed on 22-23 July and on 4 August five unexploded bombs fell on Portobello. On 27 September a bomb fell near Holyroodhouse. Others followed on 29 September. Eleven people were injured on 7 October around Marchmont. Six 250 lb bombs fell around Corstorphine Hill on 5 November. There were no serious attacks till 14-15 March 1941 with 70 incendiaries at Abbeyhill. On 7 April two landmines were parachuted down on David Kilpatrick School, Leith and on an embankment nearby. Corstorphine and Cramond Brig then received 34 incendiaries: three died and 131 were injured. On 6 May 1941 a second 1,000 lb bomb was dropped on Milton Crescent and 100 incendiaries at the Jewel Cottages: four were killed and two injured. On 6 August 1942 four 500 lb bombs fell near Craigentinny.

July 12th

1802: 'The depredations committed by nocturnal thieves, about the New Town call loudly for redress. Of late the knockers have been wrenched off many doors, and thermometers have been stolen from gentlemen's houses … We hear, the officers of justice … have got a tolerable scent of the thieves, as well as of the receivers, who may obtain a free passage to Botany Bay for their industry.' (*Caledonian Mercury*)

'Valuable Subjects for Sale. Upset Price further reduced. To be sold at Leith by public auction on Saturday the 17th day of July, at twelve o'clock noon, in the house of Mrs Bambrough, Vintner, at the foot of the shore of Leith. These large Vaults, containing 276 catacombs, besides about one half of the Vaults, which are appropriated for Wine, &c. in casks, together with the large Cellars and Granaries above the same and on the opposite side of the close, with a very large Counting House and Counting Room, and fire proof closet; also the Malt kiln, Shops and Warehouses … lying near the Green Tree, being the property of Alexander Sommervail & Co. … In the meantime intending purchasers may apply to Mr Bisset or James Hall, merchants in Leith, for further particulars.' (*Caledonian Mercury*)

July 13th

1846: 'Campbell's Livery, Job & Post-Horse Establishment, 13 Clyde Street, Edinburgh, where, upon the shortest notice, Gigs, Dog Carts, Phaetons, Minibuses, Broughams, Britskas, Omnibuses, Chariots, Tandem and Gentlemen's Four-in-Hand 'Bang-up' can be had with Horses, for business, Pleasure Parties, Marriages, &c. in good style, with clean, careful, and steady post-boys. Also, Carriages and Horses taken in for Sale or Livery. This Establishment affords accommodation for fifty or one hundred horses; has lock-up Coach-houses, Smithy, Veterinary, &c.; and being in the immediate vicinity of the Grand Centre Stations in this city for the North British, Berwick-upon-Tweed, Newcastle, Edinburgh and Glasgow Railways, &c &c. will be found very convenient for those requiring such. Letters, post-paid, addressed to the Mail Coach Office, 2 Prince's Street, or 13 Clyde Street, will be attended to.' (*Caledonian Mercury*)

July 14th

1830: On this day, an article with the title 'Promenade' was printed in *The Scotsman*:

On Saturday, this novel fete took place in the Caledonian Horticultural Society's Experimental Garden, at Inverleith, and was honoured with a truly numerous, highly respectable, and splendidly fashionable attendance of nobility and gentry. The company began to arrive about noon, and by half-past two o'clock there were not fewer than from 450 to 500 ladies and gentlemen in the garden. The general effect produced by so many groups of ladies and gentlemen promenading the garden, was admirable, particularly when viewed from the eminence near the centre ... the more rare exotics were principally arranged on stages at each end of an awning, which was constructed for the company partaking of a collation. In this tent were placed two rows of tables, which, when viewed from the western extremity through the trees and shrubs, presented a vista of apparently a mile in length ... The chief contributors of these were Mr Mcnab of the Botanic Garden, Professor Dunbar, Mr Cunningham of Comely Bank, Mr Patrick Neill, Messrs Dickson & Sons ... Messrs Peacock of Leith Walk Nursery supplied nosegays for the company, in each of which there was either a moss, a crimson, or a blush rose.

July 15th

1693: On this day, Mr James Sutherland, keeper of the Physic Garden, submitted a petition to the council explaining that since he had taken up residence at the garden in the Gardener's House attached to it, he had paid his rent punctually. However, over the past two years the Gardener's House had been completely dilapidated. This had a serious effect on him, in that when it rained or it was stormy, he had neither a house for his gardener to stay in nor one to which he could retreat. His daily attendance at the garden was essential for most of the year, particularly in winter and spring, for protecting and nourishing the more tender or foreign plants, and in summer for dealing with his pupils who had to come to the garden at four or five o'clock in the morning so that they could be back to open and staff their masters' shops. Mr Sutherland added that he had developed the garden to the point where, for quantity and rarity of plants, it was inferior to few gardens in Europe. He had achieved this largely by his own efforts on his annual salary of £20 sterling which the town provided. (*ERBE*)

July 16th

1859: The Prince of Wales, a reluctant scholar, was sent to Edinburgh to prepare for entrance to Oxford. He stayed there until 10 September, being tutored by Dr Lyon Playfair, Professor of Chemistry at Edinburgh University and by the German classical scholar Dr Leonhard Schmitz, rector of the nearby Royal High School. The *Caledonian Mercury* printed this report:

Arrival of the Prince of Wales in Edinburgh. His Royal Highness the Prince of Wales arrived here last night shortly before nine o'clock by the mail train from London. He was received at the station of the North British Railway by the Lord Provost and Sheriff Gordon, and proceeded to his carriage amidst hearty cheering from the favoured parties in the station and the crowd outside. The Prince, who was accompanied by Colonel Bruce, Captain Keppel, his equerry, and the Rev. Mr Travers, immediately proceeded to Holyrood Palace. The streets through which the Prince passed were much crowded, and at the Palace a large crowd assembled, and testified their loyalty by enthusiastically cheering his Royal Highness ... Mr Matheson, of Her Majesty's Works, was in waiting, and conducted his Royal Highness to the apartments which had been prepared for him in the Palace.

July 17th

1819: 'Articles for the Toilette, used by most of the Nobility. Atkinson's Ambrosial Soap is offered to the Public as a very great improvement in that article of general utility. It is entirely freed from those impure substances which occasion the common soaps to act so injurious to a delicate skin. It removes redness, hardness, freckles, sunburn, &c. from the skin, prevents its chapping, and makes it soft, white, and even. Price one shilling the square.—It is also prepared with Naples Soap in Shaving Cakes, and is peculiarly adapted to gentlemen who have strong beards or tender faces. Price one shilling and nine pence and one shilling and sixpence each.' (*Caledonian Mercury*)

'Atkinson's Curling Fluid restores the Hair where it has fallen off from illness, perspiration, change of climate, or any cause occasioning premature decay; it preserves it from changing colour or falling off, and keeps it in curl during exercise or in damp weather. Price three shillings and sixpence.' (*Caledonian Mercury*)

July 18th

1859: This letter was printed in *The Scotsman*:

Sir,—Having read in your paper a letter headed 'Railway Incidents', I beg to offer a few remarks in reply to the charges brought against the Railway Company by [your anonymous correspondent known as] 'Public Safety'. The facts of the Portobello case are simply these, that the goods train arrived here at 7.45pm, and when coming out of the siding with a load of wagons the leading pair of wheels on the engine came off the rails, and consequently it took some time to replace them. The main up line of rails at the station was shut when the passenger train by which 'Public Safety' travelled arrived, and the train had to be shunted across on to the down line of rails, and brought across again in front of the goods engine, so as to proceed to Edinburgh on the proper (up) line of rails. This was quickly and safely done, and the train dispatched to Edinburgh ... I took every means and precaution ... In fact, as far as human means and experience can devise, everything is done for the protection and safety of the public.—I am, &c. Andrew Tait, Station-Master.

July 19th

1800: These announcements appeared in the *Caledonian Mercury*:

Miss Dale's Concert. Miss Dale takes this opportunity of returning her most grateful thanks to her Patronesses ... and the rest of the Nobility and gentry who honoured her Concert with their presence on Thursday last, the 17th instant ... and likewise with due acknowledgements to those Gentlemen of the Band, Messrs Stabilini, Urbani and Schetky, who obligingly lent their assistance gratis.

Inniskilling Dragoons. Wanted for the above old respectable Regiment, a Person to enlist as a Trumpeter, and who can play the first Horn in a Band. Any person answering this description, will meet with every encouragement, by applying to Messrs Shippard & Gow, North Bridge Street, Edinburgh. NB.— Any spirited young men of 5 feet 7 inches, age 16, and well made, will meet with every encouragement, by applying to the Recruiting Party at Edinburgh.

Dung to Let. One half of the Dung of the streets of Bristo and Potterrow, to be Let in Tack for four years, from 20th August next. Sealed offers, addressed to the Commissioners of the District, will be received by James Sandison, Bristo Street. The highest offer will be accepted. The conditions of lease may be seen by applying as above, and offers received immediately.

July 20th

1822: On this day, *The Scotsman* reported on the council proceedings, stating that on Wednesday a report was read from the committee appointed to confer with the subscribers to the proposed new high school. They found the subscribers willing to give up their scheme, on condition that the city would build a school in a convenient situation at the north side of the New Town, which was agreed to on the part of the committee. It was decided that as soon as a proper site was chosen, and other necessary arrangements made, the building work would commence. The money was to be raised by a tax of one guinea a year on each scholar at the old school as well as the new. It was to be justified on the principle that those who reap the benefit of an establishment should bear the expense. The plan proposed to reduce or cut off various salaries and charges, by which it was calculated that a saving of nearly £2,000 a year would be effected.

July 21st

1521: Close to the Netherbow Port, at seven o'clock in the evening, the notary public Vincent Strathauchin recorded that the following persons presented themselves to him: the priest Master Adam Otterburn; Nichol Carncors; Eduard Kincaid; James Preston; Johan Davidson; Francis Spottiswod his son-in-law; the Deacon of the Fleshers (butchers) Richart Cristeson and the flesher John Stevinson. They came to show themselves ready to defend the King, his castle and the town of Edinburgh against rebels and traitors, with their bodies. They protested against the proposed removal of the head of the Chamberlain and his brother from the end of the Tolbooth, saying that they or their heirs did not take any responsibility for whatever danger, damage or hurt might ensue if this was done. (*ERBE*)

July 22nd

1650: The English Parliament, foreseeing that the treaty between Charles and the Scots would probably terminate in an accommodation, sent into Scotland an army of 16,000 men under the command of Oliver Cromwell. In order to sow divisions among the Scots, the army sent before them a declaration, addressed to 'all that are saints and partakers of the faith of God's elect in Scotland' ... Cromwell's army crossed the Tweed and, marching by Haddington towards Edinburgh, they encamped near the Pentland Hills within a few miles of the city. The Scottish army, commanded by Lesley, was drawn up at Corstorphine from where the chancellor (who was with them) wrote to the magistrates of Edinburgh for a supply of provisions, requesting them at the same time 'to ply the Lord and his throne with strong prayers and supplications in their behalf', without whose help they were utterly ruined. The Scottish army afterwards entrenched themselves in a fortified camp between Edinburgh and Leith, Cromwell, having endeavoured in vain to provoke the Scots to a battle, and having suffered several skirmishes, retired to Dunbar. (Arnot, *The History of Edinburgh*)

July 23rd

1637: On this Sunday, the new service-book started to be read at Edinburgh, in St Giles. Both the Archbishops, Privy Councillors, the Lords of Session, the magistrates of Edinburgh, besides a great concourse of people of inferior rank, were assembled. Among this multitude, not a murmur was heard, till the Dean of Edinburgh, arrayed in his surplice, opened the service book. Instantly a tumult arose. 'Out!' cried an old woman, 'out, thou false thief: dost thou say the mass at my lug?' But the clapping of hands, the hisses, the curses and exclamations which immediately followed, rendered every sentence, or attempt at speech, unintelligible. The Bishop of Edinburgh, with a view to appease the tumult, ascended the pulpit, but had not a friendly hand averted the stool which was thrown at his head, that member of the Episcopal order would have been silenced for ever. At last, the magistrates, descending from their seats, got the unruly part of the audience thrust out of the church, but still their devotion was disturbed by the rude multitude outside, raising loud clamours, rapping at the church doors and throwing stones through the windows. (Arnot, *The History of Edinburgh*)

July 24th

1593: At eight in the morning, the Earl of Bothwell, the Laird of Spott, Mr William Leslie and Mr John Colvill, came into the King's bedchamber heavily armed with pistols. The Earl and his accomplices did not come with pistols and drawn swords to harm the King in any way, but because Bothwell had been unable to gain access to the King; they were determined not to hold back until they had spoken to him. Fearing the worst, the King was coming out of the rear stairs with his trousers in his hand. But Bothwell and his accomplices fell on their knees and begged for mercy. His Majesty, being a wise, merciful and noble Prince, not looking to spill blood, granted them mercy and received them favourably. At four o'clock that afternoon he had them all proclaimed free subjects. On 27 July a similar proclamation of the King's peace with the Earl of Bothwell was renewed at the Mercat Cross, with heralds and trumpets sounding out for joy. However, on 20 September, the same Earl of Bothwell was charged by a proclamation from the Mercat Cross not to come within ten miles of the King, under pain of death. (*Diarey of Robert Birrel*)

July 25th

1923: 'Edinburgh Unemployment Schemes. Proposed Open-Air Sea Bath. The Unemployment Committee of Edinburgh Town Council had under consideration at a meeting yesterday a letter from the Unemployment Grants Committee regarding schemes of work to be undertaken by Local Authorities, with State assistance, for the relief of unemployment during the coming winter ... various schemes were considered, including the construction of a new intercepting sewer at Seafield in place of the one now at Portobello; road widening schemes at Fair-a-Far, Slateford and Saughton; and the entrenchment of a bank at Fairmilehead. Another proposal was one for the construction of an open-air swimming bath at Portobello, to be supplied with hot water from the new electric power station. It was agreed to ask whether the work would be regarded as eligible for the subsidy as a revenue-producing subject. Councillor Buchanan reported having visited Blackpool to see the recently opened bathing station in operation, and spoke to its evident popularity. Provision was made there for bathing and swimming, and for spectators, and the view was expressed that the provision of a station at Portobello would be a great attraction to the public and helpful to Portobello.' (*The Scotsman*)

July 26th

1643: Robert Haliburton Jr was fined £160 for buying a great quantity of tobacco from Jacob Janson, a stranger who had arrived from the West Indies, before the tobacco was declared and handed over for weighing in Leith. Likewise, the skipper of the vessel concerned was fined £54 when he handed in the tobacco for weighing. The council ordered the inhabitants of the burgh to take their share of the tobacco because Robert Haliburton had bought it from a complete stranger. (*ERBE*)

In his *A counterblaste to Tobacco* (1604), King James VI had written of 'the manifold abuses of this vile custom of Tobacco taking', calling it 'this filthy custom' and asking, 'is it not both great vanity and uncleanness, that at the table, a place of respect, of cleanliness, of modesty, men should not be ashamed to sit tossing of Tobacco pipes, and puffing of the smoke of Tobacco one to another, making the filthy smoke and stink thereof, to exhale athwart the dishes, and infect the air, when very often, men that abhor it are at their repast?' For such reasons, Andro Makghe, last Roman Catholic vicar of Gullane in East Lothian, was deposed by King James for smoking tobacco.

July 27th

1681: At Holyroodhouse, before His Majesty King James VII's Commissioner, James Duke of Albany and York, Sir Alexander Erskine of Cambo was vested with the surcoat as Lord Lyon King of Arms by the Duke and then crowned by him. Having also received the baton of office and the collar, Sir Alexander swore his solemn oath: 'I shall defend the Catholic faith to the uttermost of my power. I shall be loyal and true, secret and serviceable, to our Sovereign Lord the King and to all estates – to Emperor, Kings, Princes, Archdukes, Dukes, Marquesses, Earls, Viscounts, Lords or Barons, Knights, Esquires, Gentlemen, Ladies, widows and maidens of good repute, and shall forward their lawful business at their expense. What ambassage or message I take in hand to do, I shall do the same truly, without adding or taking from. I shall avoid all open vices, all bordellos, betting and drinking in taverns. I shall fortify and defend the privileges of the noble office of arms with all my power, and shall never reveal any man's secrets, treason excepted.' (Arnot, *The History of Edinburgh*)

July 28th

1828: On this day *The Scotsman* reported on this startling railway accident:

On Thursday evening a distressing accident occurred on the Railway, near Musselburgh. A young man, named Rintoul, belonging we believe to Edinburgh, was thrown from one of the carriages by a person with whom he had quarreled, and falling beneath the wheels, one of his thighs was broken, and the other limb severely injured. He was removed to one of the colliers' houses in the neighborhood, where he has received the utmost attention, but we understand he continues in a precarious state. The individual who occasioned the accident is described as an elderly man, apparently in good circumstances. He was immediately taken into custody.

July 29th

1554: Mary of Guise, the Queen Mother, took over the governing of Scotland and also political control of her daughter, Mary Queen of Scots. Within a fortnight, the Queen had dismissed the provost of the burgh and replaced him with Lord Robert Maxwell, who then took over complete responsibility for the administration of Edinburgh. Her husband, King James V had become king in 1513 after the Scottish defeat in battle against an English army at Flodden in Northumberland, where his father, King James IV, died, along with large numbers of Scots, who included the flower of Scottish nobility. James V died in 1542. (*ERBE*)

———— •◆• ————

1809: Two years after his death, the birthday of William Pitt the Younger (1759-1806) was celebrated by a magnificent banquet at the Assembly Rooms. So many attended that the large adjoining tea-rooms had to be used for the guests as well. The Duke of Buccleuch presided in one room and the Duke of Atholl in the other. Pitt, at the age of twenty-four, was the youngest-ever prime minister (1783-1801) and followed his father, also William Pitt (1708-78). He was also a Whig politician, in the office of prime minister. His statue by Sir Francis L. Chantrey (1781-1841) stands in Edinburgh at the junction of George Street and Frederick Street.

July 30th

1496: Mr William Forbes, provost of the Collegiate Kirk of St Giles, granted a charter to the burgh. The charter gave them the north part of his *mansio* (manse) and the *glebe* (ground) lying next to the kirk, namely the land and chamber of the curate and the school below … The purpose of this charter was to enlarge the churchyard and the parish burying-ground. In return, the council promised to construct a new room for the curate with a school below it. (*ERBE*)

———◆———

1588: Sir William Stewart was killed in Blackfriars Wynd by the Earl of Bothwell. It started with an argument. Sir William told the Earl to 'kiss his arse'. Hearing that answer, the Earl made a vow to God that Sir William would 'kiss his arse', but with no great pleasure. So, meeting Sir William by chance in Blackfriars Wynd, the Earl told him he would now 'kiss his arse' and with that drew his sword. Sir William took up a defensive position with his back to the wall. The Earl thrust at him with his rapier, striking him in the lower back and out at his belly and so killed him. (*Diarey of Robert Birrel*)

July 31st

1871: Dom Pedro II, the Emperor and Empress of Brazil, visited the city: 'Dom Pedro was the second emperor, his father having ascended the throne in 1822 after leading the revolution which accomplished the independence of Brazil, before a colony of Portugal. Dom Pedro II was born in 1825 at Rio de Janeiro, and since 1840 has been the Emperor of Brazil. In 1842 he married Theresa Christina Maria, daughter of Francis I, King of the Two Sicilies.' Dom Pedro was an Honorary Fellow of the Botanical Society of Edinburgh and was awarded an Honorary Doctorate of Laws by the University of Edinburgh. He set up his own laboratory in Brazil to work at Physics and Chemistry; he spoke six modern languages and was well versed in five ancient languages. In spite of his encouragement of industrialisation (especially the Brazilian railway system), Dom Pedro failed to tackle effectively the widespread problem of slavery in Brazil. He was eventually overthrown by a military coup in 1889. A republic was declared and the Royal family exiled. Pedro II died in Paris on 5 December 1891. (*Transactions and Proceedings of the Botanical Society of Edinburgh, February 1892*)

August 1st

1560: The sacred utensils belonging to the Church of St Giles were made lawful prizes by the magistrates of Edinburgh at the Reformation. They were as follows: the arm of St Giles (a relic) enshrined in silver; a silver chalice or Communion cup; the great eucharist (a monstrance for displaying the host) decorated with gold and precious stones; two cruets (small water-vessels); a golden bell, with a clapper; a golden unicorn; a golden pix (small container for communion wafer); a golden heart with two pearls; a diamond ring; a silver chalice; paten (plate) and spoon; a Communion tablecloth of gold brocade; the coat of the statue of St Giles; a round silver eucharist; two silver censers; a silver ship for incense; a large silver cross; a triangular silver lamp; two silver candlesticks; another two candlesticks; a silver chalice gilt; vestments of gold brocade, crimson velvet embroidered with gold, and green damask. All these were sold and the money applied in the first place to necessary repairs upon the church. The surplus became a part of the funds of the corporation. (Arnot, *The History of Edinburgh*)

August 2nd

1800: 'Foreign Spirits. Wines, whisky and shrubs, Whitehead's Porter,—Burton and Edinburgh ales, Hereford Cider and Perry, wine and pickling vinegars, with black beer, at Sheppard's Spirit Shop, opposite St Cecilia's Hall, Cowgate. Old Jamaica Rum, Old Coniac Brandy, Hollands Gin, Cinnamon Waters, Jamaican Rum Shrub, Capital Old Whisky, Whisky Shrub, Port, Sherry, Lisbon, Mountain Malaga and Madeira Wine, Cyder in pipes, Perry in pipes. N.B.—Samples of fifteen puncheons Old Jamaica rum, large over proofs, lying in bond at Greenock, will be sold at a reasonable price. Orders, with money, or Bank bills to the nett amount, or change returned in goods, or orders for payment on delivery, will be strictly attended to.' (*Caledonian Mercury*)

August 3rd

1659: The ministers Mr James Hamilton and Mr John Sterling met the council and reminded them of the articles that had been agreed upon on 20 July with the Lord Provost, the bailies and the kirk treasurer on the problems of: restraining the activities of Quakers; punishing swearers; administering the number and qualifications of schoolmasters and school mistresses in vulgar (lower-level) schools and their fees; the assistance by the Kirk Sessions of poor scholars from outside the burgh; the imprisoning of beggars. With respect to the Wednesday collections at the kirk doors for the support of those who had recently been made homeless by the fire in Steven Law's Close, the council allowed the collections to continue. On this day also, the council had to deal with the repair of the highway in St Cuthbert's parish and the great breach of the bottom dam-head on the Water of Leith caused by the violent storm of wind and rain some days before, which destroyed the dam walls, the spate carrying the stone away down the river. The council appointed nine persons to inspect the damage and form a plan of action so that the thirteen watermills belonging to the town and the Hospital did not lie inactive. (*ERBE*)

August 4th

1482: The provost, bailies and council of Edinburgh agreed to repay Edward IV the dowry already partly advanced by him for the betrothal of his daughter Cecily and James III's son, James. (*ERBE*)

This was the result of the presence of English forces in the burgh. Richard, Duke of Gloucester (later, Shakespeare's 'Richard III') led an English army into Scotland on behalf of his brother, Edward IV. He captured Edinburgh at the end of July 1482. Although Edward's daughter Cecily had just earlier that year been betrothed to James III's brother, the Duke of Albany (who accompanied Gloucester's army), Albany agreed to cancel the contract. The Scots asked for the restoration of an earlier marriage contract made in 1474 by Edward IV with James III for the future marriage of his (then) one-year-old son (the future King James IV) and five-year-old Lady Cicely of York, Edward's daughter by Elizabeth Woodville. The dowry agreed was 20,000 English crowns (payable over seventeen years). Gloucester, however, would have none of it and demanded the surrender of the town of Berwick with the return of the dowry monies already paid to the Scots. Cicely went on to have three husbands.

August 5th

1600: The King was invited by the Earl of Gowrie to a banquet at his house. The Earl and his brother still had malice and deadly hatred in their hearts. When they saw that the King's nobles and courtiers had gone out they asked the King to go and see their private apartment. Then they seized him and attempted to kill him with their daggers. However, he manoeuvred the Master of Gowrie under his feet. Before the Earl's brother reached the King, he cried out 'Treason! Treason!' As the two brothers and the King wrestled with each other, Thomas Erskine and John Ramsay, the King's page of honour, came running up to the private apartment and the two conspiring brothers were finally put to death. The following day the news reached Edinburgh that the King had escaped this threat to his life. There was such joy that the cannons roared, the bells rang, the trumpets sounded and the drums rolled! The whole town was up in arms, with muskets firing, fireworks thrown and bonfires blazing as was never seen in Scotland, such was the merriment and dancing. (*Diarey of Robert Birrel*)

August 6th

1825: On this day, the *Caledonian Mercury* printed these announcements:

The Duke of Atholl, being desirous to preserve the Game this Season on his Estate in the county of Perth, requests that no Gentleman will Shoot thereon without a written permission from himself. Gamekeepers are stationed to protect the game, and all trespassers will be prosecuted according to law. Former permissions are hereby recalled.

The Earl of Hopetoun requests that no gentleman will Shoot or Course on his Estates in the Counties of Linlithgow, Haddington, Fife, Lanark, or Dumfries, without his permission in writing. Poachers or others trespassing will be prosecuted.

Sir Evan J. M. Macgregor of Macgregor, Baronet, being desirous of preserving the Game on his Estates of Lanrick, Ruskie, and Balquhidder, in the parishes of Kilmadoch Port, Callander, and Balquhidder, and county of Perth, withdraws every permission that may have been formerly granted; and requests that no gentleman may shoot on his Estates this season. The gamekeeper, the tenants, and their servants, have received instructions to warn off all intruders, and to give up the names of trespassers, in order that they may be prosecuted.

August 7th

1851: An article about the Edinburgh Gymnastic Games featured in the *Caledonian Mercury*:

These sports, which, since their first establishment a year or two ago, have, on their annual recurrence, excited so much interest among the working-classes, took place yesterday under circumstances as auspicious as their most zealous promoters could desire. The ground this year selected for the display of the strength and skill of the Athlete was every way well adapted for the purpose, being the field known as Mr Hume's Park, on the Dalkeith Road. Situated close to the base of Salisbury Crags, and occupied by an assemblage which must at least have numbered several thousands, with a sun which shone forth throughout the day ... The games were of the usual character, consisting, besides some rifle-shooting, which took place on Leith Sands, of running, leaping, vaulting, &c. ... At the conclusion of the games ... Sheriff Gordon ... placed before him the prizes to be distributed to the successful competitors—consisting of a fowling-piece, a number of silver snuff-boxes, a pair of telescopes, and various ponderous-looking purses of money— the effect of all which was considerably heightened by their being displayed among a tasteful collection of flowers.

August 8th

2008: The Royal Bank of Scotland traces its origins to the collapse of the Company of Scotland Trading to Africa and the Indies, which had failed not long after the failure of the Scottish Darien colony in the Isthmus of Panama. As part of the 1707 Acts of Union, compensation was allocated to the investors who transferred it into the newly-established Society of the Subscribed Equivalent Debt. In 1724, the Equivalent Society changed its name and began to trade as a bank. This organisation was chartered in 1727 as the Royal Bank of Scotland.

In August 2008, the Royal Bank of Scotland posted pre-tax losses of £691 million for the first half of the financial year. When the American investment bank, Lehman Brothers, filed for bankruptcy, a collapse in the value of banking shares was triggered. By October it was clear that RBS were going to need £20 billion extra capital just to stay afloat. RBS failed to raise £15 billion from shareholders and the government took a 57.9 per cent share in the bank. On 19 January 2009, RBS shares collapsed as the bank estimated its losses at £28 billion, the biggest ever recorded by a British company.

August 9th

1806: On this day, the *Caledonian Mercury* printed an article about a violent storm witnessed in Edinburgh on the previous Saturday. According to the report, the morning was uncommonly sultry, the thermometer stood at 73 degrees Celsius in the shade and the air was very still. The wind in the morning was easterly, but about midday it changed to the south-west. At two o'clock, indications of an approaching storm appeared in the west, and at three it came on with a most violent hurricane, which seemed to darken the atmosphere by the quantity of dust it hurled into the air. A tornado of rain, accompanied by tremendous peals of thunder, with vivid and incessant flashes of lightning, continued with very little intermission till near nine o'clock at night, during which time it was supposed more rain fell than had done in an equal period for many years. As Saturday was the principal day for tradesmen and their families attending the races, immense multitudes were at Leith when the rain commenced. Those who stopped to see the race were completely drenched. Apparently there were no serious accidents, but towards evening time many ludicrous scenes of drunkenness were exhibited on Leith Walk.

August 10th

1832: *The Scotsman* reported on the Grand Procession of the Edinburgh Reform Jubilee, which took place on this day. It was said that to celebrate the triumph of reform, the different trades and public bodies formed a triumphal procession in honour of the occasion, which, for numerical strength and magnificent display, immeasurably surpassed any pageant of the kind ever witnessed in Edinburgh, or perhaps on the face of the 'yet discovered globe'. It stated that the morning dawned most propitiously, and the different trades and public bodies were early astir, preparing for the day's proceedings. At nine o'clock they began to assemble in Bruntsfield Links, taking their stations around the hustings according to the priority of arrival, and by half-past ten the Links were completely covered by marshalled bodies, with their standards flaunting in the breeze, and insignia flashing to the sun. The meeting was opened with the national anthem of 'Rule Britannia', sung by upwards of fifty professional gentlemen. As the 'voluptuous swell' echoed over the commons and among the meadow trees, the people at a distance rushed in a continuous stream to the spot whence the music proceeded. After a hearty round of applause, the business of the hustings was continued.

August 11th

1804: 'Prize Money. Established Office in Scotland: Navy and Army Agency Office, Clerk & Ross, at Merchants' Hall, Hunter's Square, Edinburgh, Prize Money. Officers, Seamen, Soldiers, and the Relations of those deceased, entitled to Prize Money for Ships and Captures, may now have their claims immediately attended to. *Tribune*, *Hydra* (for captures made in January 1804); *Dreadnought* (May 1803); *Pheasant* (Sept. 1799); *Argo* (Sept. 1803); *Swiftsure, Iphigenia, Leviathan, Cormorant, Africa, Lark, Ceres, Severu, Le Serin, Maria Antoinette; Constance, Penelope, Fortune, Princess of Wales* (Sept. 1808); *Sirius, Lark* (May 1803); *Hector, Mondovia* (July 1801); *Culloden, Transfer, Minotaur, Perseus, La Mutine* (Sept. 1799) … Third payment, *Holland.* Land Forces under the command of General Sir Thomas Trigge, K.B. Proceeds of Ordnance Stores taken at the Island of St Eustatius. Head Money and net final Proceeds of the Stores taken at the surrender of Calvi, in Corsica, August 1794. Parties interested will be particular to send forward their Certificates; relations, or next of kin of those deceased, such checks, or other vouchers, as may be in their possession; and Clergymen or others, when applying, will please be particular respecting the transmission of papers. All letters, addressed as above, must be post paid.' (*Caledonian Mercury*)

August 12th

1947: 'Sir,—If ever a nail was hit on the head, it certainly was by your correspondent, Mr Macdonald, in his description of the Princes Street so-called decorations. If these reflect modern Scottish art, then modern Scottish art would seem to have gone stern and wild, and supporting evidence on this point is to be seen at the Enterprise Exhibition. Reference to the scheme of decorations in happier times when Edinburgh said it with flowers, recalls a humorous incident which I was lucky to witness. The electric light standards then had little square platforms about ten feet up, bearing a choice display of flowers and plants. It was a beautiful sunny day and there wasn't a cloud in the sky. The city gardeners ... had been busy and profuse with their watering pots, and overflow drops were still falling to the pavement. Standing under one of these dripping platforms was a dear old lady with her umbrella up!—I am &c. W. Richardson.' (*The Scotsman*)

August 13th

1456: King James II confirmed a charter in favour of the provost, bailies, and community of the burgh of Edinburgh, for the valley and low ground lying between the rock commonly called Cragingalt to the east, and the common way and passage towards Leith on the west (known as Greenside) to be used for presenting tournaments, sports and other appropriate martial arts, at the pleasure of the King and his successors. This grant was made before the Bishops of St Andrews and Brechin, the Lords Erskine, Montgomery, Darnley, Lyle and others. (*ERBE*)

This was the catalyst that unleashed not only pageants and tournaments, but also Lord Lyon King of Arms, Sir David Lindsay's biting *Ane Pleasant Satyre of the Thrie Estaites*, staged between 1539 and 1544. However, in 1558, because this work savaged the corrupt lives of some of the senior Scottish clergy, Sir David's books were ordered to be burnt by the public executioner. However, adapted by Robert Kemp, with music by Sir Cedric Thorpe Davie, Lindsay's play was staged at the Edinburgh International Festival in 1948, 1949, 1951 and revived in 1959 by director Sir Tyrone Guthrie, staged at the Assembly Hall.

August 14th

1943: 'The New Edinburgh; A Master Plan Required. The case for the redevelopment of Edinburgh has been stated in the current exhibition at the National Gallery, and a challenge thrown to the citizens of Edinburgh. The time has come when they must see to it that a better city is planned. When peace comes there will be vast constructional arrears to be made up; and it is the duty of the people of Edinburgh to consider the results of the building which has taken place in the last 50 years … The house-wife is apparently content to wage everlasting war with smoky dirt; the parent is apparently content that his children should live in constant danger from vehicular traffic. The tenement-dweller has not rebelled against climbing high flights of stone stairs, when the efficiency and convenience of lifts have been established for more than a quarter of a century. The breadwinner in the bungalow accepts the daily struggle for transport to and from his work, and rarely inquires why he has to live so far from his office or factory in order to find comparative peace and quiet amid healthier surroundings.' (*The Scotsman*)

August 15th

1816: 'Convictions. Tuesday the following convicts were sent off from Edinburgh jail for Newhaven, from hence they were put on board the *Prompt,* a London smack, to be conveyed to the hulks, previously to their being transported to Botany Bay, viz.— From Edinburgh—William Honeyman and John Smith, condemned to death for breaking into and robbing the warehouse at Carron Works, sentence changed to transportation for 14 years. Thomas Methven, *alias* Wallace, *alias* Watson, theft, at Cupar, Fife, 14 years. James Duff, theft, seven years. John Mackenzie and William Mackay, house-breaking and theft in Leith, 14 years. William Robertson, *alias* James Mitchell, and John Liddell, theft, 14 years. James Hutchinson, house-breaking and theft in East Lothian, 14 years. Thomas Macdonald, robbing ships in Leith Dock, seven years ... Thomas Macdonald, William Mackay, John Mackenzie, and John Liddell, some time since made an attempt to break the jail, which, had it not been for the vigilance of the keeper, might have succeeded. Since that period, their conduct has been outrageous, so that it was found necessary to keep them constantly in irons, notwithstanding which they broke and destroyed everything within their reach in the apartment where they were confined.' (*The Caledonian Mercury*)

August 16th

1800: 'The Lord Provost and magistrates having been informed, that the present scarcity of Potatoes in the Edinburgh Market has been occasioned by reports insidiously circulated, with a view to enhance the Market Price—Do hereby offer a premium of Five Guineas, to be paid by the city Chamberlain, to the person who shall, during the course of the ensuing eight days, bring into and retail in the City, either from their carts or in the Market Place, the largest quantity of Potatoes of the growth of this season, at the most reasonable prices. Given at Edinburgh, this 13th August 1800, James Stirling, provost; William Fettes, bailie; David Willison, bailie; Robert Bow, bailie; Archibald Menzies, bailie.' (*Caledonian Mercury*)

'Wanted. A gentleman lately retired from business wishes to procure a situation in any of the Public Offices in or about Edinburgh, yielding from £100 to £200 per annum. Any person disposed to resign, or who may have interest to procure such a situation, will receive an adequate premium. For further particulars, apply to John Patison, W. S.' (*Caledonian Mercury*)

August 17th

1621: The council instructed the treasurer, Peter Somervell, to give Mr John Hay to deliver to Richard Liver, of the London Customs, the sum of ten pounds sterling as the price of a large quadrant which belonged to him, which he had sent to the mathematician and inventor, John Napier. This was delivered to Mr Andro Young, professor of Mathematics at King James' College. It was added to the inventory of the College and stored in a specially-constructed wooden housing for the use of the teachers and the improvement of the pupils. (*ERBE*)

———◆———

1642: The Convention approved the draft of the Solemn League and Covenant, which had been passed by the General Assembly. On 13 October, after the agreement of the English Parliament had been received, the Covenant was sworn by the Estates and the Assembly in Edinburgh. Thus England and Scotland were bound by a treaty, impossible of fulfilment, which was to breed endless ill-feeling between the nations and bring disaster upon Scotland. By the will of the Estates and the Assembly and of the Presbyterian majority in the English Parliament, Presbyterianism was to be enforced on a country which, for the most part, did not desire it. (*ERBE*, 1604-1626, ed. Marguerite Wood, 1931)

August 18th

1812: Owing to an extraordinary rise in the price of oatmeal, a crowd of people assembled in the Cowgate and Grassmarket for the purpose of intercepting the supplies on their road to the market. Several carts were accordingly seized, and their contents distributed among the populace; after which the mob proceeded to the Dalkeith road, where they seized several more carts, and retailed the meal at two shillings per peck, which they gave to the drivers. The shops, also of the victual-dealers and bakers in Nicholson Street and places adjoining, were threatened by the populace, and were in consequence prudently shut up. In the evening, the houses of several meal-sellers in different parts of the town were attacked and the windows broken. In Leith there were also considerable tumults. The magistrates, with a party of constables, made every exertion to quell the tumult. As a necessary precaution, a party of soldiers was ordered from the castle. (*Caledonian Mercury*)

August 19th

1826: 'Police Court. On Thursday a young Irishwoman … was accused not only of refusing to pay a debt which she had lawfully incurred, but of maltreating and abusing her creditor …The defender, with the thoughtless levity of her country, had borrowed, it appeared, a bawbee from the complainer, about a fortnight ago, and as she seemed entirely to have forgotten the transaction, the latter ventured to remind her of it, and to express an opinion that it was now high time the debt should be liquidated. Instead of meeting with gratitude … she was assailed by a torrent of abuse … and latterly her person was assaulted. The Irishwoman having advanced to the bar, surveyed the judge with a look of calm composure … and then scowled on her accuser a look of defiance and scorn … The complainer declared … that unless some punishment was inflicted on the defender, she need never think of going home. The Magistrate, therefore … bound her over to keep the peace under a penalty of forty shillings.' (*The Scotsman*)

August 20th

1669: A Virginia merchant was admitted as a burgess, one of an increasing number of foreigners whose commercial contribution to the town was appreciated. The goldsmith Zacharias Millons, long resident in Edinburgh, was admitted on 4 September 1670 at a nominal fee. On 7 March 1673, four foreigners were made gild brothers and burgesses: John Madorf (a Pole), Henry Choll (a Swedish merchant), David Amya (a merchant in Gothenburg) and William Blacket (a merchant in Newcastle). On 6 September 1676 a French watchmaker, Paul Romieu (Rewmer), was admitted gratis – except for a contribution to the poor box, as there were no other watchmakers in the town. On 10 October 1679, a Hamburg merchant, a Scot merchant in Cadiz and the Major in Tangiers (also a Scot) were admitted. There were also mass admissions: the Duke of Buccleuch and Monmouth, General of the King's army, was given the burgess ticket (in a gold box), along with his retinue of 72 persons. The King's Commissioner, the Duke of Albany and York, was admitted on 26 December 1679, along with 117 of his attendants, as was the diarist Samuel Pepys, who accompanied the Duke in 1682. (*ERBE*)

August 21st

1806: 'General Post-Office, Edinburgh. Under the patronage of Robert Trotter, Esq., of Castlelaw, Postmaster-General of Scotland, this day is published, price 2 shillings and sixpence, the Post-Office Annual Directory, from Whitsunday 1806 to Whitsunday 1807, containing an Alphabetical arrangement of the Noblemen, private Gentlemen, Merchants, Traders, and others, in the City and Suburbs of Edinburgh and Leith, with their Residence. The Publishers have spared no pains to render this Directory of real general utility. Besides the Tables of Fares for Hackney Coaches and Chairs, Rates of Porterage, &c. ... To be had by applying to any of the Letter-Carriers in Edinburgh and Leith, or at the Lobby of the General Post-Office.' (*Caledonian Mercury*)

'City of Edinburgh Militia. At a General Meeting of the Lieutenancy of this City, and of the County thereof ... orders were issued to the Constables to make up the Annual lists, in manner directed by the said act, of the Names of all the Men within the several parishes and places for which they shall respectively act, between the ages of eighteen and forty-five years ... Those neglecting to state ... Appeals are liable to a penalty, and in case of non-payment thereof, to be imprisoned.' (*Caledonian Mercury*)

August 22nd

1582: Having seized King James VI at his house in Ruthven, William Earl of Gowry, with other Lords, kept his Majesty in confinement and directed affairs at their pleasure. The pulpit resounded with applauses of the godly deed. An act of assembly was passed, declaring the conspirators to have done a good and acceptable service to God, their Sovereign and the country and threatening, with ecclesiastical censures, those who, by word or deed, should oppose the good cause. The Lords brought the King to Edinburgh. The solemnity of his reception was characteristic of the manners of the times. He was met by the ministers of Edinburgh. The whole procession walked up streets, singing a psalm expressive of their critical escape from danger and the great deliverance they had obtained by the captivity and subjection of the King. The news of James' confinement spread all over Europe. They even pierced the walls of her prison and reached the unfortunate Mary Queen of Scots, whose maternal feelings they extremely agitated. King Henry III of France sent an ambassador to Edinburgh with instructions to exert his utmost endeavours to restore the King his freedom and independence. (Arnot, *The History of Edinburgh*)

August 23rd

1681: John Duke of Rothes, Lord High Chancellor of Scotland, died in the Palace of Holyroodhouse, and his body was brought up to St Giles, accompanied by a train of coaches. From there it was conveyed to the Royal Chapel at Holyroodhouse, in the following order of procession: the Commander-in-Chief of the Forces, accompanied by two Adjutant-Generals; a regiment of guards, with their weapons reversed; The Governor of Edinburgh Castle, who was also General of the Artillery, with a baton in his hand, at the head of a company of soldiers; a train of artillery, with wagons and ammunition, led by horses in military harness, the gunners walking beside them. Then came two undertakers, each holding a long staff, two mourners, one carrying a small death's-head banner, the other an hourglass with wings on which was written the motto *Fugit hora* (Time flies). Then came fifty-one poor men, corresponding to the age of the deceased, wearing hooded gowns, each carrying the Duke's coat of arms on a staff, on their shoulders the interwoven letters and numbers of his name and age. (Arnot, *The History of Edinburgh*)

August 24th

1947: *The Scotsman* printed two stories relating to Paris on this day:

Paris, Sunday.—Edinburgh was described ... by a special correspondent of the Paris evening paper, *Paris-Presse*, in a dispatch from Edinburgh ... Festival Notes. The list of distinguished artists in Edinburgh was brought nearer completion yesterday by the arrival of the Sadler's Wells Ballet Company, and, later, members of the Jacques Orchestra and the Old Vic Theatre Company ... The 8.18 pm *Flying Scotsman* ... brought the other artists ... and a Corporation bus carried musicians and players to their hotels and hostels. Among the Old Vic players who arrived at the Waverley Station in the evening were Miss Pamela Burke (Katharina in *The Taming of the Shrew*) and Miss Renée Asherson (Bianca in that play, and the Queen in *King Richard II*). Mr Trevor Howard (Petruchio) and Mr Alec Guinness (Richard) travelled by other routes. Mr John Burrell, producer of *The Taming of the Shrew*, said he knew and liked Edinburgh's theatres.

Economic Plan for Europe. This week should see completion of the European Plan which the 16 nations have been framing in Paris ... The French want a Customs Union ... If Britain wrecked the prospects by staying aloof ... the French ... might cheerfully denounce British obstructionism.

August 25th

1513: On this day, the council ordered that, after nine o'clock in the evening, no fruit seller should sell fruit or other goods at the Mercat Cross or in their own homes. The punishment for a contravention of this order was the confiscation of their fruit and physical punishment of their persons. Additionally, no vagrant person should be on the High Street after nine o'clock in the evening, unless they were carrying out lawful business, carried a lighted candle and declared themselves to the watchmen. Persons found by the watchmen not following these instructions would be imprisoned overnight and then brought before the magistrates in the morning, who would hand them over to the King's army. (*ERBE*)

1838: 'Royal Hotel. The following distinguished personages have arrived:—The Prince and Princess of Schwarzenberg; Prince Windeschgratz; Count Grunne and Count Erdody, from a tour in the Highlands. Lord and Lady Willougby D'Eresby, on their way to Drummond Castle, Perthshire. On Tuesday afternoon the *North Briton,* a fine ship of 400 tons burthen, bound for Australia, left Leith Harbour in gallant style. There are a number of twenty-seven passengers amongst whom are a number of highly-educated young men who intend making Australia the land of their adoption.' (*Caledonian Mercury*)

August 26th

1809: 'Hercules Insurance Company. The Directors of the Company beg leave to intimate to the Public, the approbation of the General Meeting of Proprietors, upon the 12th curt. To an extension of Capital, application for Shares may therefore be made, as formerly either to the Agents or the Manager, by whom they will be submitted for the consideration of the Directors. Insurance is done at their Office against Fire, upon Lives and Survivorships, and Annuities granted, upon the most liberal terms ... Nicol Allan, Manager.' (*Caledonian Mercury*)

'Royal Exchange. Extensive and Elegant Premises to Let, for such number of years as can be agreed upon, to be entered to at Martinmas next. The Whole Building presently possessed by the Court of Exchequer, within the Royal Exchange, consisting of a great variety of rooms, large and small, with kitchen, closets, garrets, &c. ... They are well adapted for a public banking-house or elegant hotel, or for any extensive business that requires a central situation ... Mr William Allan, the present house-keeper, will show the house on Mondays, Thursdays, and Saturdays, from eleven till two o'clock; and the City Chamberlain will give information on further particulars.' (*Caledonian Mercury*)

August 27th

1463: Pope Pius II (1405-64) granted a 'plenary indulgence' (cancelling all the punishment due to sin) to all who, being profoundly sorry for their sins, visited Trinity Collegiate Church during the festival of its dedication (10 July) every year for five years, or during the following week (known as the octave), for a period of up to fifty years. A third of the value of offerings made by each penitent during these octaves was sent to the papal treasury in Rome to help in the campaign to make the Holy Land accessible to Christians. The rest went to pay for the completion of the church building. (*ERBE*)

As the layman, scholar and poet, Aeneas Silvius Piccolomini (the future Pope Pius II) had visited Scotland in 1435, having been shipwrecked near Dunbar while on a covert mission to persuade King James I to attack England so as to distract the English from attacking the French. In thanksgiving, he walked five miles barefoot to Whitekirk. Although he thought Scottish women were rather ugly, he had a relationship with a Scots girl and she gave birth to a son (who died soon after). He noticed with amazement that outside the churches, monks handed poor people 'black stones' (coal).

August 28th

1491: Following the cruel slaughter of the cordiner (shoemaker) Robert Malyson, recently murdered in Edinburgh, the bailies and sheriffs ordered a search for the perpetrators – William of Bog, John of Schele (a shield-maker) and the skinner John Taitt, all of whom had escaped from the burgh. Accordingly, they were denounced at the Mercat Cross to the sound of horn. Anyone who sheltered or hid them would suffer the death penalty. (*ERBE*)

1809: On this day, the *Caledonian Mercury* reported on a legal case from the Friday before. The sitting magistrate fined an innkeeper, for infringing the regulations respecting goods delivered at the quarters of carriers. The Magistrate, on Saturday, confiscated and sent to the Charity Workhouse of this city, a quantity of fresh butter, which had been seized by their officer of the market, for being deficient in weight. In the report it was speculated that the intention of the magistrates was to publish the names of those who would in future be convicted of exposing butter short of weight.

August 29th

1623: A number of complaints had been made about the regulations for Bellmen (undertakers) and grave-diggers and the prices they charged. As a result, the town council fixed the prices: forty pounds Scots to the Bellman and twelve shillings to the grave-makers when the best velvet mortcloth pall was used; forty shillings to the Bellmen and nine shillings to the grave-makers; thirty shillings to the Bellman for carrying the corpse and six shillings to the grave-makers for children when the velvet mortcloth was used; three pounds Scots to the Bellmen and twelve shillings to the grave-makers when a cloth mortcloth was used; thirty shillings to the Bellmen and nine shillings to the grave-makers when the middle-quality cloth was used; eighteen shillings to the Bellmen and six shillings to the grave-makers for children using the small cloth mortcloth. The Bellmen should carry the bodies of children of four years and under. Persons in receipt of Church alms would be buried free of charge. A register was to be kept by one of the Bellmen of all burials and prices. The Bellmen were required to pay the ordinary yearly allowance to the ringer of the town bells. This was to be proclaimed and a table of prices printed. (*ERBE*)

August 30th

1876: 'The Fire at the Caledonian Distillery. The worst fears as to the fate of the stillman, Muir, who was in the still-house at the time the explosion occurred, have unfortunately been realized—his dead body, black and charred with the smoke and fire, and scarcely recognizable, having been found among the ruins early yesterday morning. The staging on which he worked had been entirely burned away, and the body had fallen to the next floor, a distance of twelve or thirteen feet. Muir, who was between thirty and forty years of age, and had been in the employment of the company for a considerable time, leaves a wife and two children. He resided in Dalry Park Terrace. The fire smoldered until between two and three o'clock yesterday morning, when it was completely extinguished. In the still-house were two stills—one on the south side, built on two columns, and known as the coffey still, which was capable of producing about 50,000 gallons in a couple of days, was the principal still in the distillery. It is about fifty feet in height, with a framework of wood in which the copper pipes were riveted; and it has suffered most, the woodwork about it being entirely destroyed.' (*The Scotsman*)

August 31st

1842: On this day, a piece titled 'Revisiting the Trial of Thomas Muir for Sedition (1793)' appeared in *The Scotsman*:

The Prosecutor's speech betrays a spirit of bitter animosity, which a Prosecutor at this day would be ashamed to manifest … It is entirely composed of either open charges—to support which, there appears not a tittle of evidence—or of abusive epithet. He told the Jury that 'a wider range of diabolical mischief would appear in this man [Muir], than ever was seen in England or anywhere else!'—that, 'like the demon of Sedition, he recommended that club government has produced all the anarchy we see in France,' though not one single witness deposed to a single act or word that could be so construed! …having referred to a book-shop, which Mr Muir used to frequent, he elegantly characterised it as —'A cathedral of sedition, where he sat like a spider weaving his filthy web to catch the unwary.' He told the Jury further, if they were loyal to their king, they would find Muir guilty.

September 1st

1804: 'Safe and Expeditious Travelling. The elegant Stirling Long Coach, with four horses and a Guard, continues to set out at nine o'clock in the morning, from J. Mackay's, White Hart Inn, Grassmarket; and returns at the same hour, from J. Masson's, Saracen's Head Inn, Stirling ... this Coach was built purposely for the roads in this country, and that no conveyance can surpass it for safety and expedition.—Likewise, the Old Stirling six-seated Coach, with four horses (a safe, easy and expeditious conveyance), continues to set out at nine o'clock in the morning from M. Oliver's, Grassmarket; and returns at the same hour from John Gibb's, Golden Lion, Stirling.— The Proprietors of the above Coaches, to accommodate the public, have now reduced their Tickets to 8 shillings.—Falkirk, 6 shillings.—and Linlithgow 4 shillings. Outside, 5 shillings. Falkirk, 4 shillings.—and Linlithgow 3 shillings.—Uptakes, 3 pence per mile.' (*Caledonian Mercury*)

September 2nd

1839: 'Serious Accident from Foul Air.—On Monday evening an accident occurred to one of the workmen belonging to Mr Phillips's Distillery, Yard-heads, Leith, while cleaning one of the large tuns belonging to the establishment, which was nearly attended with fatal consequences. It is customary, it appears, before proceeding to cleanse the tuns, to allow a stream of water to flow through, in order to dispel the carbonic acid gas which collects within them. On the present occasion, however, this had been neglected; and, consequently, no sooner had the man descended than he was seized with faintness and fell down. Two other men who were present instantly attempted to get down to remove him, but the smell was so strong that they were both driven back. One of them, however, ran for the Humane Society's drag, by the help of which they were enabled to lift him out, but by this time he was quite senseless, having been more than fifteen minutes exposed to the influence of the noxious vapour. Drs Craigie and Lawrie having been sent for, were speedily on the spot, and after working several hours with him, fortunately succeeded in restoring animation.' (*Caledonian Mercury*)

September 3rd

1808: 'Masonic Procession. Grand Lodge of Scotland. The Lord Provost, Magistrates, and Council of Edinburgh, having signified their desire to the Grand Lodge of Scotland, that the Foundation Stone of the New Gaol, should be laid by the Grand Master of Scotland, and having appointed Thursday the 8th inst. at 12 o'clock, for this purpose, a Grand Masonic Procession will take place on that day, from the College of Edinburgh to the Highland Society Hall … and from thence to the site of the intended Gaol in Forrester's Wynd. The Grand Master, and the other Office Bearers of the Grand Lodge, will be in the College at eleven o'clock precisely; and they particularly request that the Brethren attend there exactly at that hour. Tickets will be delivered to the Masters of Lodges for distribution among their respective Members — And none will be admitted to the Procession without tickets, or who do not attend the Grand Master at the hour appointed. William Guthrie, Grand Secretary.' (*Caledonian Mercury*)

September 4th

1611: The council ordered the burgh treasurer to plan the construction of a school for Mr Patrik Henrysoun, master of the Song School. On 1 May 1612, the council instructed the treasurer to build and equip a song school in the Over Kirk yard of the burgh in the same place where there was one many years before. The council appointed Alexander Clerk, Patrick Whytelaw and James Arnott to oversee the work, receive funding from the treasurer, buy the materials, pay the workmen and engage the stonemasons within fifteen days. (*ERBE*)

———◆———

1808: This day marked the death at Merchiston Bank of the playwright Revd John Home. Born at Leith on 22 September 1722, he graduated from the University of Edinburgh and was licensed by the Presbytery of Edinburgh in 1745. In the same year he fought against the Jacobite forces and was taken prisoner at the Battle of Falkirk. He escaped to become the Church of Scotland minister at Athelstaneford near Haddington in East Lothian. His greatest claim to fame is his play *Douglas*, which opened in Edinburgh. At its Edinburgh premiere in the Canongate Theatre (14 December 1756), an enthusiastic challenge came from the audience: 'And where's your Willie Shakespeare noo?'

September 5th

1513: Preparations for an engagement against the English were made in Edinburgh, which was on high alert. The provost, bailies and council ordered all combatants staying in the burgh to rejoin the King's army and all inhabitants due to bear arms to present themselves before the provost on pain of forfeiting their life, land and goods, in order to ensure King James IV's victory and safe return. (*ERBE*)

But it was not to be. Fought on 9 September 1513 at Flodden, Northumberland between a Scots army under King James IV and an English force under Thomas Howard, Earl of Surrey, this was the numerically largest battle between the two nations. For the Scots, the price of defeat was devastating: the English lost 1,500 men but the Scots around 10,000, including twelve Earls, fifteen Lords, many clan chiefs, an archbishop and above all, King James IV himself. It is said that every great family in Scotland mourned the loss of a relative at the Battle of Flodden. The dead were remembered 200 years later by Jean Eliot (1727-1805) in her lament, 'The Flowers of the Forest', where she set her own poignant words to a seventeenth-century tune. (Dick Gaughan: www.youtube.com/watch?v=cJIrAkJnS1I)

September 6th

1941: On this day *The Scotsman* featured some intriguing advertisements:

Matrimony.—Gentleman (32), would like to meet small lady with plump figure; Protestant; genuine.

Men Old at 40! Be as young as you were at 25. Oystrax Brand Tonic Tablets contain revitalisers, rejuvenators, invigorators. Vitamin B1, Iron, Calcium, Phosphorus. First dose starts new life, vigour, vital force. At all Chemists—only 1 shilling and ninepence (plus Purchase Tax).

How to stop Smoking. Overcome Tobacco Craving. Booklet of world-famous method free. Mr G. M. Stanley, 255 Strand, London, WC2.

House of Refuge for the Destitute, 64 Canongate. Donations of Unwanted Clothing, boots and shoes for either sex, specially wanted for the Destitute; also books and magazines. Messenger will be sent on receipt of postcard to the Governor.

September 7th

1736: At the execution of a smuggler in the Grassmarket, John Porteous, captain of the City Guard, fired twice upon the mob and ordered his men to do the same. The Captain's orders were obeyed and six people were killed and eleven severely wounded. Porteous was prosecuted, convicted by the unanimous verdict of a jury and condemned. But Queen Caroline (then Regent) indulged the criminal with a reprieve and the people were enraged to a degree of fury. They surprised and disarmed the Town Guard and blocked up the gates of the city, to prevent the admission of troops quartered in the suburbs. The prison doors, which would not yield to the force of their hammers, they consumed by fire. The prisoners they dismissed, Porteous excepted – whom they threatened with the tragic catastrophe which he dreaded. They marched with lighted torches to the Grassmarket, opened a shop, took out a coil of ropes and paid for them ... they proceeded to a dyer's post, near the spot where the unfortunate people were killed. After reproaching him with his barbarity, they hanged him on the post and dispersed. (Arnot, *The History of Edinburgh*)

September 8th

1519: On this day, the Lords of Council sent letters under the signet (the Royal seal) to the provost and bailies of the burgh of Edinburgh directing that all placks (a four pence coin made of silver and copper) issued during the reigns of the late and present Kings should be accepted by the general public regardless of the metal of which they were made, and that searchers would be appointed in every burgh to destroy all false placks, and to pass all good placks, which should subsequently be accepted under pain of death. Two timber shops would be erected, one in the Meal Market, and the other between the Tron and the Fish Market, in which shops the searchers would sit every day. (*ERBE*)

1820: The Associate Presbytery (later known as 'Seceders') left the Established Church of Scotland in 1733 and in 1747 divided into two parties over the issue of oaths taken by town burgesses to support the National Church, which they saw as suffering from abuses. Those who thought such oaths unlawful became known as the Anti-Burghers, and the remainder became the Burghers. After seventy-three years of separation, both parties were reunited in the Bristo Street meeting-house.

September 9th

1802: On this day, the *Caledonian Mercury* reported on a crime that occurred on the previous Sunday night at about eleven o'clock. As two gentlemen were coming up the Canongate they met four young men near the Canongate Church, one of whom struck a dog. This produced some altercations. The two gentlemen, however, soon left the other party, but were followed by the group to the Netherbow, where the four fellows took up stones, and threw at the gentlemen, and unfortunately struck one of them so severely on the head as to fracture the skull. The gentleman, however, walked home and went to bed; but early on the Monday morning it was found necessary to call a surgeon, who, on examining the wound, discovered a severe fracture. The operation of trepanning was found absolutely necessary ... but, in spite of every exertion, the gentleman lingered in great agony until the Tuesday night, when he died. As soon as the magistrates were informed of this, they adopted every measure to discover the offenders. Parties of peace officers patrolled the streets on Monday night, to discover any lurking predators, but a very accidental circumstance led to the discovery of the whole gang. The newspaper revealed that three of them were apprehended and committed to jail.

September 10th

1547: Scots were defeated by the English at the Battle of Pinkie Cleugh (or Falside), near Edinburgh. The battle was sparked by English demands that Edward VI of England (aged 10) should marry Mary Queen of Scots (aged 5) – an event known as the 'Rough Wooing'. It is estimated that 15,000 Scots were killed, 1500 captured and English losses amounted to only 500.

———•◆•———

1604: Following the accession of King James VI to the throne of England, the general master of the Scottish Mint sailed to London to defend the minting of Scottish coins before the Council of England. He defended the separate Scottish coinage as hard as he could, so much so that the wit and knowledge of the general master astounded the Englishmen. And he returned home on 10 December. (*Diarey of Robert Birrel*)

———•◆•———

1883: This day saw the opening of the Lyceum Theatre by the actor Mr Henry Irving and the London Lyceum Company. As a young actor, he changed his name from 'Brodribb' to Irving. He came to Edinburgh in 1856 and by the time he left in 1859 had played a wide variety of roles.

September 11th

1800: 'Ten guineas of Reward. The three following young lads, Indented Apprentices, have absconded from Aberdeen, viz. John Diack, aged fifteen, fair complexion, and brown hair, went off about three weeks ago ... James Brown, aged about fifteen, dark hair, and dark complexion, stout made for his age, went off early on the morning of the 5th current ... John Grant, aged fourteen, ruddy complexion, and much pitted with the smallpox, brown hair, absconded along with Brown ... They are all natives of Aberdeen, and may be known by their dialect. A reward of Ten Guineas will be paid for their apprehension, or for such information as shall lead to it, on applying to Mr Robert Morice, advocate in Aberdeen.' (*Caledonian Mercury*)

'Indentures of Apprenticeship, made upon improper Stamps, rendered invalid. His Majesty's Commissioners ... do hereby give notice, that ... in respect of indentures of apprenticeship made for the binding of poor children and others, which have, through mistake or inadvertency, been executed upon stamps of a different denomination ... the persons who have incurred any penalty by such neglect or omission, are indemnified against the same ... By order of the Commissioners, John Bretell, Secretary.' (*Caledonian Mercury*)

September 12th

1423: A document of indenture was drawn up between Dean John of Leith, formerly Abbot of Holyrood, and the alderman, bailies, and other officers of the burgh on behalf of the community. In this document, the Dean made over the Canons' Mills and their associated works for five years, with the payments from tenants required to grind their grain in the mills and the additional fixed levy imposed on them, along with all the other associated freedoms. (*ERBE*)

———◆———

1829: 'Contractors Wanted. The Commissioners of the Bridewell for the City and County of Edinburgh hereby give notice, that they are ready to receive offers for supplying Bridewell with the necessary quantities of the following articles ... Bread.—In loaves ... made from wheat ground overhead, without any of the bran being taken out; Meal.—Best Mid Lothian oatmeal; Barley.—ordinary pot barley; Cheese.—of a quality not inferior to soft Kanter; Beer.—good small beer; Salt.—of the best quality; Flesh.—Cow or Ox heads ... to be made up with an equivalent in Houghs; Coals.—best Jewel coal; Soap.—Best hard soap ... the above provisions to be delivered free of charge ... Such estimates to be lodged with Mr Murray, Clerk.' (*Caledonian Mercury*)

September 13th

1753: The foundation stone of the proposed Royal Exchange was laid by George Drummond, Grand Master of the Freemasons. A triumphal arch was constructed, with theatres for the magistrates and officers of the Grand Lodge and galleries for the other lodges and spectators. However, the contract for the work was not settled until 12 June 1754, with work beginning on the site the following day. (Arnot, *The History of Edinburgh*)

1871: 'At the Police Court yesterday, Sheriff Hallard disposed of the following cases:—James Cunningham, Washington Street, Dalry, was sentenced to fifteen days' imprisonment for stealing a coat and vest from a cart in the Lawnmarket on the 18th inst. James Gray, residing at St John's Hill, was remitted to a higher court, as was also John McCartney, Cowgate, the former on a charge of assaulting his wife in a brutal manner on the 9th, and the latter on a charge of cruelly ill-treating his father on the 11th inst. Both prisoners had been twice previously convicted of assault. Louis Hennessey was sentenced to forty days' imprisonment, with hard labour, for behaving in an outrageous manner in the High Street on the 11th inst., and assaulting two police-constables in the execution of their duty. Hugh Keenan ... was sentenced to fifteen days' imprisonment, with hard labour, for breach of the peace, committed in the High Street, and also with assaulting a man named Hindford. William Wallace was sentenced to forty days' imprisonment, with hard labour, for assaulting his wife in Shoemaker's Close on the 10th inst.' (*The Scotsman*)

September 14th

1128: Four years after he had become King of Scotland, after the death of his brother Alexander I in 1124, King David I (1084-1153) left Edinburgh Castle to go hunting. He did so against the wishes of his chaplain, who had advised him to stay at home as it was the Feast of the Holy Cross (*Hali Rude*). David's mother, Queen (Saint) Margaret, had handed down to him a precious relic of the True Cross of Christ: keeping the feast day holy was a family tradition. However, David's love of hunting got the better of him and he rode out. All went well until he was surprised by a huge stag. David's horse reared up in terror and as the King struggled to control his mount the stag lunged at him with its sharp antlers. David was knocked to the ground and lay, half-dazed on the earth. As he recovered, his guilty conscience at the words of his chaplain got the better of him and he interpreted the accident as a warning from Heaven. One of his first actions was to invite the Augustinian canons to Scotland and provide them with a monastery of the Holy Rood. (*ERBE*)

September 15th

1595: On this day, Bailie John MacMorran was killed. It started when the children at the school followed the usual custom of coming to the town council once a year to ask for a special holiday. This was refused by Bailie MacMorran. Accordingly, a number of the scholars, being the sons of gentlemen, mutinied. They came out at night and took over the school building, having provided themselves with food, drink, guns, small pistols and swords. They barricaded the doors of the school and they refused to allow their master in, nor anyone else. The council, hearing this, ordered John MacMorran to go to the grammar school and establish order. MacMorran, accompanied by council officials, went and told the scholars to open the doors. They refused. The bailie and the council officers took a large wooden joist and ran at the back door. One scholar told him to stop battering the door otherwise, he vowed to God, he would shoot two bullets at his head. The bailie, thinking he would never shoot, continued to run at the door with his officers. A scholar named William Sinclair, son of William Sinclair Chancellor of Caithness ... killed the bailie with a shot to the head. (*Diarey of Robert Birrel*)

September 16th

1745: Upon the approach of the Pretender's (Prince Charles Edward Stuart) army, which a few days before had crossed the Forth above Stirling, the cash of the banks and other public offices was removed into Edinburgh Castle. The King's forces who, with the Town Guard, were posted at Corstorphine and Coltbridge, fled. The Town Guard retreated into the city, which was seized with general consternation. Early next morning, a coach drove to the Netherbow Port and the sentinels, suspecting no bad consequences, permitted a porter to let the coach pass. But, upon the gates being opened, a party of Highlanders who had reached the gate undiscovered rushed in, secured it and the other gates of the city, took possession of the main guard, made the soldiers on duty prisoners, and seized the arms and ammunition belonging to the city. About noon, the Highland army, headed by the Chevalier, arrived in the King's Park and encamped near Duddingston. The Chevalier himself took possession of Holyroodhouse. They were met by an immense multitude of spectators, whom the novelty of the fight or affection to the cause had drawn together. (Arnot, *The History of Edinburgh*)

September 17th

1745: At the Mercat Cross, with the ceremonies customary at royal proclamations, the heralds and pursuivants were obliged (by the Jacobites) to publish a declaration, a commission of regency and a manifesto. In these the subjects were promised the free exercise of the Protestant religion and full enjoyment of their rights and privileges. Proclamations were also published, commanding the inhabitants of the town and county of Edinburgh to deliver up their arms at the Palace of Holyroodhouse and prohibiting the soldiers, and others in the Highland army, from molesting the people or pillaging their effects, under pain of being punished by martial law, with death or otherwise, according to the offence. A message was sent to the city requiring, under pain of military execution, a certain quantity of stores for the army, of which payment was promised as soon as the present troubles should be over. They were furnished accordingly and an assessment of two shillings and sixpence upon the pound was imposed on real rents within the city, for defraying that expense. (Arnot, *The History of Edinburgh*)

September 18th

1817: 'Demolition of the Old Jail. The subscription for the relief of the debtors in the old jail has fully answered the purpose intended. The subscribers will be gratified to learn that their generosity enabled the Committee on Tuesday to throw open the door of the jail, and liberate every prisoner confined there for debt; and a small balance still remains, which is to be applied in aid of the families of those most in want. The criminals, twenty-five in number, were removed to the new jail on Monday morning. The two McIlvogues, McCristal and Janet Douglas, under sentence of death, were sent to the lock-up-house.' (*Caledonian Mercury*)

'Conviction. A complaint was made by several respectable inhabitants against a man of the name of Dunlop, for keeping a riotous and disorderly house in Stevenlaw's Close, which was attended by the most abandoned company, and open at all hours of the night. The complaint was fully proved, and the Magistrate forfeited his licence, in terms of the 21st section of the last Police Act. This is the first conviction under the act, and, it is hoped, it will operate as a warning to retailers of spirituous liquors what company they admit to their houses.' (*Caledonian Mercury*)

September 19th

1815: The *Caledonian Mercury* printed this article on the Grand Masonic Procession:

On Tuesday last, the day appointed for laying the foundation-stones of the Regent's Bridge and New Gaol, the inhabitants of this place were gratified with the most brilliant procession which ever adorned the annals of Masonry ... This procession, containing upwards of 2,500 persons, took its way down the High Street, whence it moved along the North Bridge by Leith Street to the Low Calton. Having reached the site where the foundation-stone of the Regent's Bridge was to be laid, Lord Provost, Magistrates and Council, the Sheriff, and Parliamentary Commissioners, and the Grand Master ... entered the respective platforms prepared for them ... The grand Master ... then descended from the platform into the pit where the stone was placed, and there ... concluded the ceremony of laying the foundation of the Regent's Bridge ... the brethren again formed themselves in their proper order, and the procession moved off to lay the foundation of the New Gaol on the Calton Hill ... the ceremonies of depositing the coins, &c. of fixing the inscription-plate, &c. were again gone through with the greatest solemnity, the band of singers performing the air 'Great Light to Shine'.

September 20th

1904: 'The Autumn Holiday. This was celebrated in Edinburgh under specially pleasant weather conditions. The morning was cold and hazy, but by nine o'clock the sun dispelled the mist, and there was warm and almost uninterrupted sunshine during the remainder of the day. Almost all classes of the community observed the holiday. Open shops were the exception, and all the banks, insurance offices, and public departments were closed for the day. The Stock Exchange, however, remained open as usual. The railway companies offered special trains and cheap fares. Many people, taking advantage of the extended weekend, left the city on Saturday, but the great majority confined their holiday-making to yesterday. Both the Waverley and Caledonian Railway Stations were exceptionally busy, even for a public holiday. Beginning as early as four o'clock—the early starters being bound for distant towns—the rush of traffic continued until well on in the day. At the Waverley Station, five special trains left in the early morning for Inverness, the passengers, numbering something like 2,500, being connected with the Shopkeepers' Association. Another special left about seven o'clock, conveying 700 excursionists to Aberdeen, and this train was followed by another carrying 300 passengers to Dundee.' (*The Scotsman*)

September 21st

1848: On this day, the *Caledonian Mercury* printed these advertisements:

Institution for Drawing, Painting and Perspective, 54 North Frederick Street. Mr. Simson & Son beg to intimate, that their Classes will be resumed on Monday, 2nd October.

Musical Education. Mr & Mrs Eager have the honour to announce, that their Academy, 54 Frederick Street, for the Musical Education of Young Ladies, and the Tuition of the Art of Piano Forte Playing, will re-open on Monday the 2nd of October.

Mr Rampini has resumed giving instructions in Italian. His classes will open on the 2nd of October. Young Ladies who attend from the commencement of the Session ... will find it also more economical. Classes and private lessons to Governesses on moderate terms. 10 Gloucester Place.

French Institution, 8 Nelson Street. Monsieur Surenne's Classes, consisting of two distinct Departments—namely, Senior and Junior, will open on Monday 2nd October. The former comprises various degrees of attainment in the Languages; but the latter is entirely devoted to the Young Ladies just beginning their English Studies. Conversation is carried on in both departments.

September 22nd

1497: The King commanded the provost and bailies of the burgh to put the following proclamation into effect so as to prevent the imminent danger of the infection of the community by the contagious disease known as the grandgore (syphilis): 'By our authority we immediately charge and command that all persons in the burgh who are now infected ... leave the burgh and gather on the Sands of Leith at 10 am where they will find boats ready and stocked with food to take them to the nearby Inchcolm Island in the River Forth. They will remain on the island as long as God provides for their well-being. All persons who are being treated for the disease will accompany them. Anyone found within the burgh after sunrise on Monday will be branded on the cheek. If they still remain in the burgh after this punishment, they will be placed under the threat of banishment.' (*ERBE*)

1896: On this day, Czar Nikolai Aleksandrovich of Russia and his Czarina, Alexandra of Hesse, disembarked at Leith on their way to Balmoral. The Czarina was the grand-daughter of Queen Victoria. He was the last Czar of Russia, abdicating in 1917 before being executed by the Bolsheviks, with his family, in 1918.

September 23rd

1809: This notice appeared in the *Caledonian Mercury*:

Five Hundred Pounds Reward. A forgery of the Guinea Notes of the Governor and Company of the Bank of Scotland, having recently appeared, the Directors hereby promise a Reward of Five Hundred Pounds Sterling, to anyone who shall, within three months from the date hereof, give such information as may lead to a conviction of any person or persons concerned in forging the said Notes, or in uttering them, knowing them to be forged. The reward to be paid on conviction. The engraving, the paper, and the seals of the forged Notes, are much coarser than those of the true. In the forged Notes the ink is browner, and the words 'One Pound One Shilling' fainter, and less distinct than in the real Notes. There are more minute differences, which the Bank's officers and agents will point out. Bank of Scotland.

September 24th

1943: 'Home Guard Absentees.—For failing to attend Home Guard duties, in accordance with instructions, two men appeared before Sheriff Gilchrist, K.C., at Edinburgh Sheriff Court, yesterday, and were fined. David Patterson Barrie, carter, 1 Dean Street, Edinburgh, admitted absenting himself without reasonable excuse from duty between April 12 and August 10 this year, during which period he should have attended parades twice a week. Mr J. Gibson, the Depute Fiscal, said that Barrie had omitted about 40 attendances. He was fined £5. Thomas Jinks, sugar warehouseman, 22 Bothwell Street, Edinburgh, was attached to an anti-aircraft battery of the Home Guard, and he pleaded guilty to failing to attend Home Guard duties, with one exception, between July 29 and September 16. He had a previous conviction and was fined £10.' (*The Scotsman*)

September 25th

1843: The *Caledonian Mercury* contained a rather grim selection of news stories on this day:

Accidents.—On Saturday night, Robert Howden, baker, fell from the window of a common stair in Niddry Street, and was severely hurt. He was carried to the Royal Infirmary.— Yesterday morning, a man named O'Brien was found lying on the street, near the County Hall, with a severe cut on his head, supposed to have fallen from intoxication. He was also sent to the Infirmary.

Suspicious Death.—Between seven and eight o'clock on yesterday morning, a child belonging to Joseph Emley, tailor, St Mary Wynd, was found dead in the house, having a severe cut in the head. It had been heard crying a good deal at an earlier period of the morning. But the father and mother, who were the worse of liquor, were taken into custody by the Police constables, and are kept for further examination.

Death from Starvation.—We have seldom had occasion to record a more horrible case of destitution than one that occurred here on Friday morning, when Dr Tait of the Police Office was called to attend an old woman who was found lying in a kind of closet at the bottom of the Old Fishmarket Close. She was in a state of utter nudity, and quite dead.

September 26th

1357: A Council held at Edinburgh confirmed the obligation of the Three Estates (first, Bishops and Abbots; second, Dukes, Earls and lay tenants; third, burgh commissioners) to provide a ransom for the King. (*ERBE*)

———◆———

1506: The provost and council ruled that no pigs of any kind should be kept within the burgh, under the pain of slaughter and confiscation by the public executioner, Patrik Fessail, who had been ordered to kill any pig whenever he found one out-of-doors and untethered. (*ERBE*)

———◆———

1801: 'Anatomy & Surgery. Mr John and Mr Charles Bell will begin their Winter course of Lectures on Anatomy and Surgery, on Tuesday the 10th of November, at their Anatomical Rooms, Surgeon's Square. Mr Charles Bell will deliver his usual Course of Lectures on the Principles of Midwifery and that part of Pathology connected with it, at seven o'clock in the evening.' (*Caledonian Mercury*)

September 27th

1509: Thomas Johnston, stonemason and road engineer, and salt merchant John Brown, put forward an application to the provost, bailies and council to be given a contract to sweep and clean the High Street. This work would entail the purchase of horses, covered carts, wheel-barrows and other necessary equipment. They also needed a clear description of their duties and work routine. This proposal was accepted by the burgh authorities and the two men were directed to clean the High Street from Castlehill on both sides of the street, to the top of Leith Wynd on the north side and St Mary's Wynd on the south. In every part of the burgh they were required to supply and install ten sections of stone roadway per annum to improve the accessibility and appearance of the burgh. In return, to cover the expenses of these duties and render a profit to themselves, they would be licensed to collect from residents, on both sides of the High Street, one penny per quarter for every booth, vault, cellar or bedroom and from every seller of meat or fish, four pence a quarter to clean up their waste and rubbish on Monday market days. (*ERBE*)

September 28th

1660: The council granted liberty and tolerance to William Woodcok, former officer in Leith, to set up and fit a hackney coach service between Leith and Edinburgh at the following rates: coach hire up or down for a single person twelve shillings if the person desired to travel alone. If the person who hired the coach would wait for another to go along with him, then the fee was no more than twelve shillings. If three people travelled together then the fee was also no more than twelve shillings. If more people travelled together then each person paid four shillings Scots for the hire. Coming up to Edinburgh, passengers would be dropped off at the foot of Leith Wynd on the pavement. This arrangement would continue until otherwise notified. William Woodcock had licence to transport other passengers to and from outlying country districts according to agreed private contracts. On 20 August 1673, new regulations were issued: Coachmen who refused a hire would pay double to the would-be hirer; coaches should not trot nor gallop in the streets of the town or suburbs. Carters and sledders were to lead their horses and carts in the streets. (*ERBE*)

September 29th

1832: On this day, the *Caledonian Mercury* advertised classes for these cultured pastimes:

Dancing. Mr McGlashan & Son respectfully intimate, that they will re-open their Classes, at 23 James's Square, on Monday the 1st of October. Boarding Schools and Families attended.

Dancing. Mr Howison, Professor of Dancing, most respectfully intimates to the Nobility and gentry, that he will resume his Classes on Monday the 1st of October. NB Schools and Families attended. 44 Howe Street.

Dancing. Mr Bryson has the honour of announcing to the Nobility and gentry, that he will resume his Classes on the 1st of October. Families and Schools attended. 29 Frederick Street.

Music. Mr Robertson having returned from completing in London his annual selection of Piano Fortes, will resume teaching the Theory and Practice of Music, in his Academy, No 4, Queen Street, on Monday the 1st of October. Terms, &c. may be known at the Music Saloons, 39 and 47 Prince's Street, where may be seen a most extensive collection of new and second-hand Piano Fortes, and a large assortment of the newest and most fashionable music. The lovers of our National Music are also respectfully informed, that ... the Vocal Melodies of Scotland, have just been reprinted and may be had as above.

September 30th

1862: On the final day of September in this year, *The Scotsman* reported on the 'Police Prosecutions of the Clubs':

At the Police Court yesterday, before Bailie Russell, several cases of illicit spirit selling, under the new Public-houses Act Amendment, of 1862, were brought up for trial. Mr James Bell, SSC, conducted the defence in each case. William Rose and Ralph Bates, both residing in Castlehill, were charged with trafficking in spirits and other excisable liquors, and selling spirits and ale to Thomas Godfrey, residing in Milne's Court, Lawnmarket, and selling ale and porter to William Cairns, residing in Cowan's Close, East Crosscauseway, on the 7th September last, without either of the accused having obtained a certificate on that behalf—such an offence being their first offence. Thomas Godfrey deponed [stated] that he knew Rose's house, and was in it on 7th September with a man named Davidson, a fiddler. He had a glass of whisky and a pint of ale, which he paid for. He did not see Rose in the house, but was served by Bates. Cross-examined by Mr Bell—He knew Rose's house to be a club, and was a member of the club. He knew as a fact that parties not members of the club were refused drink.

October 1st

1560: On this day, the Dean of Guild accounts recorded the sale of the liturgical treasure (the jewels) of the Collegiate Kirk of St Giles: a Eucharist hung with four little golden bells, a blue bell of gold, two little hearts, two little crosses; the relic of the Arm of St Giles with a ring on one of its fingers; a silver cross and base; four silver candlesticks; two censers; an incense boat; a container for oil of Chrism; a chalice; a plate and spoon. The combined weight of the silver was two stone 15 pounds and eight ounces. Two stone 6 ounces was sold to John Hart at twenty-one shillings an ounce, giving a total of £652 and 12 pence. Eight pounds 11 ounces was sold to Michael Gilbert, a total of £145 and 19 shillings. John Hart bought 5½ ounces of gold for £53. The combined sale value of the gold and silver was £854, 7 shillings and 6 pence. The diamond ring that was on the finger of the relic of St Giles was sold to Michael Gilbert for £9, 6 shillings and 8 pence. (*ERBE*)

October 2nd

1654: The provost produced a letter from the military Governor of Scotland, General George Monck, containing printed copies of the declarations of Oliver Cromwell, the Lord Protector and of the Parliament of England, Scotland and Ireland, ordering a day of solemn fasting and humiliation in the three nations. The council was asked to publish these instructions immediately and make them known to the various parishes and congregations in Edinburgh, and ask the ministers and pastors to inform their congregations the following Sunday before the Day of Humiliation (Wednesday 11 October throughout Scotland and England) and to give an account of the main points and how they should be observed in the parishes and congregations. To implement these instructions, the provost went into the Kirk Session after the sermon and handed over a printed copy to the minister, Mr James Hamilton and read out the letter. This instruction was generally disregarded by the Scottish clergy. A letter from two ministers to General Monck in 1656 on the subject of another Fast, stated that Fasts had only been kept by the appointment of, and for the causes agreed by, kirk legislation. They objected to any Fast other than those prescribed by the Church. (*ERBE*)

October 3rd

1477: King James IV ordered the provost, bailies and council to make use of the open spaces in the burgh for regular markets and fairs: hay, straw in the Cowgate between Forrester's Wynd and Peebles Wynd; the fish market on both sides of the High Street from Blackfriars Wynd to the Netherbow; the salt market in Niddrie's Wynd; the travelling salesmen's (chapman's) stalls between the Tolbooth and the Tron, hatmakers and shoemakers' markets from Dalrymple's Yard to the Greyfriars; capons and chickens at the Mercat Cross; grain and corn between the Tolbooth and Libberton's Wynd; all metalwork to be sold in the Friday market in front of the Greyfriars; butter, cheese and wool at the Over Bow. (*ERBE*)

1505: The council took action to prevent any outbreaks of plague, ordering that whenever a person fell sick in the burgh, the master or mistress of the house should bring the sickness to the attention of the bailies within twelve hours, under pain of branding and banishing. No person dwelling in the burgh should harbour anyone from the countryside, or their belongings, without the permission of the bailies. No one should go to see or meet with anyone in a place where disease was active. (*ERBE*)

October 4th

1848: 'Scottish Institution for the Education of Young Ladies, 9 Moray Place, Edinburgh. The fifteenth Session commenced on Monday the 2nd of October. Branches taught in the Establishment—1. History & geography; use of the Globes, Grammar, Composition, Literature and Elocution; 2. Junior English Department, including Reading, Grammar, Derivation, History and Geography (Mr Graham and his assistants, 78 Queen Street); 3. Writing, Arithmetic and Book-keeping (Mr Trotter, 10 North St David Street and assistants); 4. Singing (including Psalmody) and, 5. Theory of Music, and Elements of Composition (Mr Finlay Dun, 41 Heriot Row and assistants; 6. Pianoforte (Mr Charles Hargitt, 56 Queen Street and Assistants); 7. Drawing and Perspective (G. Simson, RSA, 54 Frederick Street & Mr D. Simson, 25 India Street and Assistants); 8. Natural History and Physical Science and Mathematics (Mr Anderson, 7 Gayfield Square); 10. French Language and Literature (Dr Dubuc, 121 George Street and Mlle. Boules); 11. Italian Language and Literature (Signor Rampini, 10 Gloucester Place); 12. German Language and Literature (Dr Aue, 16 South Charlotte Street); 13. Dancing and Deportment (Mlle. Angelica, 61 Queen Street); 14. Elementary Gymnastic Exercises (Mr Roland, 17 Dublin Street).' (*The Scotsman*)

October 5th

1832: The *Caledonian Mercury* reported on the proposal of a monument for Sir Walter Scott:

One of the largest assemblages of gentlemen that ever met within the walls of the Great Assembly Room, and certainly the most conspicuous in respect of rank and talent, which ever assembled in Edinburgh on any public occasion, took place at one o'clock, for the purpose of doing honour to the memory of Sir Walter Scott, and of taking measures for the erection of some lasting monument of the gratitude and imperishable esteem of his fellow-countrymen ... The Lord Advocate, Francis Jeffrey confirmed, 'That this meeting ... are of the opinion that a Public Memorial should be erected in the metropolis of Scotland to the Memory of Sir Walter Scott, on a scale worthy of his name ...' Sir John Forbes rose and said, that he was deputed by the Bank of Scotland, and the other Banks and Banking Companies in Edinburgh, creditors of Sir Walter Scott, in token of their admiration of the honourable feelings which induced Sir Walter Scott, after his embarrassments in 1826, to dedicate his talents, during the remainder of his life, to insuring the full payment of his debts, to subscribe in their names the sum of £500 towards the object of the meeting.

October 6th

1508: In a charter under the great seal, King James IV gave the provost, bailies and council of the burgh of Edinburgh power to rent or feu the common muir (grassland) and common myre (rough land) to increase the public purse, provided that the persons to whom the lands were let were subject to burgh regulations. He also granted the same lands for the construction of houses and the making of parks and pleasure grounds on them. (*ERBE*)

1648: Four bailies, the former provost, the deacon of the surgeons and their clerk, were appointed to go down to the Canongate in the afternoon and, in the council's name, salute the Lord Cromwell, Lieutenant General of the English forces. The council ordered all those who had been in arms to pursue the recent fight against England. They were to depart out of the city and suburbs within forty-eight hours of the publication of this order. The inhabitants were warned not to hide or harbour any strangers within their houses, box-beds or rooms without first handing in the names of such strangers to the constables every day, with information on their social status, their arms and tackle and condition of life. (*ERBE*)

October 7th

1819: 'A Fresh Supply of the following excellent Antidote to a Scorbutic Habit is just received by John Deuchar, chemist, 27 Lothian Street, and R. Jamieson & Co., chemists, 33 Prince's Street. Price 4 shillings and sixpence a Box, or six in one for 21 shillings. Dr Venel's Antiscorbutic Vegetable Pills, as an alternative medicine for purifying and sweetening the blood, is patronised by the first families in England. By circulating with the blood it promotes a genial warmth, and removes in its passage every infection. Scorbutic Ulcers and Eruption, Scrofula, Leprosy, the ill effects of Mercury, obstructed perspiration, &c. invariably yield to the wholesome effects of this vegetable preparation.' (*Caledonian Mercury*)

October 8th

1518: The provost, bailies and council issued statutes and orders governing the management of their College Kirk of St Giles. It stated that the officers of the Guild of the Holy Blood should keep the choir of the kirk free of all ordinary people during the time when Matins (between midnight and 2.00 am) was being sung, during the High Mass and during Evensong (Compline and Vespers). They should be responsible for the whole kirk and not allow any kind of beggars to enter the kirk during these services, under pain of losing their office and being replaced … The inhabitants of the burgh were ordered by the provost, bailies and council to wash and clean the street as far as the centre of the roadway in front of their houses or booths, as well as the vennels (passages) in the High Street and the Cowgate from all kinds of rubbish and filth by Monday evenings, under pain of a fine of eight shillings. All tar-barrels and waste-pipes should be removed from the High Street during the time when street cleaning was in progress. No muck, manure, piles of stones, nor middens should be placed near the common walls of the burgh, neither inside nor outside. (*ERBE*)

October 9th

1843: 'Music Festival. The performances of this Festival commenced on Monday evening, in the noble Music Hall recently added to the Assembly Rooms ... the expense of the room, including the organ, has exceeded £10,000. Some dissatisfaction has been expressed at the exclusive nature of the management of this Festival ... the vast expense necessarily incurred in the engagement of performers, of whom no fewer than 80 have been brought from London, Liverpool, Manchester, York ... rendered a considerable charge requisite ... the effective choral force [is] 199 strong ... First Performance, October 9.— This evening's performance consisted of a miscellaneous selection of secular music, chosen with excellent discrimination ... On entering the room, we were struck by the painful contrast between the crowded orchestra and the desolate appearance of the Hall ... We have since been informed that the attendance was 600, and the room being seated for 1,500 ... Second Performance, Tuesday morning, October 10.—The grand oratorio of *The Messiah* ... The choruses were admirably executed ... The fugued passages were taken with great exactness and given with much force ... The attendance was considerably better than on the preceding evening, but the room was still not much above half full.' (*Caledonian Mercury*)

October 10th

1867: *The Scotsman* reported on a great fire in Edinburgh:

Last night, between ten and eleven o'clock ... a most alarming
fire, and one attended with considerable destruction of property,
broke out in Messrs Hewit & Son's tannery, situated at the
bottom of North Gray's Close and Bailie Fyfe's Close to the
east ... The whole of these adjoining buildings were placed in
the most imminent peril by the fire. Crowding upon each other
in pestilential confusion, and towering in all directions to most
unwieldy heights, it seemed all but hopeless ... For much of the
property, as regards its worth, it might matter little how soon
it was demolished; but when the lives and small possessions of
so many poor people were at stake, the danger and suffering
implied in the spread of the fire was great and oppressing ... The
lurid and fitful glare in the sky apprised the whole city of the
disaster, and the spectacle, as such, was grand in the extreme. The
night was very dark, some rain falling during the continuance
of the fire, and as the broad sheets of flame shot out and wove
into each other, the illumination became at once magnificent and
terrible.

October 11th

1593: While the King was riding to a meeting on the laws of Scotland, the excommunicated Lords met him. He received them favourably. On 2 November, a proclamation was made that no one should trouble these papist Lords but receive them and entertain them as the King's faithful and true subjects, or be answerable to the King. On 27 November, a proclamation was made of absolution in favour of the papist Lords. (*Diarey of Robert Birrel*)

———•◆•———

1802: 'Overseer Wanted.—A steady intelligent man, to take the charge of conducting a considerable Lime Work, which is drained by a small Steam Engine, and sometimes employs above twenty hands.—The person must understand keeping accounts correctly, and write a good hand.—None need apply who cannot bring sufficient testimony of honesty, sobriety and diligence. Apply to Mr Hugh Bremner, accountant, No 1 Ramsay Garden, Castlehill.' (*Caledonian Mercury*)

———•◆•———

1855 'Dietetic Reform.— A lecture was delivered last night in the Queen Street Hall, under the auspices of the Edinburgh Vegetarian Society, by James Simpson, Esq., of Lancashire … [who] stated that he was anxious to impress them with the belief that the vegetarian system of diet was the best and most natural that could be adopted.' (*Caledonian Mercury*)

October 12th

1950: On this day *The Scotsman* delivered bad news about further cuts to rations:

> Another Cut in Bacon Ration. — 3 ozs from October 22. The Minister of Food announced yesterday that the bacon ration will be temporarily reduced from four ounces to three ounces a week from October 11, 1950. The fall in supplies which normally occurred at this time of year has been more marked and has lasted longer than usual this year, chiefly because Continental importing countries have been buying large quantities of pig meat, the Ministry stated. Supplies to the United Kingdom are expected to recover before the end of the year. From ration week No. 23, beginning on October 22, bacon coupons in ration books RB1, RB2, RB4, and on temporary ration card RB12 will each be worth three ounces. Coupons for ration week No. 22, which are not used until ration week No. 23, will keep their present value. The value of bacon coupons in the weekly card RB8A will be unchanged.

October 13th

1604: The Chancellor of Scotland sailed from Berwick to London, to be present at the Union of the Crowns. However, he left for home and so there was no consensus about the Union. On 31 October, a proclamation was sent from the King that the ministers should not come together in an assembly, under the pain of the sanctions contained in the Acts of Parliament. On 19 November, a proclamation was made that the countries should no longer be called Scotland and England but 'Great Britain', so fulfilling the ancient prophecy that the Lion would be lord of all. (*Diarey of Robert Birrel*)

———— • ◆ • ————

1801: The ratification of the proclamation of peace between Britain and France saw the Edinburgh Volunteers on parade in the meadows and then marching down to Princes Street. Facing the castle, they let off what was known as a '*feu-de-joie*' – a joyful rat-tat-tat of rifle fire, and the big guns on the Castle Rock thundered out the Royal salute. Edinburgh was full of spectators. In the evening, the church bells rang and the centre of the city was brilliantly illuminated. To mark the day, 208 French and 24 Dutch prisoners were sent off from Leith to return to their homelands.

October 14th

1512: The provost, bailies and council took steps to counteract the contagious disease described as 'pestilence', which had recently broken out. If anyone in the burgh fell ill, children or adults, the adult responsible, man or woman, was required to report the illness to the provost and bailies under pain of banishment and the burning of their property and whatever other physical punishment was thought appropriate. If anyone was ordered to remain in their house, they could not attempt to come out, under pain of punishment. If anyone came from an infected place and entered the burgh they were punished by burning – branding on the cheek (if a woman) and (if a man) another punishment as thought necessary. No one in the burgh could give shelter to a person coming from a location believed to be infected. With respect to the crowds of beggars who were able-bodied and fit for work, they were either given employment or sent away from the burgh. Poor people who were physically incapable or old who showed signs of infection could remain within the burgh, but young people fit for work were employed or sent away from the burgh. (*ERBE*)

October 15th

1475: The Wrights (carpenters and joiners) and Stonemasons of Edinburgh were granted their Seal of Cause and the use of the aisle and chapel of St John the Baptist in St Giles' College Kirk, to enable them to offer daily divine service. They were also given authority to repair and reconstruct any features of the craft altar where necessary. Two wrights and two stonemasons were to be chosen to inspect the work of each craft and to act on any complaints. Craftsmen who came for the first time to work in Edinburgh had to present themselves to the inspectors and show proof of their ability. If they were passed as proficient to work, they had to give an offering of one merk towards the upkeep of St John's chapel. (*ERBE*)

———— •◆• ————

1818: The American Indians, who were performing in the theatre here, went out, at the request of the Royal Company of Archers, to shoot with them at the Company's Butts. The distances at which the Indians were accustomed to shoot were so much shorter than the distance practised by the Royal Company, that no just comparison could be formed of the merits of the shooters. (*Caledonian Mercury*)

October 16th

1939: Just off May Island in the Firth of Forth, HMS *Mohawk* was in a convoy of destroyers and cruisers when it was attacked by a German aircraft, including Junkers 88 bombers. The ships engaged the enemy but lost seventeen killed, including the skipper. Four German aircraft were shot down, the first by George Pinkerton of 602 Squadron (City of Glasgow). Spitfires from 603 Squadron (City of Edinburgh) were also responsible for shooting down at least one other German bomber. One Heinkel lost its tail and crashed into the water near Inchgarvie. On 28 October 1939, the so-called 'Humbie Heinkel' was shot down by 602 and 603 Squadrons and crash-landed on the moors near Humbie in East Lothian, the first to do so on British soil. Later, on 9 February 1940, a Heinkel 111 crashed near North Berwick, with three survivors and one dead. Two of the German airmen were buried with full honours at Portobello Cemetery. Later, their bodies were moved to Cannock Chase, Staffordshire. An hour before the German surrender was to come into force on 7 May 1945, two British vessels were sunk off May Island by a U-boat. (www.aircrewremembrancesociety.com/luft1939/pohle.html)

October 17th

1805: This was printed in the *Caledonian Mercury*:

Proclamation for Pardoning Deserters from His Majesty's Regular Forces.— Whereas it has been represented to the King, that there are at this time several Deserters from His Majesty's Regular Land Forces, who might be induced to return to their Duty by an offer of His Majesty's gracious Pardon, and that such an instance of his Royal Clemency would have a due influence upon their future behaviour; His Majesty has been graciously pleased to grant his Free Pardon to all Deserters from his Regular Land Forces, who shall surrender themselves, on or before the 8th day of December next, to any of His Majesty's Civil Magistrates, to the Commanding Officer of any regiment, to any of the Superintending Field Officers of the Recruiting Service ... or to the Inspector-General of the Recruiting Service in the Isle of Wight ... No Soldier, who may Desert after these His Majesty's Gracious Intentions are made public, shall be included in the above Pardon, but be proceeded against with the utmost severity; nor shall any Soldier, who surrendered himself upon any former Proclamation of His Majesty's Pardon, and who afterwards again deserted, be included in the above Pardon.

October 18th

1824 'House of Refuge.—The Lord Provost had very handsomely agreed to preside at a public meeting, to be held soon, for the purpose of naming a Committee to conduct an experimental House of Refuge on a scale for about thirty boys; the expense to be defrayed by subscription in the first place, but afterwards, it is expected, chiefly by the labour of the boys. The following is a calculation of the expense for the first six months, as prepared by practical men, for a committee of the Commissioners:— thirty second-hand looms, at 30 shillings (£45); Six months board of 30 boys at 3 shillings per week (£117); Wages and board of a Cook for half a year (£120; Wages of Overseer for half a year (£19 and 10 shillings); Wages of Assistant Overseer for half a year (£15 and 12 shillings); Clothing for half a year (£30); Hammocks, bedding (£42); Schoolmaster for one hour each day (£30). The Committee found strongly on what has been realized in the Glasgow and Belfast Bridewells, in assuming the practicability of making boys from 12 to 18 years of age support, or very nearly support themselves by their own labour.' (*The Scotsman*)

October 19th

1687: Alexander Hay, a carpenter burgess, informed the council that he had constructed and outfitted six sedan-chairs, each to be carried by two men in handsome livery coats. He proposed to make a charge of seven shillings Scots per hour for passengers uplifted between the Castle and Holyrood Abbey. For transportation beyond the city he would negotiate a fee. He was happy to provide more sedan-chairs if needed, emphasising that the service he offered would enable the nobility, ladies and persons of quality (as well as those sick or infirm) to pass through any close or wynd in the city where coaches could not go. He asked for a monopoly of the sedan-chair service and this the council granted for eleven years. He was allowed to build a timber shed in the back-close of the council house to keep his sedan-chairs at night. On 3 April 1700, the council considered the petition received from Euphane Ross, widow of Alexander Hay. She asked for her husband's monopoly to be renewed in order to maintain and educate her children. The council granted her the request on condition that the sedan-chairs were kept clean and in good order. (*ERBE*)

October 20th

1830: 'King Charles X.—We noticed ... that the Ex-King of France arrived at Holyrood on Wednesday. The Duke and Duchess d'Angoulême are expected to arrive on Tuesday. They proceed hither via Carlisle. In the event of His Majesty King William carrying into effect his intention of visiting this metropolis next summer, it is King Charles' intention to take a tour through the north of Scotland, so as to have the coast clear for the reception of our own court. Lieutenant Eyton, R.N., who brought Charles X from Poole, has been presented by the Ex-King with a superb gold snuff-box ... It was the Duc de Polignac, brother to the ex-Minister, and not the Duc de Duras, who came on shore at Newhaven with Charles X on Wednesday. Yesterday forenoon King Charles, with one of his suite, walked through various streets for about an hour, and was everywhere noticed with the greatest civility and politeness by the citizens. Only one exception occurred in the Canongate, where a drunken fellow used some rude expression, which was so highly resented by the crowd, that the police were obliged to take him into the watch-house to secure him from serious maltreatment.' (*Caledonian Mercury*)

October 21st

1807: On this day, the *Caledonian Mercury* printed a warning from the magistrates:

> The Magistrates of the City of Edinburgh. —Whereas, notwithstanding of His Majesty's Royal proclamation for 'the encouragement of Piety and Virtue, and for preventing and punishing of Vice and Immorality;' subsequent Act of Council, and of repeated orders issued by the Magistrates for preventing the Profanation of the Lord's Day, by the improper practice of keeping open Ale or Tippling Houses during the time of Divine Service, and also Shops, at all hours on Sunday, still exists, to the disturbance of the orderly and well disposed inhabitants—The Magistrates being resolved to use every endeavour to put a stop to a practice of so immoral and dangerous a tendency, do hereby strictly prohibit and discharge all Persons within this City and Liberties thereof from having Ale or Tippling Houses open for the reception of Company during the time of Divine Worship on the Lord's Day, or the Keepers of Shops, Vaults, Warehouses or Cellars, from Retailing Liquors, Fruits or Goods of any denomination therein, during any part of Sunday; certifying all those who [do] shall be convicted of acting in the contrary, that they will be liable in a Penalty of Five Pounds Sterling.

October 22nd

1589: King James VI began his sea journey, sailing from Leith around ten o'clock at night, and sailed to Norway. On 23 November he was married to Anne of Denmark in the town of Upslo (modern Oslo) in Norway. This news was sent to the Duke of Lennox and the Earl of Bothwell, who were left to govern Scotland in the King's absence. The King travelled with his new Queen in Denmark where he remained until the following year. On 1 May 1590, the King and Queen landed at Leith, having set sail from Denmark. On 7 May, Anne of Denmark was crowned Queen of Scotland at Holyroodhouse. On 19 May, the Queen made her entry into Edinburgh with great triumph and joy. Pageants were celebrated in every corner of the city, which was adorned with all appropriate ceremony. Young boys, with artificial wings, raced towards her when she entered Edinburgh and presented her with two silver keys of the city. The castle loosed cannons in five separate salvos. At night the town was full of bonfires. (*Diarey of Robert Birrel*)

October 23rd

1706: A mob attacked the house of Sir Patrick Johnston, a strenuous promoter of the Treaty of Union (between the Scottish and English Parliaments), their late Lord Provost and one of their representatives in Parliament. By a narrow escape, he saved himself from falling victim to popular fury. The mob increasing, rambled through the streets, threatening destruction to the promoters of the Union. By nine at night they were absolute masters of the city, and a report prevailed that they were going to shut up the ports (the gates). To prevent this, the Commissioner ordered a party of soldiers to take possession of the Netherbow and afterwards sent a battalion of Foot Guards, who posted themselves in the Parliament Square and in the different lanes and avenues of the city, by which means the mob was quelled. The panic which seized the Commissioner and others was not, however, allayed. The whole army was brought into the neighbourhood of Edinburgh. The Commissioner walked from the Parliament House to his coach between a double file of musketeers, and he was driven at full gallop to his lodgings, hooted, cursed and pelted by the rabble. (Arnot, *The History of Edinburgh*)

October 24th

1694: Alexander Monteith, surgeon and burgess, petitioned the council for a gift of bodies for medical dissection from among those who died in the Correction House and foundling babies who died upon the breast. He asked to be permitted to be provided with a convenient place to carry out dissection and for the use of the College kirkyard for their eventual burial, for which he offered to serve the poor of the town free of charge. The council considered his request and decided that it was both convenient and necessary to make a start to the practice of anatomy in the city. Therefore they granted the petitioner's request but under the following restrictions: only the bodies of those sent by the courts to the Correction House for serious breaches of the moral code and the bodies of foundling children who died while suckling should be available for dissection: dissection of dead bodies should only take place between one equinox to the other, including the winter season exclusively; the large intestines of those dissected should be buried within forty-eight hours and the entire body burnt in the same place within ten working days on the petitioner's expense. (*ERBE*)

October 25th

1809: The Jubilee of the accession of King George III to the throne was celebrated with a series of ceremonies. At dawn, the church bells of Edinburgh and Leith began to ring without ceasing. At 8.00 a.m. the Lord Provost, magistrates and council drove to Leith where they laid the foundations of a new defensive construction – King George III's Bastion and Military Works to protect the docks, harbour and the town of Leith. Soon afterwards, breakfast was served at Leith Assembly Rooms. At noon the bells began to ring out again. The Edinburgh Volunteers fired a *feu-de-joie* from Princes Street and the Royal salute was given from the castle guns and from the warships in Leith Roads. At two o'clock, churches and chapels held services of thanksgiving and at five o'clock there was a grand public dinner in the Assembly Rooms, attended by 500 gentlemen. At seven in the evening there was a display of fireworks and illumination of public buildings, a feature of which was the many pictorial transparencies painted by Mr W.H. Lizars. (Gilbert, *Edinburgh in the Nineteenth Century*)

October 26th

1660: Captains and colours were allotted to the Town Companies: Orange, John Fullerton (merchant); White, John Dunbar (skinner); Blue, Robert Baird (merchant); White and Orange, Thomas Wilson (merchant); Green and Red, William Hamilton (tailor); Grey, Thomas Crawford (merchant); Blue and White, John Johnston (merchant); Green, Thomas Brand (shoemaker); Green and White, John Mein (merchant); Red and Yellow, James Scott (wright); Yellow, James Currie (merchant); Red and Blue, David Boyd (merchant); Blue and Orange, Edward Cleghorne (goldsmith); Red and White, Alexander Pearson (merchant); Grey and Red, Robert Gray (merchant); Red, George Turnbull (baker). Citizens aged between sixteen and sixty years of age were required to provide sufficient arms such as swords, pikes, muskets, bandoliers, gunpowder and ball, partisan (double-bladed pole weapon) and gather when called by beat of drum. The penalty for non-compliance was imprisonment. The town companies had to patrol the streets at night, watch for robberies at burials and public birthday celebrations, and parade at the Riding of Parliament. On such occasions they would assemble at the Mercat Cross, each man armed with twelve shots which they would discharge when given the order. Then, with two drummers and four trumpeters, they marched down to Holyrood Palace. (*ERBE*)

October 27th

1823: This report appeared in the *Caledonian Mercury*:

A Melancholy Case. Adamson, the carter, who was drowned on Wednesday week in the pond between Leith Walk and the Easter Road, lived in the Abbeyhill ... He was occupied in drawing goods from Edinburgh to Leith, on Wednesday week, and having met with some of his companions, went into a public house in Leith Walk, to drink ... a bumper of cheap whisky. He remained to a late hour, when he found that his horse and cart were missing. From Leith Walk he had then taken his direction by that road which leads to Abbeyhill by the Quarry Hole, and it is supposed he had leapt over the wall to take a nap, as was his custom, for the purpose of sleeping off the effects of the drink before he went home; but, unfortunately, that which he supposed was a field, proved to him a watery grave ... his wife, or widow, as it proves, sent on Sunday morning for a relation, and requested him to go and seek for her husband in the old Quarry ... after a minute search, he found a hat floating amongst some willows, which proved to be the hat of poor Adamson.

October 28th

1941: 'Apprentice Plumbers—Edinburgh Strike Continues (New War Bonus Terms). Apprentice plumbers engaged in the building trades in Edinburgh remain on strike. The strikers' demand for increased wages was discussed by the Edinburgh, Leith and District plumbers' Association at their general meeting, held in Dowell's Rooms, George Street yesterday and they unanimously endorsed the finding of the Scottish Federation of Plumbers' and Domestic Engineers' (Employers) Associations regarding the apprentices' war bonus. The Federation had met in the North British Station Hotel, Edinburgh during the weekend, and heard a report from the Committee appointed to examine the revised conditions of training, education, wages and war bonuses of apprentices, which had been under the consideration of the Federation for some months. They then unanimously decided that all apprentices should be given a minimum war bonus of 50 per cent on the pre-war basic rates of wages, which will include all war bonuses previously given—the new rate of remuneration to start as and from October 27. Further, as from January 1 next, in respect of every halfpenny per hour of an increase in wages granted to journeymen, apprentices, it is stated, will receive 1 shilling per week as additional war bonus.' (*The Scotsman*)

October 29th

1624: Janet Hunter, widow of the late John Mure, a tailor, was called in front of the council because she had been repairing a number of her thatched houses contrary to the Act of Parliament issued against the use of thatch in roofing. The council withdrew her obligation to make any further repairs of houses using thatch. John Gilmour, a solicitor and heritor of a number of thatched houses in the Cowgate, was likewise forbidden to continue repairing them with straw and thatch. (*ERBE*)

———— ◆ ————

1647: The council ordained the treasurer to pay the account to Monsieur Montreuil, agent for the French King, extending to the sum of £178 and fifteen shillings, six pence and gave its permission for M. Montreuil to be created a burgess of the city. This ceremony was accompanied by a 'collation' (light meal).

Jean de Montreuil had been sent to England in July 1645 by Cardinal Mazarin, nominally as agent to the Scottish government, but in reality to see that a settlement satisfactory to France should be reached. The General Assembly concerned themselves with the fact that he had a priest, and that mass was said in his lodgings. (*ERBE*)

October 30th

1806: This letter was printed in the *Caledonian Mercury*:

To the Public. From the numerous accidents which happened during the storm on Saturday, by the blowing down of smoke cans, slates and projecting ticket-boards—the Dean of Guild finds it necessary to caution the proprietors of houses immediately to have a survey made of their chimney tops and roofs, in order that the smoke cans and slates, which have been loosened by the violence of the gale, may be repaired without delay; and as a notice was published in September last, relative to the projecting sign and ticket-boards being limited to within twelve inches of the wall ... unless this notice is attended to between now and the 1st of the month, they will have themselves to blame for the consequences. The Tron-men are particularly called upon to give notice of whatever may appear dangers on the roofs of the houses ... persons neglecting to comply with this notice will not only be fined, but subjected in whatever expense may be incurred by enforcing compliance. One half of the fines will be given to informers; and information on this subject will be received by Mr Sprott, Procurator-fiscal, and immediately attended to. William Coulter, Dean of Guild.

October 3-1st

1815: 'Musical Festival. On Tuesday morning, the long expected musical entertainment commenced with a selection of sacred music in the Parliament House. As the time approached for this grand display of musical talent ... the anxiety of the public increased, and it was at last raised to the highest pitch ... By the liberality and good taste of the people of Scotland, this scheme for the display of music on a greater scale than was ever before attempted in this country, has met with unparalleled success ... However high the expectation of the public was raised, it was completely gratified ... The concourse of company in town is very great. Those who were to attend the morning concert on Tuesday, began to assemble between eight and nine in the morning, and the row of carriages in waiting reached from the Parliament House to the Post Office. The road was kept clear by parties of horse and foot, and also by parties of the police ... the police officers who were stationed to keep order, conducted themselves ... in the most disorderly manner. They not only stopped people who were going through the Parliament Square on business ... they were abused and insulted.' (*Caledonian Mercury*)

November 1st

1591: The Acts and Statutes of the town were proclaimed at the Mercat Cross. Item, because fornicators and harlots daily came from various locations to Edinburgh and were given employment by a number of residents of the town prior to their proving their repentance and making satisfaction to the kirk, it was ordained that no such persons should be employed within the burgh unless they first showed valid documentary evidence of their repentance. Item, because the Sabbath day was desecrated and deliberately misused by holding markets for a variety of products and also by inn-keepers, publicans and brewers, who had more respect for their dirty bellies than to God's service and the health of their own souls, it was ordained that there should be no market on the Sabbath day, no taverns or alehouses should be found open at the time of preaching and prayers and no one should eat or drink on the Sabbath between sunrise and sunset. No taverns should be open after the ten o'clock night bell had rung. The penalties for breaking these regulations were confiscation of goods, imprisonment and punishment at the discretion of the magistrates. (*ERBE*)

November 2nd

1507: King James IV sent a letter of gift signed with his privy seal to the provost, bailies, council and sheriffs on the question of the All Hallow (All Saints) Fair, traditionally proclaimed on the eve of All Hallow's (31 October), lasting for eight days. The problem was that the fair interfered with the celebration of other holidays that fell within that time – the mass of Holy Souls and the feast of the dedication of St Giles' Kirk (3 November), for example. The King was anxious that such popular customs as the All Hallow Fair should continue to be celebrated for the honour and love of God and all the saints, as well as for the benefit of the whole burgh. So he confirmed the All Hallow Fair to the burgh and also the Trinity Fair on the Monday after Trinity Sunday, with all their various 'customs, tolls, fees, privileges, freedoms, profits and duties'. All loyal subjects were required, under the pain of the most severe punishment, to keep the peace at those times and obey the burgh authorities. (*ERBE*)

November 3rd

1865: On this day, theological questions regarding the Reformation were expressed in *The Scotsman*:

> The Influence of the Reformation on Scottish Character.—The winter season of the Philosophical Institution was opened with an inaugural lecture by Mr James Anthony Froude … 'The heart of the matter which the Catholic Church had taught was the fear of God; but the language of it, the formulas of it, were made up of human ideas and notions about things which the mere increase of human knowledge gradually made incredible … Thus the Catholic formulas, instead of living symbols, became dead and powerless cabalistic signs. The religion lost its hold on the conscience and the intellect, and the effect, singularly enough, appeared in the shepherds before it made itself felt among the flocks. From the chair of St Peter to the far monasteries in the Hebrides or the Isle of Arran, the laity were shocked and scandalised at the outrageous doings of high cardinals, prelates, priests, and monks. It was clear enough that these great personages themselves did not believe what they taught; so why should the people believe it?—And serious men, to whom the fear of God was a living reality, began to look into the matter for themselves.'

November 4th

1601: On a public Fair Day in Edinburgh, a pitched battle was fought between two Border families, the Kers and the Turnbulls. Much blood was spilt. On 16 December 1601, Andro Turnbull was beheaded at the Mercat Cross for killing Thomas Ker. (*Diarey of Robert Birrel*)

———•◆•———

1809: 'A Reward. Whereas, on the evening of Saturday last the 28th ult. some evil-disposed Person … intentionally put into the Mill Lead, at the Water of Leith, several pieces of wood, which had the effect of breaking the Outer Wheel of one of the Mills belonging to the Incorporation of Bakers.—If any person will give such information to Robert Henderson, writer, Fife Street, or to Mr Metcalf, Superintendant of Police for that district, as will lead to a discovery of the person or persons guilty of the above, will, upon conviction, be entitled to a Reward of Fifteen Guineas.' (*Caledonian Mercury*)

November 5th

1807: These announcements appeared in the *Caledonian Mercury* on this day:

> By the Council. All Hallow Fair of this City is to begin on Monday the 9th day of November, to be continued the usual time, and to be kept and held in the Poors House Park, west end of Prince's Street.

> Horse Engine, for Drawing Water. To be sold at Ravelston on Tuesday 15th November at twelve o'clock. It consists of two Yetling Pumps, several large lead pipes, and beams of wood, &c. and was erected by Messrs Moodie, engineers, about four years ago. Enquire at the House of Ravelston; or at 43 Queen Street.

> For a family in the neighbourhood of Edinburgh. Two English women servants, one as Nursery Maid, the other as Lady's Maid. Mrs Dumbreck, St Andrew's Square.

November 6th

1899: On this day *The Scotsman* printed a letter about noisy trains from a disgruntled local:

Sir,—It would be a great boon to the inhabitants of Osborne Terrace and neighbourhood if some householders would combine for the purpose of protesting against the distracting whistling that goes on during the night on the North British lines. Whistling is no doubt a necessary evil, but not to the extent to which it is carried on. The requisite warnings might be given without occasioning the terrible discomfort that they now entail, for it is absolutely impossible for any but the heaviest sleepers to get an unbroken night's rest under the present conditions ... I fail to see, if some engines whistling on comparatively low and therefore less disturbing notes are considered sufficiently protected and protective, why others need be endowed with shriekingly high ones ... it is just these last that are turned on for forty or sixty seconds at a time, or give a long series of shrill sounds which, in the otherwise silence of night, cannot be necessary—to be so prolonged, I mean. If, Mr Editor, by the publicity you give this letter, anything is done towards the abatement of the nuisance complained of, you will merit the cordial thanks of your obedient servant, 'Osbourne Terrace'.

November 7th

1945: *The Scotsman* reported on the results of the Edinburgh Municipal Elections:

Seven Labour Gains in Edinburgh ... Early results showed successes for the Labour Party, although the swing to the Left appeared to be less pronounced than in England. In Edinburgh, Labour advanced their strength in the council by seven gains— four at the expense of the progressive party, who will still hold an emphatic majority; one from an Independent, who was generally included in the Progressive calculations; one from Protestant Action in Gorgie, the only seat they were defending; and one from an Independent Protestant in South Leith, where Mr J. Trainer, who had left the Protestant Action group and has now retired from the Council. Labour had a notable gain in Calton, where Mr J. B. Stewart Lamb, who was Chairman of the Education Committee and a Progressive, was defeated. The other Labour gains were in Canongate, where Mrs Esta Henry (Independent) was beaten; Gorgie, George Square, South Leith, Central Leith and Liberton. In Edinburgh, the Progressive Party ... still retain an emphatic majority ... Thirteen of the 20 Progressives were returned, 13 of the 27 Labour candidates, and one of the three Independents. Two Communists and two Protestant Action candidates were defeated.

November 8th

1806: 'Police.—On Friday, Janet Mason, a very young girl, was committed to Bridewell, for stealing clothes from a house in Thistle Street; and, being the third time of her being committed for theft, the Judge ordained her to be confined in a solitary cell, and fed on bread and water.' (*Caledonian Mercury*)

1810: 'General Mourning. James Spittal conceives it his duty to inform his Friends, that he is at present well supplied in Sarsanets, velvets, Bombazeens, Lustres, Crapes, Bom-Bazets, and every article proper for the present mourning, with which he will be happy to supply them on the most reasonable terms. Fashionable Gallery, No 84, west side of South Bridge Street.' (*Caledonian Mercury*)

1838: 'Morning Concert of Mr [Johann] Strauss. This concert, which took place on Tuesday, was very numerously attended, and produced the most lively symptoms of delight … The precision and vigour with which the burst of the whole orchestra at the commencement of the introduction was played, delighted us beyond measure, and, indeed, the entire performance of the piece left nothing to be desired … Of the beautiful waltzes played on this occasion we are quite at a loss to say which is the best as a composition.' (*Caledonian Mercury*)

November 9th

1614: Mr John Rea, master of the town's high school, was ordered to follow these regulations when instructing his scholars: one teacher should be in charge of the rudiments class, basing his teaching on the Despauter grammar book of Jan de Spauter (c. 1480-1520), a Flemish academic whose name was latinised as 'Despauterius'. The second class should study a work of the Dutch priest and humanist, Desiderius Erasmus (1466-1536) and letters of the Roman orator Cicero. The third class should continue with more of Cicero's letters and an introduction to the poems of Ovid. The following class moved on to Julius Caesar's 'Commentaries' and the poet Virgil. Finally, the top class studied rhetoric (the art of public speaking), writing speeches and verses, and began to learn Greek grammar. They were also trained to repeat parts of these works from memory and to engage in debates and were publicly examined every year in front of the ministers and magistrates, at the beginning of May and on 20 October before they passed on to the College (Edinburgh University). Only those who passed these examinations were allowed to move up the school or go on to the College. (*ERBE*)

November 10th

1811: The *Caledonian Mercury* reported on the fire in the Exchequer:

Early yesterday morning, the upper part of the Exchequer Chamber, Parliament Square, was discovered to be on fire. On the first alarm, the engines belonging to the different offices, and also the city engines, repaired to the spot. At five in the morning, the conflagration presented an awful spectacle, and to a distant beholder from the south, it seemed as if the whole Parliament Square had been in one blaze. The exertions of the firemen were somewhat impeded by the height of the buildings; so that it was nearly seven o'clock before they were able to stem the fury of the flames. At that time the roof of that part of the building where the fire began, gave way; and about nine o'clock, the fire was completely got under.—Great praise is due to the unexampled exertions of those who wrought the engines, and to several persons who volunteered their assistance. Every obstacle arising from the situation of the fire was overcome by the enterprising zeal of some individuals, who mounted up ... to the most commanding stations, and from thence directed the engine-pipes ... with such effect, that the fire began visibly to abate.

November 11th

1608: The council instructed that a proclamation should be made for lighting bonfires on 5 November to recall the recent escape of the King's Majesty, the Queen, their children and all the estates of the realm and the Parliament of England from the treason intended that day in 1605 by certain English Catholics, detected through the mercy of God. People who did not build bonfires would be stripped of their citizenship. (*ERBE*)

———•◆•———

1816: 'A genteel young man called at a jeweller's shop in Union Place, a few days ago, and priced some silver spoons, and, on Wednesday evening, called again to [buy] them, when having got four of them into his hands, he ran off with them. He was immediately pursued by the jeweller, and overtaken in York Place, and the property recovered. He was then given over to the police. On Saturday last, about six o'clock in the evening, a watchmaker's shop, in Leith, was robbed of three watches … by means of a newly glazed pane in the window, which the thieves contrived to get loose … without making the least noise, and although the people were in the shop at the time, they got clear off with their booty.' (*Caledonian Mercury*)

November 12th

1831: 'Statue. Workmen, brought by Mr Chantrey from London, have been busied for the last few days in erecting machinery at the crossing of Hanover Street and George Street, for the purpose of depositing the statue of his late Majesty. This erection, which consists of two huge beams reared triangle-wise, and steadied by ropes on each side, has itself an impressive appearance.' (*Caledonian Mercury*)

'Footpath Soldiers. Yesterday at noon, the 90th Regiment marched through several of our streets, and in passing along Waterloo Place, instead of the causeway, as usual, chose the pavement. This is a practice which must not be allowed to [continue].' (*Caledonian Mercury*)

'Theft. On Tuesday night a farmer-looking person, in liquor, was observed by a police officer in company with a loose female; the officer took him to the Police Office, where a large sum of money was found upon him, which was retained till next morning, and the owner went to sleep at Ambrose's Hotel, but for which prudential step he would most likely have been minus £65.' (*Caledonian Mercury*)

November 13th

1857: These news stories were printed in the *Caledonian Mercury* on this day:

The Monetary Panic.—It is gratifying to be able to state that the excitement so intense on Wednesday has completely disappeared. Yesterday all the banks in Edinburgh, with the exception of the City of Glasgow, which remained closed, did business in the customary manner, and without the slightest indication, on the part of those calling, of the previous want to confidence ... We are authorised to state that all the banks in this city have agreed to accept the notes of the Western and City of Glasgow Banks in the ordinary course of business.

Apprehension of the Yorkshire Drover.—Sergeant Reid, of the Edinburgh County Police, who was sent in pursuit of the Yorkshire drover and the fifteen bullocks with which he had absconded ... traced the runaways from Kelso to Hawick. He there found that a party answering to the description of the one he was after had taken the road to Carlisle. With praiseworthy alacrity he set off on the moment, and discovered the object of his search about fifteen miles from Carlisle. He apprehended the man, whose name is Edmond Apple, and brought him into Edinburgh. The cattle are also on their way back.

November 14th

1601: Thomas Armstrong and Adam Steill, known as 'The Peckit', were both hanged at the Mercat Cross. Armstrong had his hand cut off with a single stroke of the axe before he was hanged, because he had killed James Carmichael. 'The Peckit' was one of the most notable thieves that ever rode a horse. (*Diarey of Robert Birrel*)

———•◆•———

1818: 'Hallow Fair.—At All-Hallow Fair of this City, which commenced on Tuesday, there were 3,500 head of black cattle, chiefly lean stock, which sold very briskly, at prices about 30 per cent above those of last year; this rise is chiefly owing to the fine crops of turnips; fat cattle [were] much about the [same] prices in Edinburgh market last week. There were 740 horses; good ones sold high, but inferior were little in demand. Sheep were few in the market, and sold quickly at from 10 shillings and sixpence to thirty-seven shillings and sixpence per head.' (*The Scotsman*)

November 15th

1824: On this Monday night the most disastrous fire recorded in the history of Edinburgh broke out in a large seven-storey house at the head of Old Assembly Close. Every building on the south side of the High Street from the head of Old Assembly Close to the Exchequer buildings in Parliament Square, including most of the property running back down to the Cowgate was destroyed, with the exception of one tenement left standing opposite the Mercat Cross. Twenty-two fire engines belonging to the insurance companies attended. As a result of the 1824 Great Fire almost four hundred people left their homes, eleven residents and two firemen of the newly-formed Edinburgh Fire Establishment lost their lives. This tragedy did have some positive effects: 24 year old James Braidwood, recently appointed Master of Fire Engines for Edinburgh, was galvanised by what he saw a more effective training for firemen. He was the first municipal fire-master in the world and went on to set up the London Fire Brigade. Admirers of the poet Robert Fergusson, author of 'To the Tron Kirk Bell', collected pieces of the bell which had melted in the fire and lay on the ground and made them into little mementoes of the poet.

November 16th

1093: Having been seriously ill for some time, Queen Margaret died at Edinburgh Castle on this day. It was just three days after her husband and her eldest son were killed at the siege of Alnwick. The grand-niece of King Edward the Confesssor, Margaret, was born in 1045 probably in Hungary, where her family had escaped after the Danes invaded England. They returned to England in 1057 but moved north after the battle of Hastings (1066). In 1070 she married King Malcolm, with whom she had six sons and two daughters. Besides being a woman of great personal piety, Margaret is credited with being a civilising influence on Scotland. She also showed the important role that women should play in every sphere of life. She worked to help integrate Celtic monastic life into the wider Christian communion and so prepared the way for her son, King David I, to bring new monastic orders into Scotland with religious houses such as Holyrood, where Margaret's own collection of precious relics, including the Black Rood relic (said to have been part of the Cross of Christ), which had pride of place at Holyrood Abbey. Queen Margaret was canonised in 1250 by Pope Innocent IV.

November 17th

1498: The provost, bailies and council issued a statute to combat the threat of plague which had now spread to many parts of the country. In the name of the King, they commanded that any resident of the burgh who harboured within their house or stable any person, without first advising the bailies and receiving their permission, would be banished from the burgh and have all they owned confiscated and used for the common good of the burgh. Anyone who travelled to Glasgow without the explicit permission of the bailies would be refused re-entry to the burgh for forty days.

Also discussed was the importing of English cloth into the burgh; whether by an English person or a Scot, this was forbidden by the provost, bailies and council. The penalty for those found with any English cloth was that it would be confiscated and burnt.

It was again confirmed by statute that no children whatsoever were allowed to wander unaccompanied in the streets or inside the churches (kirkis). In the case of children under thirteen years of age, punishment for this offence would be a fine of forty shillings payable by parents to the community welfare fund. Those who had no parents would be put into custody. (*ERBE*)

November 18th

1815: The *Caledonian Mercury* featured these articles:

Accident. A brewer's servant in Leith met with a shocking death on Wednesday, his head being crushed by a cart of which he had charge, the horse having been frightened and starting suddenly off with it. He has left a widow and several young children.

Waterloo Fund. In reviewing the contributions ... we are struck with the mass of money which the general patriotism of the people has produced, but our attention is arrested in particular, by the sum collected in the island of Islay. There is no quarter of the kingdom where a greater degree of prosperity exists, and in evidence of this, the contribution amounted to two hundred and three pounds, fourteen shillings and three pence halfpenny, and came from all classes of the people with the most hearty welcome.

Musical Festival. We understand that a meeting of the directors of the late Musical Festival is to take place today ... We hear that £1,500 will, in the mean time, be paid to the public charities.

November 19th

1519: The provost, bailies and council reminded the community of the privileges of Edinburgh with respect to Leith. All inhabitants of Leith and those who were not freemen were forbidden to buy wine, wax, food, iron, timber, lint, pitch, tar or any other staple goods imported or brought by foreigners into the Port of Leith or any other port within the burgh's jurisdiction, unless the merchants and ship-masters had gone to the burgh officers and registered their goods in the burgh ledgers. Upon which, the burgh officers would set the prices of the goods according to the Act of Parliament. The Royal Comptroller or Treasurer should take what the King needs from the cargoes, paying at the statutory rate. No inhabitant of Leith or those who were not freemen should buy herring, seals, salmon or other fish arriving at the Port of Leith. Nor should they salt or pack any fish, nor export them to England or other countries, before the Royal Comptroller had inspected them and, if necessary, taken his portion of the catch. Lastly, no inhabitant of Leith, be he freeman or not, was permitted to bring any merchandise to market within the freedom of Edinburgh. (*ERBE*)

November 20th

1616: John Moir of Leith, having been brought before the burgh council accused of assaulting Francis Hay, son of the late Sir Alexander Hay of Whitburgh, a Knight and Clerk of the Royal Register, by striking him with a golf club and kicking him, was fined £50 Scots to be paid to the burgh treasurer and was ordered to be taken into custody and put into irons, shackled and manacled. (*ERBE*)

———◆———

1806: 'Corri's Rooms. To-Morrow, 21st November, 1806. Grand Military Promenade & Ball. The public are respectfully informed, that the whole suite of the above Rooms will open for the Season on Friday the 21st instant, with a Promenade and Ball. During the Promenade military Music will be performed by that truly excellent Band of the Dumfries-shire Militia, by permission of the Right Hon. the Earl of Dalkeith. The side rooms will be laid out for Cards. To begin at half-past eight o'clock.—Admission Four Shillings.' (*Caledonian Mercury*)

November 21st

1827: 'Oysters.—The oyster dealers of every description are complaining that this is the worst season they have had for a number of years. The demand is still good, but purchasers will not give former prices. There are fifty boats daily employed on the two beds at Newhaven. On an average they rake about 800 each, making a total of 40,000. Besides these about 4,000 come daily from Prestonpans, making the daily consumption of Edinburgh and vicinity 44,000. The fish-women get on the whole 1 shilling and 4 pence a hundred, and hence, by this valuable shell-fish alone, they daily turn upwards of £260. The mussels, as wholesome, though not so delicious or so fashionable, do not cause the turn of a fortieth part of the above sum.' (*The Scotsman*)

1829: 'Accident.—On Tuesday, one of the workmen employed at the Dean Bridge had his leg broken by the heavy iron nippers, with a large stone attached, separating from the crane and falling upon him.—The same day, a child in Jamaica Street, about twenty months old, while its mother was engaged in washing, unperceived drank boiling water from the spout of a tea kettle, which caused its death, on Thursday forenoon.' (*Caledonian Mercury*)

November 22nd

1595: Four heralds were sitting drinking. Two of them were John Purdie and John Gladstanes. John Gladstanes stabbed John Purdie at the table. Gladstanes was arrested and beheaded on 25 November for the murder. (*Diarey of Robert Birrel*)

———•◆•———

1648: The kirks of the burgh considered the regulations given to them by the great Session on 4 October last in relation to: curbing the excessive feasting at the baptising of children on the Lord's Day; the closure of wine and ale outlets on that day; restraining vagrant persons who spread the dangers of the plague to outlying areas mainly on the Lord's Day; stopping dirty lodging-houses; controlling the numbers of strangers and able-bodied beggars; the guarding of the town gates on the Sabbath day; dealing with those who refused to pay the monthly contributions for the poor of the town; the payment of church preceptors. Thanks were given to the council for proclaiming these measures throughout the burgh so as to prevent all these public disorders and restraining all such vices according to the penal statutes of the burgh. (*ERBE*)

November 23rd

1846: 'Interesting Atmospheric Phenomena.—On Tuesday night there was a very beautiful and rather uncommon display of *aurora borealis*. About eight o'clock it formed two very distinct arches across the sky; one, as usual, low down in the magnetic north, the other so far south as to obscure the stars near the ecliptic. The whole northern part of the sky between these two arches was covered by a luminous haze, through which only the brighter stars were visible. The light of the aurora was almost equal to that of the moon at the first quarter. Later in the evening, the southern arch broke up into clouds and disappeared, but the northern arch was visible till after midnight. On the same evening, shooting stars were more than usually numerous. One very brilliant meteor fell about half-past eight, and seemed to be within the auroral haze.' (*Caledonian Mercury*)

November 24th

1624: Alexander Speir was ordered by the council to satisfy and pay William Newman, one of the instructors at St Paul's Work (originally a medieval hospital but at this date a manufactory for training poor children in spinning, weaving and knitting and a Correction House for incorrigible vagabonds), the sum of £133, six shillings and eight pence in payment for the items he had supplied for the good of the burgh, namely a broad bay loom with all its ancillary equipment; a small loom with its equipment; ten large quills, nine small quills with spindles and toothed guiders; a pair of warping sticks; ten wooden racks for drying wool; sixty bobbins; a new large plaid for storing the wool; a wooden rack with a trestle table attached to it; an iron chimney brace; two pairs of shelves and planks; four iron spools for the looms; seven wooden pins (some of which for the boys); two sieves; a mechanical screw; a bobbin-wheel with rods and other fixtures; three finishing-stools; three wool barrels; two pairs of finishing combs; three iron keys for the carding combs. (*ERBE*)

November 25th

1879: 'The Midlothian Campaign. Mr Gladstone, who was so full of energy and vigour that those who listened to him must have found it hard to realize ... that he has entered on his seventieth year [and] was perfectly at home with the meeting from the first words he spoke, and he kept their attention and their interest riveted to the end. The plan of his speech was masterly. Constituting, as it did, the opening of a great electioneering campaign, it was necessarily comprehensive in its scope, and surveyed not only the general issues at stake, but the personal grounds which had induced the orator ... to enter into such a contest. There was an unmistakable ring of sincerity and dignity in the opening sentences, in which Mr Gladstone repudiated all petty and personal motives, and referred to the strong sense of patriotic duty which had brought him to Mid-Lothian. Even his bitterest critic could not deny the good taste of his brief allusion to the Duke of Buccleuch. His powerful denunciation of the endeavours of the Tories to swamp the constituency by means of faggot votes naturally elicited as hearty a response from his hearers as any other passage of his speech.' (*The Scotsman*)

November 26th

1801: On this day, the *Caledonian Mercury* reported on Andrew Lawrie, late letter carrier in the general Post Office. He was accused of abstracting money-letters and was apprehended at Greenock, on board a ship bound for Liverpool. He was brought to town by Mr George Williamson, messenger. The following circumstances were reported to have led to this detection: A woman with whom he cohabited had accompanied him ever since the period of his elopement, and when they went to Greenock he engaged to work his passage on board a ship bound for Liverpool, and then to America. Not having money to pay her passage, he left her behind, and the ship began to hove off. She immediately went to a messenger, whom she informed that Lawrie was on board. The messenger took a boat and went with her on board the ship, where she pointed him out. He was secured and brought on shore.

November 27th

1824: News of a devious robbery appeared in the *Caledonian Mercury*:

In the Police Court on Thursday, two men, named Glass and McLean, were put to the bar, on a charge of stealing from one of the houses which has been rendered uninhabitable in Borthwick's Close, in consequence of the late fire. These miscreants having learnt that property of considerable value remained in the deserted habitation, went and procured permission to get out at a garret window of an adjoining land, under pretence that they had been sent by one of the sufferers to remove part of the property. On Monday, they took away two feather beds, and a variety of other articles … the owner discovered his loss, and made the approaches all secure … On Wednesday the thieves returned, and fell into a trap which had been laid for them. The … prisoners … were sentenced to sixty days confinement in Bridewell, and to be kept at hard labour at the tread mill.

November 28th

1589: Following an order of the council, the burgh controller paid for the repairing and reforming of the town brass weights. David Rowen re-cast the weights and adjusted them, using the old brass weights, augmented by some counterfeit weights found in among the open stalls. The weights were made from brass mixed with lead and were stamped with the three-castle symbol of the burgh by the goldsmith John Bartane. Part of the metal came from the potters, John Padein and John Hog, who supplied three stones of brass to make a new Tron two stone weight. David Rowen, who cast the weights, was paid £6 and 14 shillings and a choppin of wine. (*ERBE*)

Measures in Scotland at that period were different from those in England. The Scots 'choppin' was an English half pint, while the Scots pint was three times the English pint. By a statute of 1618, the Scots pint was 26,200 English Troy grains of the clear Water of Leith, at 50 degrees Fahrenheit. Scots weights and measures were abolished by the Treaty of Union (1707).

November 29th

1387: A contract was drawn up between, on the one hand, Adam Forrester (the Laird of Nether Libberton), Andrew Dickson, Provost of Edinburgh, and the community of Edinburgh, and, on the other, the stonemasons John Primrose, John of Scone, and John Squyer, over the construction of five new chapels on the south side of the Collegiate Kirk of St Giles. (*ERBE*)

1681: The Royal College of Physicians was incorporated by a charter of Charles II, which was ratified by Parliament in 1685. Formerly the College of Physicians had a meeting-room and some other property near the Cowgate Port but, the house having become ruinous, they chose not to build in that location and sold the ground, then feuing from the town of Edinburgh a large area in George Street.

1802: Because robberies and street offences had become common, a meeting of Edinburgh citizens was held where resolutions were agreed that the use of a Town Guard to police the city was no longer effective. A recommendation was made for an Act of Parliament to provide better policing of the city and its suburbs and that the establishment of a new police force should be paid for by increasing the local assessment.

November 30th

1818: The *Caledonian Mercury* revealed details of a revenue court held by the Justices of the Peace, in their new court-room. The report described several cases of adulterated coffee that were brought before them. Samples of the articles were produced, the chief ingredients of which appeared to the Court to consist of burnt beans, and was called by the traders 'American vegetable powder'. It was pretended that it had come from Liverpool from America, and sent without orders from that place for each invoice. The trader could not produce the invoice, and alleged he had returned it, and had refused to take the article; there was little doubt, however, that it was the manufacturer of this neighbourhood that had committed the crime, and there was much reason to believe that it was a practice that had long been carried on. The two Justices before whom the cases came, with a proper consideration to the health of the lieges, as well as the protection of the revenue, recommended them to be laid before the Lord Advocate, and in the mean-time delayed proceedings.

December 1st

1678: An account for painting work submitted to the town council by the contract painter George Porteous shows the variety of work involved – gilding and painting a worn wooden board on the Leith Tolbooth steeple; colouring a small carved wooden decoration in the Parliament House with oil paint; repairs in the High Council house for the Lords of Justiciary; colouring green the benches and walls around the High Council house for the Justice Court; painting white the roof of the Inner room; painting the benches red and marbling the fireplace; painting the middle room where the Lords put on their gowns, with the roof and walls whitened, the fireplace marbled and the entry to the Inner House; the washing-boards in olive wood graining and a chest to hold the Lords of Justiciary's gowns, in olive wood graining and red inside; two cellars in the Tolbooth white; five seats in the West Kirk painted with the town coat of arms for the millers of the Water of Leith; the flag of the Regiment of Colours, eight banners for the pipers, with a scroll reading *Nisi Dominus Frustra* and heraldic balls; four trumpeters' banners, two pairs of colours for Portsburgh and Potterrow. (*ERBE*)

December 2nd

1768: The roof of Holyrood Abbey finally fell to the ground. This was the last of many indignities. After the English burnt down the palace in 1544, both church and palace were speedily repaired. At the Restoration (1660), King Charles resolved to rebuild the palace and, at the same time, to give the church a complete repair. However, the populace gave vent to their fury at the Revolution (1688) and despoiled the ornaments of the inside of the church, leaving nothing but the bare walls. They even broke into the vault which had been used as the royal sepulchre, in which lay the bodies of King James V, of Magdalene of France his first Queen, the Earl of Darnley and others of the monarchs and royal family of Scotland. They broke open the lead coffins, carrying off the lids. A new roof was installed in August 1768 but its weight could not be supported by the ancient walls. In 1776, the body of James V could still be seen in the lead coffin. Then the coffins were stolen. The head of Queen Madgalene, at that time entire and beautiful, was stolen, as was the skull of Darnley. Only his thigh-bones remained. (Arnot, *The History of Edinburgh*)

December 3rd

1897: *The Scotsman* printed this letter about cruelty to animals:

Sir,—Last night I happened to be coming down the Mound about nine o'clock, and there saw an exhibition of cruelty the like of which I have never seen before ... A 'bus belonging to the Edinburgh Tramway Company was coming up the Mound, crammed inside and out with women and males (I cannot call them men); this was being drawn by three wretched horses, slipping and struggling in their efforts to haul the over-weighted vehicle up the incline. In spite of the ... vigorous application of the whip the 'bus stopped, and would never have started again if a number of so-called 'roughs' had not shoved bravely behind; these poor men had far better hearts than the people who lolled on the 'bus, and they had pity on the wretched animals ... Now, sir, I really think it is time the Society for Prevention of Cruelty to Animals moved in this matter ... as each of those horses was pulling more than half a ton over what it should be asked to pull on level ground. Some frosty day one of those buses will skid at the corner, lock, and overturn—I am, &c. 'A Lover of Animals'.

December 4th

1800: 'Dancing.—Madame Bonnet, late M. Marcucci, begs leave to acknowledge, with gratitude and respect, the great favour and encouragement she has received from the Nobility, Ladies and Gentlemen, during several years she has taught Dancing in this city. Having resided most part of last summer in London for the purpose of acquiring the present fashionable and improved modes of Dancing, as taught by Sir J. Gallini, Mr Wills, &c. (who have obligingly favoured her with written testimonials) she with some degree of confidence, presumes to solicit a continuance of the public favour, which her utmost abilities shall be exerted to deserve. She continues to teach in that very central and accessible School in James's Court, which was built purposely for a Dancing School, and was last summer repaired and fitted up in an elegant manner.' (*Caledonian Mercury*)

December 5th

1805: On this day, these announcements appeared in the *Caledonian Mercury*:

Reward.—Whereas on the night between Friday the 22nd and Saturday the 23rd November last, the Counting-Room of James Milne, tanner, south back of the Canongate, was broke into, and one £10 note of Sir William Forbes & Co. and a £5 note of the Bank of Scotland, together with some other papers, taken from a desk in the said Counting-room—This is to give notice, that any person who can give such information as will lead to the conviction of the offenders, shall be handsomely rewarded by applying to H. R. Brown, coach-maker, York Place, treasurer to the Canongate Association for the Prosecution of Thieves.

Employment for Families.— Cleanly, industrious, and well-behaved families, in which there are three or more children, upwards of ten years of age, natives of the Highlands or Lowlands of Scotland only, and who can procure properly authenticated testimonials of their good character, may have constant employment, with every comfort that work people can desire, by applying at the New Lanark Cotton Mills.

December 6th

1949: On this day, this sports news was printed in *The Scotsman*:

Baird plan for Scottish Football. The new financial deal for Scottish football, proposed by Mr Tom Baird, Motherwell F.C. director, was discussed in Glasgow yesterday by the Management Committee of the Scottish League, but no statement was issued, at the close of the meeting. In a recent letter to the League, Mr Baird suggested, among other things, the institution of a maximum wage, a limit to the number of players a club might engage, and a share in the profits for players. He also proposed that the books of all clubs be examined annually by auditors appointed by the League. The committee agreed not to fill meantime a vacancy in the referee inspectors' list. When this was drawn up by the League a few weeks ago four names were listed but before the scheme came into operation Mr Robert Ferrier, ex-manager and player, withdrew his nomination. Approval was given to the draft constitution prepared at a conference between members of the League, the Scottish Football Association and the Players' Union.

Powderhall Sprint. Three hundred and six [professional] runners have entered for the Powderhall 130 Yards New Year Handicap. Eight previous winners are included in the record entry.

December 7th

1597: On this, the first day of Parliament, Archibald Jarden, servitor and master stabler to the Earl of Angus, was accidently killed by Andro Stalker, a young goldsmith living at the head of Niddry's Wynd. Stalker was arrested and put in prison. The young men of the town were all armed, as was the custom at the time of a Parliament. They went to the King and asked for clemency for Stalker. The King told them that if they went to Lord Angus, the man's master, to satisfy him and calm his anger, then he would grant him his life. James Williamson, leader of the young men, went to Lord Angus and offered him a bond of manrent, to make himself available to serve him when needed. Lord Angus agreed and gave Stalker his life, and so he was released from prison that evening. (*Diarey of Robert Birrel*)

December 8th

1821: *The Scotsman* printed an 'Assessment for Broken Windows':

The Council have resolved to levy seven or eight hundred pounds upon the inhabitants of this city, to make good the damage done by the mob at the illumination for the Queen's acquittal ... It will be recollected, that ... the Magistrates thought proper to issue a proclamation, urging the inhabitants not to illuminate and threatening, if an illumination took place, to fill the city with soldiers and constables, and to make our purses pay for any damage done ... it turned out, too, that our rulers, after promising protection to those who did not illuminate, were quite unprepared to repress the spirit of mischief which their own absurd conduct had provoked. A mob of three or four hundred apprentices and sailor boys traversed the streets from 9 till near 11 o'clock, and broke windows at pleasure, undisturbed by police, constables or military. The source of all the mischief done was unquestionably the factious, irritating and blundering conduct of the magistrates ... But this is one of the blessed fruits of the rotten burgh system. Magistrates, generally, instead of being the representatives of the citizens, are the tools of men in power, and are ever ready to serve their purposes.

December 9th

1950: 'Builders to Resume Work. Two hundred Edinburgh building trade workers—among them 61 bricklayers—who came out on strike on Thursday because of the dismissal of four shop stewards, are expected to resume work this morning. The stoppage was at Old Saughton, where new government buildings are being erected. The dispute started because the stewards and 24 bricklayers and 11 labourers were to be 'paid-off' last night as redundant. Following discussions with the Union officials, the Ministry of Works, and the contractors yesterday, it was finally agreed that two of the stewards should be retained in their jobs. The other workers, the 24 bricklayers and the 11 labourers, however, were given notice last night. Because negotiations are to continue on the position, the rest of their colleagues at Old Saughton are to resume work. It is understood that Union efforts were made throughout yesterday to try and absorb the 24 bricklayers and the 11 labourers on to other sites in the city where Corporation houses are being built. At the present time, however, this was found impossible because of shortage of bricks to keep them going.' (*The Scotsman*)

December 10th

1688: The Chancellor, the Earl of Perth, fled from Edinburgh and the government fell entirely into the hands of revolutioners. A mob rose, drums beat through the city, the inhabitants assembled in great multitudes. They proceeded to demolish the chapel of Holyroodhouse but were opposed by a party of about a hundred men stationed in the Abbey. The mob, who pressed forward, were fired upon by this party. About a dozen were killed and thrice as many wounded, upon which they fled for the present but quickly returned with a warrant from some Lords of the Privy Council. They were headed by the magistrates, the Town Guard, the trained bands and heralds at arms who required Wallace, the captain of the party, to surrender. Upon his refusal, another skirmish ensued in which Wallace's party were defeated, some being killed and the rest made prisoners. Then there was nothing to resist their fury. The Abbey church and private chapel were robbed and despoiled of their ornaments. The Jesuit school was almost pulled to pieces and the homes of Roman Catholics plundered. The Earl of Perth's cellars became a notable prey to them and wine, conspiring with zeal, inflamed their fury. (Arnot, *The History of Edinburgh*)

December 11th

1851: These advertisements were printed in the *Caledonian Mercury*:

J. W. Mackie, purveyors to Her Majesty, No 108 Princes Street, in directing public attention to the customary variety of Christmas buns and cakes, takes the liberty of recommending them, on the ground of being well raised, baked and seasoned—to say nothing of the fruit and other material being very superior, and prepared with the utmost carefulness. The acknowledged excellence of his Shortbread and Pitcaithly Bannocks renders it unnecessary to do more than convey the assurance that the quality of what is now submitted will be found, in every respect, equal to the expectation naturally raised by former experience. These articles are neatly put up in tin cases, and may be conveyed uninjured to the remotest distances. The daily increasing demand for the Royal Sandwich Loaf lately introduced, affords satisfactory evidence that nothing could better have answered the purpose for which it was intended.

Mr Thackeray's Lectures. The appearance of this distinguished author in Edinburgh to deliver a series of lectures which have already attracted much attention, on the poets of the last century, has excited an interest such as might have been anticipated from the attractive nature of the theme, and his well-known masterly treatment of it.

December 12th

1945: 'Edinburgh Bank robbed. Two men acting in concert carried out a daring robbery from an Edinburgh branch bank yesterday. One of them snatched a bundle of notes form the counter, and the men dashed out into the busy thoroughfare, dropping a number of the notes as they went, and although pursued they made good their escape. About £105 was stolen. Shortly after midday a man called at the South Side branch of the National Bank of Scotland at 30 Nicolson Street and tendered a two shilling piece which he wanted changed into coppers. Three minutes later a second man called at the bank and handed over a ten-shilling note also asking for change. He was given three half-crowns, a florin, and a sixpence. He returned this to the teller, saying that he wished single shillings. When the teller turned his back on the man in order to get his bag containing single shillings, the robber pushed aside a young lady who was waiting to be attended to, leaned over the counter, and snatched a bundle containing one hundred pounds in one-pound Bank of England notes and some ten shilling notes. The man then bolted out of the bank and into the street.' (*The Scotsman*)

December 13th

1813: 'House of Industry, Canongate. The managers ... solicit the attention of the public to the following short statement of the advantages which have resulted from the institution ... This charity ... is divided into two different branches. 1st, *The Spinning Room*—designed, not as a receptacle for vagrants, but as an asylum for industrious women of respectable characters, who, either from being destitute of employment, or from age and infirmities, [are] incapacitated from earning a sufficiency for their subsistence, [and] were in danger of becoming burthensome to the public, or sinking into the extremes of want ... 2ndly, *The Lace School*—intended to promote habits of cleanliness, industry, and order, and to render the labour of children productive of pecuniary advantage to themselves and their parents ... The ladies who superintend the institution, have peculiar pleasure in being able to state, that of the girls who have from this school gone out to service, there are few of whom they have not heard the most satisfactory accounts.' (*Caledonian Mercury*)

December 14th

1933: 'Iraq Judge. The death has occurred in Edinburgh of Mr Alasdair Iain Maclaren, W.S., who occupied a number of judicial posts in the East, and was latterly for some time President of the Civil Court of Baghdad. Mr Maclaren was the elder son of the late Mr Duncan Maclaren, S.S.C., Edinburgh, and was born in 1889. Educated at Merchiston Castle School and Cambridge University, he qualified just before the outbreak of the Great War as a Writer to the Signet. When war broke out he joined the Field Artillery, and was sent to Mesopotamia, where he served until hostilities were over, winning the Military Cross in 1917. After the war he was appointed to the judicial services in Iraq, and … was finally made President of the Civil Court at Baghdad, from which, owing to ill-health, contracted in the course of his war service, he had to retire in 1929. The years of his retirement were spent partly in Switzerland and partly in Edinburgh, where he was a member of Mortonhall Golf Club. Mr Maclaren was a keen golfer, and besides winning the Championship of Iraq three times, he gained a number of competitive trophies in India.' (*The Scotsman*)

December 15th

1851: 'Disturbance by Students.—On Friday evening some annoyance was occasioned in the Theatre-Royal by two young men, apparently students, conducting themselves in a very obstreperous manner. They were, of course, ejected with as much promptitude as possible; but on being given into the custody of the police, they immediately assumed the offensive as well as defensive, the police found some further assistance necessary, a large crowd collected, kicks and buffets (of which the defenders of order received not a few) were freely interchanged. The scene of conflict even extended a good way up Register Street; and, in short, the melée was just beginning to assume a very serious aspect when the original causers of the disturbance were, with great difficulty, overpowered and taken to the Police-Office. On Saturday the two unfortunate youths were, along with a woman who appeared to have been in their company, brought before Sheriff Arkley, who ... at once sent them all for thirty days to prison.' (*Caledonian Mercury*)

December 16th

1590: John Fian, also known as Cunninghame, a schoolmaster in Prestonpans, East Lothian, was executed after being tortured in the 'buits' (the 'Spanish boot'). Along with a number of others based in East Lothian, he was accused of active complicity in witchcraft designed to sink the ships that carried King James VI and Anne, his Queen, from Denmark to Leith. First a carpenter dug a wooden post into the ground, for which he was paid ten shillings. Then ten cart-loads of coal (bought for 64s 4d) were spread around the post. Over the coals were laid two bundles of heather and two of yellow broom. Finally, six barrels of tar were poured over these combustible materials. The Lokman (executioner) was paid £5 18s and 2d. A month later, Agnes Sampsoun was burnt and on 15 June 1591 it was the turn of Euphame McCalyeane to be executed. (*ERBE*)

While in Scandinavia, it is thought that King James may have absorbed some of the Danes' preoccupation with witches. The trial of Dr Fian and his associates, and his interrogation by the King, appeared in an English publication, *Newes from Scotland* (1592) and then in the tract *Dæmonologie* (1597), written by King James himself.

December 17th

1596: Being a Friday, and the King sitting in session in the Tolbooth, some devilishly officious person entered and claimed that the ministers were coming to take his life. At once the Tolbooth doors were shut and barred. Then there arose such shouting, 'God and the King', and 'God and the Kirk' that the whole population of Edinburgh were up in arms but did not entirely know why. There was a deacon of deacons, whose name was John Watt, a blacksmith. He raised the whole Craft in arms and came to the Tolbooth and there shouted for a sight of the King, threatening to smash the gate with his hammers as if no one inside the Tolbooth would escape with his life. At length the King put his head out of a window and addressed the people. They promised to live and die with him. Eventually, the King came down after the townspeople were ordered from the gate, and was accompanied by the craftsmen to the Abbey of Holyroodhouse, where he stayed the night. Next morning the King rode out of the town and sent back his accusations. This uproar created great trouble between the King and the town of Edinburgh. (*Diarey of Robert Birrel*)

December 18th

1923: A glowing review of Waverley Market Carnival appeared in *The Scotsman*:

In the Waverley Market 'The Carnival', which opened a week ago, is in full swing. The cold, drab, prosaic aspect of the Market has vanished for the time being, as if by the waving of a fairy's wand, and the interior of the building presents an appearance of animation, brightness, and gaiety in keeping with the joyous spirit of the season. When one enters this atmosphere of dazzling delights, laughter, and music, even the most staid person feels constrained to enter into the fun of the fair. There are many sideshows of unusual interest ... A strong attraction is the platform performance, in which a large number and variety of artistes and various kinds of animals take part. There are acts by dogs, which display wonderful cleverness; there are astonishing balancing feats by sea lions; there is a boxing pony. Jugglers and gymnasts and wire-rope walkers do daring things and cause thrills. One of them does tricks at the top of an unsupported ladder. Last, but not least in importance, there is the band under the direction of Mr John Guy, which is responsible for an enlivening programme of music.

December 19th

1812: 'Duddingston Loch. The late intense frost has been very favourable for the elegant amusement of skating. On Monday and Tuesday the Skating Club mustered strong at Duddingston, and were on the latter day attended by the band of the Ayrshire militia. The company on the ice, among whom were a great number of ladies, was very numerous. There was also a keen curling match at the east end of the loch.—With the fineness of the day, and the beauty of the surrounding scenery, it is hardly possible to figure a more animated and interesting scene than Duddingston Loch presents on such an occasion.' (*Caledonian Mercury*)

'Accident. On Tuesday evening, a poor woman fell on the ice at Prince's Street and broke one of her legs; accidents of this kind are very liable to occur when the boys are permitted, for their amusement, to make it dangerous to walk the streets. The police should look to the vigilant execution of their regulations, which require the inhabitants, in times of frost, to strew ashes before their doors.' (*Caledonian Mercury*)

December 20th

1947: This account of the Christmas graduation was printed in *The Scotsman*:

Eighty-five students were capped at the Christmas graduation ceremony of Edinburgh University held in the Upper Library yesterday. As well as the native Scots, they came from Eire and Wales, Poland and Egypt, the Gold Coast, India, China, New Zealand, Canada, and, even, said Professor O. L. Richmond, who presided, from England, which still sometimes seemed to have need of us. But, he said, there was also something homely and intimate about these Christmas graduations. There was, too, something inspiring about the library in which they were held. Their late Principal, Sir John Fraser, had himself taken a great pleasure in these lesser ceremonies. Those of them who, of late years, had been living close to the Principal and watched him and come to admire his high qualities, had observed certain things which would be of help to the others. 'You must have courage,' said Professor Richmond, 'and when I say that, I mean intellectual courage, because physical courage this generation has proved itself to have. 'It was a good old Roman and a wise one who said that education ends only with death, and you must prove yourself capable of self-dedication, and there I can assure you lies the ultimate happiness of human life.

December 21st

1811: The *Caledonian Mercury* revealed the details of an unfortunate accident. It reported that on Saturday night, between eight and nine o'clock, the following melancholy accident happened in the city. A low house in Blair's Close, Castlehill, opposite the city's reservoir, suddenly blew up with a great explosion, and the inhabitants in the floor above were instantly precipitated, along with the falling ruins, into the cellar below. A room on the second floor was also blown up, in which there was luckily no person at the time of the accident. The house immediately caught fire, which was soon got under control when the persons who had fallen along with the rubbish were taken out. The house immediately above the cellar was inhabited by a man named Campbell, his mother, and three women lodgers, with three children. Campbell was much scorched; his mother was killed and one of the women had her thigh bone broken and scorched. The other two were also greatly scorched and bruised. The children were not much hurt. The unfortunate sufferers were all sent to the Royal Infirmary. The magistrates, police and firemen soon attended, and the fire was got under control in a short time. The newspaper also stated that the gunpowder which occasioned the explosion was supposedly concealed in the cellar.

December 22nd

1874: *The Scotsman* printed a letter with the title 'Assault in the Streets':

Sir.—At half-past ten, after leaving two ladies at their homes, and while passing the cab-stand at the head of Forrest Road, I heard someone running close up behind me, and seeing it was a man, asked him what he wanted. The only reply I received was a rush, bullock-fashion, at me, and a blow, which caused my nose to bleed. I had just time to strike my assailant with my walking-stick, when five or six of his fellows coming up behind me, I received a blow behind the ear which half stupefied me, and was surrounded and mauled. By dint of my hitting out freely, and at the sight of the crowd which was collecting, my assailants drew off, and I found that my watch was hanging at the end of my chain, and that my hat and stick, and as I subsequently found, the few shillings that I had in my greatcoat pocket, had vanished. But what annoyed me more than these losses was the apathy of the crowd, although they could plainly see that single-handed and encumbered as I was I could be no match for five or six men. I am, &c. 'Colonist'.

December 23rd

1696: Son of a surgeon, eighteen-year-old Thomas Aikenhead, had been a medical student at Edinburgh University for four years when he was accused of blasphemy, arrested, thrown into a prison cell in the Tolbooth and then taken to the High Court of Justiciary for trial. He was accused of having stated in conversation that 'theology was a rhapsody of ill-invented nonsense, patched up partly of the moral doctrines of philosophers, and partly of poetical fictions and extravagant chimeras'. He ridiculed the Bible, referring to it as 'fables' and claimed that Jesus Christ had learnt magic in Egypt which he used to perform miracles. He rejected the mystery of the Trinity and laughed at the Incarnation of Christ. Although he retracted these opinions, he was tried for the crime of blasphemy under Acts of 1661 and 1695. Although Aikenhead petitioned the Privy Council for clemency, considering his age and circumstances, the Privy Council only agreed to reprieve him if the Church of Scotland intervened. The Church, however, replied that only execution would provide an example to the widespread lack of respect given religion and the profanity of the times. He was hanged on 8 January 1697. (Arnot, *Celebrated Criminal Trials*, 1785)

December 24th

1828: An unsettling report appeared in the *Caledonian Mercury* on this Christmas Eve:

> West Port Murders—Trial of Burke and Hare. We have heard a great deal of late concerning 'the march of intellect' for which the present age is supposed to be distinguished; and the phrase has been rung in our ears till it has nauseated us by its repetition, and become almost a proverbial expression of derision. But we fear that, with all its pretended illumination, the present age must be characterised by some deeper and fouler blots than have attached to any that preceded it; and that if it has brighter spots, it has also darker shades and more appalling obscurations. It has, in fact, nooks and corners where everything that is evil seems to be concentrated and condensed; dens and holes to which the Genius of Iniquity has fled, and become envenomed with newer and more malignant inspirations.— Thus the march of crime has far outstripped 'the march of intellect,' and attained a monstrous, a colossal development ... No one who reads the report contained in our last of the regular system of murder, which seems to have been organized in the city, can doubt that it is almost wholly without example in any age or country.

December 25th

1680: After the Restoration, the students at the University of Edinburgh appear to have been pretty much tainted with the fanatic principles of the Covenanters. In the year 1680, when the Duke of York was at Edinburgh, they resolved to manifest their zeal by a solemn procession and a burning of a Pope on Christmas Day. The magistrates, having got intelligence of their design and being resolved to prevent a ceremony calculated to affront the Duke, as well as foment sedition, sent a party of soldiers to stop the procession. But instead of His Holiness being burned with all solemnity at the Mercat Cross, the students were keen to burn him post-haste in Blackfriars Wynd. Seven of the rioters were apprehended and committed to custody for a few days and then liberated. Violent denunciations against the magistrates were heard. But it was not supposed that these young people had been so early imbued with the furious zeal and rancorous malice which the subsequent conduct suggested. On 11 January 1681, Prestonfield House, seat of Sir James Dick, Lord Provost of Edinburgh (the family being in town), was set on fire and, with all its furniture, burnt to the ground. (Arnot, *The History of Edinburgh*).

December 26th

1600: King James made a great feast: Queen Anne had delivered of a child in Dunfermline Palace on 20 November and the cannons were shot for joy. On 23 December, the King's second son was baptised and named Charles and immediately afterwards, with a great triumph, his father created him Duke of Albany, Marquess of Ormond and Earl of Ross. Then all the cannons in Edinburgh Castle roared in celebration. (*Diarey of Robert Birrel*)

———◆———

1801: The *Caledonian Mercury* reported on a local market, saying it was very well supplied with excellent haddocks and cod. The report also described a particular practice, which was considered questionable: It was that women frequented the market and purchased large quantities of the fish, which they afterwards sold by retail at an advanced price. In order to carry out this deception, they dressed in habits similar to the Newhaven fishwomen, and thus carried off part of their trade. It was commented that this latter class were somewhat robust in their manners and rude in speech, but that still their matchless industry and hardy exertion entitled them to every encouragement.

December 27th

1836: 'Destructive Fire. Yesterday morning about three o'clock, a fire ... broke out in the workshop of Mr George Sandeman, upholsterer, No. 8, Greenside Street. The city fire-engines arrived at Greenside about half-past three, and the firemen, under the superintendence of Mr James Patterson, lost no time in proceeding to work: but, unfortunately, the flames had gained considerable strength before the engines came, and the wind blowing pretty high, every moment added to their already overwhelming violence. There was a communication between the workshop of Mr Sandeman and the showroom in front, by means of an arched passage; and there being a strong draught of air sweeping through it, the fire soon burst into the latter, defying all attempts to arrest its progress. With equal rapidity the houses right and left were attacked, and, the wind blowing from the northeast, sent the flames more particularly to the left, their advantages being only checked in that direction by the small lane between Greenside Street and Calton Street, called Nottingham Place. Several tenements and a yard, lying at the back of Greenside Street, also took fire; and at about five o'clock in the morning, the appearance which this extensive conflagration presented was awful in the extreme.' (*The Scotsman*)

December 28th

1815: One outcome of the first Edinburgh Music Festival at the end of October was the formation of the Edinburgh Institution for the Encouragement of Sacred Music in Churches. This new society was formed on 28 December with the Duke of Buccleuch as president and Lord Provost Sir William Arbuthnot as one of the vice presidents. The first step was the formation of a chorus. In response to an appeal for singers, 780 names were received and 380 were selected: 150 trebles, 58 altos or counter-tenors, 111 tenors and 61 basses. Mr Mather was appointed chorus-master and six performances were arranged for the following year.

———•◆•———

1860: The *Caledonian Mercury* printed this letter:

Sir,—As a Leith resident, I had the felicity of enjoying for the first time this season, this very day (Saturday) a dish of sprats. I sincerely trust that the arbitrary law against *garvie* fishing in the Firth of Forth will in a few months hence be numbered with the things that were; so that the poorer classes of society may be enabled to enjoy as hitherto a cheap and wholesome diet, and the hardy fishermen of Newhaven free to pursue a course of honest industry— I am, &c, 'Not a Fisherman'.

December 29th

1868: This letter was printed in *The Scotsman*:

Sir,—I send you the enclosed table, taken from Professor Playfair's eloquent and masterly Lectures on Chemistry. The table proves that the present site of the Infirmary is surrounded by a locality nearly half as filthy as a pig-sty ...

Organic Matter in Air – ammonia (ml.) per metre of air:
Pig-sty: 94.0
Cowgate: 40.0
High Street: 30.0
Princes Street: 22.0
Calton Hill: 12.0

More letters on the same theme were also printed on this day:

Controversy ... I believe the drainage for the Royal Infirmary gives little or no cause for complaint ... Dr Sanders speaks of morbid poison creeping along the corridors of the Surgical Hospital ... the drainage of this extensive [new] establishment on a dead level is to traverse the most thickly populated districts of the town.—I am &c., 'N'.

Sir,—An hospital without baths! This is the discovery which the public has made within the last two or three days. No wonder so many persons enter these gates never again to come out alive.

December 30th

1580: As no guard had previously surrounded the Scottish throne, King James applied to the town council of Edinburgh on 18 January 1581 to raise a hundred men to protect his royal person and a hundred more to convey the Earl of Morton from the castle in Edinburgh to that of Dumbarton. The council complied with his request and the King, still thinking himself insecure, demanded of the city an additional company of a hundred men to guard him in his Palace of Holyroodhouse, which the town accordingly granted. Scotland being freed from the shackles of papal usurpation, was well nigh subjected to a more formidable tyrant in the person of her deliverer. She preserved her freedom and independence but with difficulty, and to the struggle between the civil and ecclesiastical states, most of the troubles which distracted the nation for near a hundred years, may be imputed. If the Pope claimed in religious matters a supremacy over temporal sovereigns, the Presbyterian declared his independence of them, prudently choosing a head placed at a convenient distance. (Arnot, *The History of Edinburgh*)

December 31st

1596: The King came to the Abbey and a public proclamation was made that the Earl of Mar should guard the West Port, Lord Seton the Netherbow and Lords Livingston, Buccleuch and Cessford the High Street. The following morning (1 January 1597), before dawn, there were great rumours and gossip among the townsfolk that the King planned to send in the common thief Will Kinmond and many Borders men to devastate the town of Edinburgh. Hearing this, all the merchants took their goods out of their booths and shops and transported them to the best-protected house in the town and stayed in that house with their servants, expecting everything to be plundered. Similarly, all the craftsmen and common people met together in what was the strongest house they knew and best protected from pillage or burning, armed with hackbuts (guns), pistols and other arms to defend themselves. The noblemen and gentlemen, keepers of the town ports (gates) and the High Street, were at their stations with pikes and spears and armour. They stood there until the King reached St Giles' Kirk, to hear Mr David Lindsay preach. (*Diarey of Robert Birrel*)